# IN SOUTHERN INDIA

# IN SOUTHERN INDIA

## A VISIT TO SOME OF THE CHIEF MISSION STATIONS IN THE MADRAS PRESIDENCY

MRS. MURRAY MITCHELL

GYAN

*Published by*

Gyan Publishing House
5, Ansari Road
Daryaganj, New Delhi-110002
Phone: 011-47034999, 9811692060
E-mail: books@gyanbooks.com

*Distribution Network*
gyanbooks.com
India, USA, Canada, UK, Australia



ISBN: 978-93-7133-239-2 (PB)

First Published, 1885

2nd Impression 2025

*Printed at:* Gyan Press, Delhi.



**IN SOUTHERN INDIA**
Author Mrs. Murray Mitchell

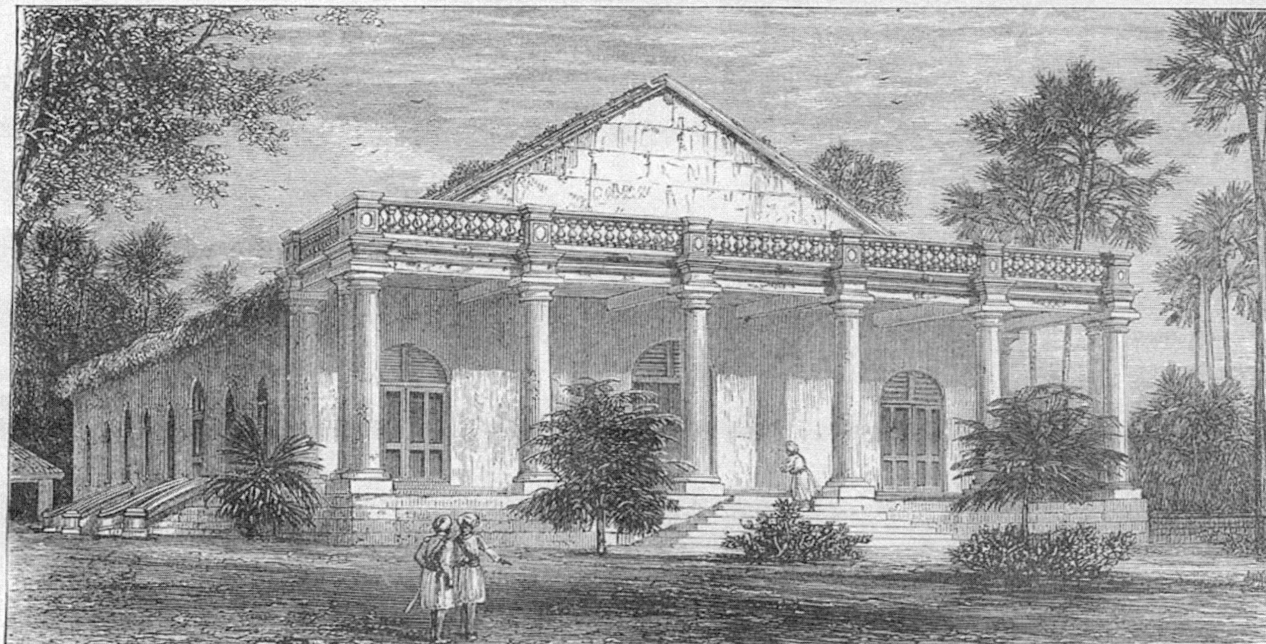

NAGERCOIL CHURCH.

# IN SOUTHERN INDIA.

## A Visit to some of the chief Mission Stations in the Madras Presidency.

BY

MRS. MURRAY MITCHELL,

AUTHOR OF 'IN INDIA,' 'A MISSIONARY'S WIFE AMONG THE WILD TRIBES OF SOUTH BENGAL,' ETC.

'Large, England, is the debt
Thou ow'st to Heathendom,—
To India most of all.'
SOUTHEY.

*WITH A MAP AND MANY ILLUSTRATIONS.*

THE RELIGIOUS TRACT SOCIETY,
56, PATERNOSTER ROW; 65, ST. PAUL'S CHURCHYARD;
AND 164, PICCADILLY.

1885.

# INTRODUCTORY NOTE.

My wife asks me to write a preface to her book, and I have agreed to do it; but I find very little to say that is not better said in the book itself.

We have many works on India, but not many written by women. This one, it is hoped, may accordingly help to fill up a blank. On several subjects, especially those connected with family life in the East, women are much better qualified to speak than men.

The book refers to Southern India—the Presidency of Madras. It is always well to remember that there is as much diversity between two parts of India as between two parts of Europe; that, for example, a native of Travancore is as different from a Bengali as a Spaniard from a Swede. Missionary work, too, has a peculiar aspect in the South of India, inasmuch as it began nearly a century earlier than in Bengal, and more than a century before its commencement in Bombay. Hence, in some respects, it has a different character in the Madras Presidency.

It will not detract from the value of these pages that the writer was able to compare one part of India with another. Missionary work, however, is by no means the only topic referred to in this little book. Mrs. Mitchell took a lively interest in nearly everything she saw; and she has endeavoured to give a faithful description of what has most occupied her attention.

We had for many years been familiar with Missionary

efforts both in the West and North of India, and it was the fulfilment of a long-cherished hope when we were at length able to visit the chief Missions of the South. What we saw awakened the deepest possible interest. We were also able to take part, to a considerable extent, in the work; so that the visit might be called an evangelistic tour. The welcome we everywhere received, both from the Missionaries and the native Christians, will ever remain with us as a delightful memory. Nor can we forget the kindly greetings of many others who were not professedly Christians, but who seemed fully convinced that they had no truer friends than the Missionaries.

India is at present in a state of transition, and not of slow transition. No change recorded in history was of greater magnitude than that which is now going on; and the issues—social, religious, political—will be in every way momentous. This little work will not have been written in vain if it may serve to extend a knowledge of Indian life and character, increase the interest felt in Missionary work—especially as carried on among women—and deepen in the mind of Britain a sense of national responsibility to God in connection with her great Eastern dependency.

J. MURRAY MITCHELL.

# LIST OF ILLUSTRATIONS.

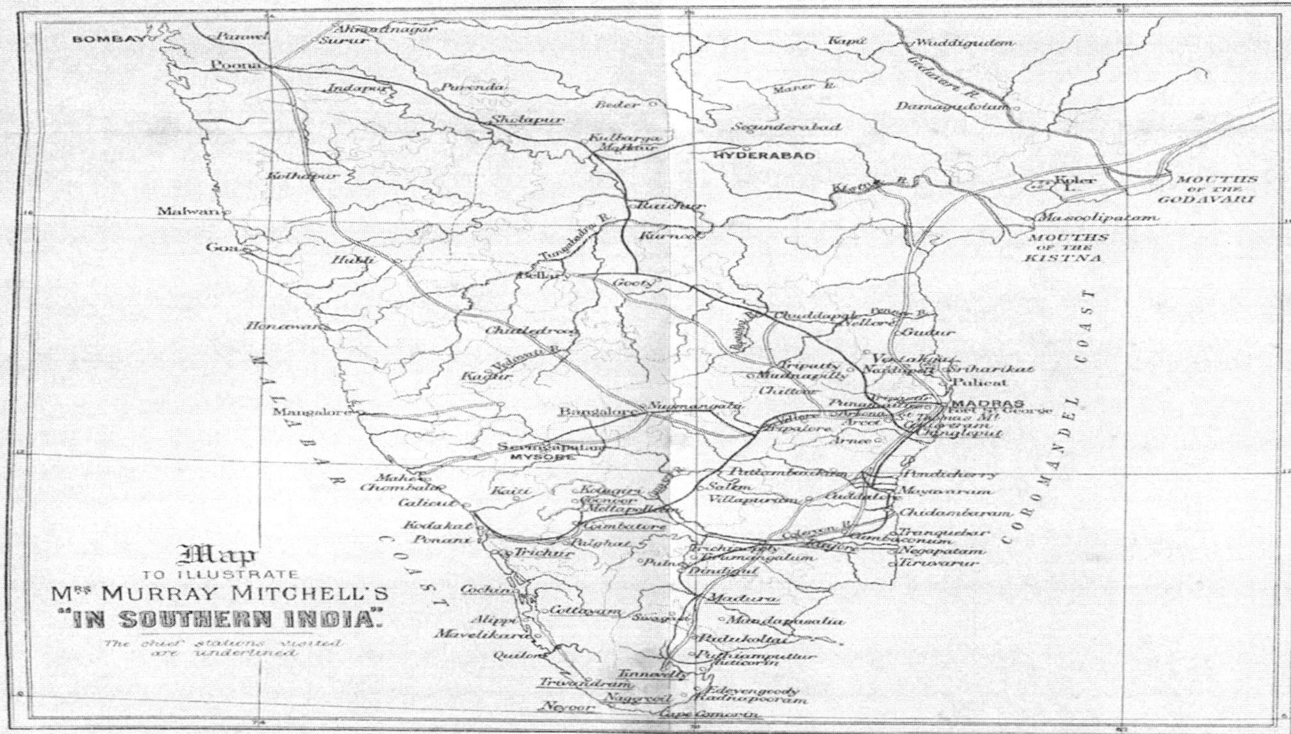

Map
TO ILLUSTRATE
MRS MURRAY MITCHELL'S
"IN SOUTHERN INDIA".
The chief stations visited are underlined
BOMBAY
Panwel
Ahmadnagar
Surur
Poona
Indapur
Purenda
Sholapur
Beder
Kulbarga
Kolhapur
Malwan
Goa
Hubli
Raichur
Kurnool
HYDERABAD
Secunderabad
Kapu
Wuddigudem
Godavari R.
Maner R.
Damagudolum
Kistna R.
Kolar
MOUTHS OF THE GODAVARI
Masoolipatam
MOUTHS OF THE KISTNA
Tungabadra R.
Bellary
Gooty
Honawar
Chitledroog
Cuddapah
Nellore
Gudur
Kadur
Tripatty
Madnapilly
Chittoor
Sriharikat
Pulicat
MADRAS
Fort St George
Mangalore
Bangalore
Arcot
Chingleput
Arnee
Seringapatam
MYSORE
MALABAR COAST
COROMANDEL COAST
Mahe
Chombala
Calicut
Kodakal
Ponani
Pondicherry
Salem
Villapuram
Cuddalore
Mayavaram
Chidambaram
Coimbatore
Palghat
Trichur
Tranquebar
Combaconum
Negapatam
Tiruvarur
Trichinopoly
Dindigul
Cochin
Madura
Cottayam
Alippi
Mavelikara
Quilon
Mandapasalia
Pudukottai
Tuticorin
Tinnevelly
Trivandrum
Nagercoil
Neyoor
Edeyengoody
Cape Comorin
A. Johnston, 6 Paternoster Buildings, E.C.

# CONTENTS.

# CHAPTER I.

## WE BEGIN OUR MISSIONARY JOURNEY.

*January 15th*, 1882.

THE dawn was spreading softly over earth and sky yesterday morning, when, after a more substantial *chota hajri*, or preliminary breakfast, than usual, we stood in the verandah, equipped ready for the start.

Our starting-point was Bombay, where we had been staying some weeks with our kind friends, Mr. and Mrs. Miller. . . . .

We had to leave early to catch the morning train for Poona and the Deccan. The morning is always the best part of our Indian day, and I am almost sure that it is also the most beautiful. As I stood watching the sweet silver dawn steal gently up and dispel the darkness and mystery of night, I thought it was not so wonderful that the impressionable, dreamy old poets of ancient India should have made her one of their divinities. The Dawn is one of the earliest Hindu goddesses. She is called *Ushas*, and is described with poetic grace as 'a mother come to awake her sleeping children.' The contemplation of Nature in her sublime and exquisite aspects no doubt led to her adoration among those old Rishis, for they were ignorant of Him who is the God and Framer of Nature, and did not hear her voice aright. Surely nothing ever declared His glory with more eloquent speech than this pure, blue, beauteous, cold-weather dawn! It is so peaceful, yet so gladsome, so fresh, and so suggestive of hope. But she would certainly have said to the sages of old in their adoration of herself what the angel said to John in the Apocalypse: 'See thou do it not; for I am thy fellow-servant!'

As I gazed on the lovely scene from the verandah, I thought our dear old Bombay had never looked more beautiful. This suburb—the Breach—is one of the prettiest. Arthur Seat, as our friend's bungalow is called, stands pretty high, on a long, wavy undulation over the rocky shore, and commands some striking and charming views of the scenery for which our Western capital is so justly famed. The gentlemen were below under the porch, having our belongings packed on to the *palki-ghari* which was to convey us to the station, and so I could take 'a last fond look' of the dear, familiar scene—familiar for many long, happy years, now gone by. The little cottage in the palm-wood, where we spent the earliest years of our missionary life, stands half a mile away, along the same shore, nearer the native town.

The chief feature in the scene was the great, calm, peaceful sea, of the deepest indigo blue, beginning now to sparkle in the rays of the rising sun, stretching to the far horizon, and rippling up on the rocks at our feet with musical murmur. An immense fleet of fishing craft, with white sails, gleamed in the distance; there were also one or two large ships, with sails set to catch the morning breeze, while, nearer the shore, here and there, a tall-masted *pattimar*, or cargo boat, glided past, helped on by the oar. Flocks of silver-winged gulls rode on the blue wavelets, hunting for their breakfast; and down among the rocks one or two tall-necked cranes stalked majestically, similarly engaged.

Along the margin, white-robed Parsis, in their high, picturesque head-gear of dark calico, stood facing the sea, muttering prayers; gentlemen and ladies galloped along the good wide road; while babies, and ayahs, and dogs, and servants, and ponies, passed in grand retinue, all bound for the early walk. Every one who is wise tries to extract what vigour is to be had from the fresh air of morning in India.

Turning to the left, our view is bounded by the lovely little Malabar Hill, of which every one has heard, though the long, low promontory running into Back Bay, with a bungalow belonging to the Government nestling amid the green at the point, is hid by the higher ground at this side. Nearer us, and divided from Malabar Hill by a valley and good road, there is another high wooded undulation, called Camballa Hill, beyond which lies our magnificent harbour, with its forest of shipping, its picturesque island-rocks, and the grand outline of the Western Ghāts not very far off. These hills and heights are one of the chief beauties of Bombay. They are wonderfully green and richly wooded, the tall palm-trees, with their glorious crowns of wavy fronds, being conspicuous everywhere, while pretty bungalows and handsome residences, belonging chiefly to the English and Parsi communities, gleam white among the trees at every elevation. Away to the right, there is the long, undulating island of Salsette, stretching as far as the eye can reach, indented with quiet bays, and covered with forests of the stately cocoa-palms, which are here in countless numbers, making the wealth of the people as well as the richness of the scene. And, finally, below at our feet, a picturesque little promontory runs out to the sea, crowned with the quaint old temple of Māhālukshmee. Here a *mêla*, or festival, was going on; queer little booths lined the road, people were beginning to congregate, and strange, grotesque figures—many of them religious mendicants decorated with tiger-skins—grouped themselves in the enclosure.

Some lines of delicate grey cloudlets lay pencilled at the horizon, now flushed with rose as the sun mounted higher, and a sweet, cool, faint breeze came gently up from the sea. As we drove away from the hospitable door, I am not sure that I was so elated as I ought to have been to think that a long-cherished dream was about to be realised, and we were indeed off to see the mission fields of South India.

We were tired; for we had had an exciting week. This was due to the visit of the famous Boston lecturer, Mr. Joseph Cook, and his charming wife. . . . The wonderfully able lectures, the crowds, the growing interest of Mr. Cook's utterances, the dinners, the meetings, and the universal entertaining, were all so thoroughly enjoyed, that our energies were naturally used up.

This most stirring visit was indeed an immense success. I never saw our native friends gather in more enthusiastic crowds than they did to every lecture, whatever the hour. Is it not a fact worth noting, and something to be thankful for, that a man like Mr. Cook can come out to India, and find at once, over the length and breadth of it, audiences of English-speaking, educated native gentlemen ready to hear, and understand, and appreciate all he has to say to them? I hope such visits from men of mark, both European and American, may henceforth be of more frequent occurrence.

One of the social gatherings held in honour of our distinguished guests was, to myself, the most interesting by far. This was an entertainment given by the Native Christian Union of Bombay. It took place in the large upper hall of the Free Church Institution, which, when all had assembled, presented quite a striking spectacle. The place was prettily decorated. Round the room sat rows of native Christians of all degrees—fathers, mothers, and children, while numerous groups occupied the centre. Many nationalities were represented, Hindus, Parsis, Europeans, Americans, East Indians, etc.; and every Mission, I think, in Bombay, contributed its quota of guests, both European and native. Many friends, too, had come from Poona and other out-stations to be present; and altogether the assemblage was large and most interesting. The costumes were, of course, very varied, and the whole scene was full of colour, and animation, and picturesqueness. It was also full of suggestiveness. One's heart could not but thrill with thankfulness and joy at such a sight.

These men and women are the fruit of missionary effort, part of the great ingathering from the Gentile world, the vision of which filled our Lord Himself with holy joy, when He said: 'I, if I be lifted up from the earth, will draw all men unto Me.'

I had the good fortune to sit beside an American stranger — a lady whose face was beaming with benevolence. 'What a sight!' she exclaimed. 'Can all these indeed be Christians? I would have come all the way from America if only to witness this scene and to meet these people. How is it,' she added, 'that people say Missions have had no success?'

How, indeed? All one can say is, that it is as if a man went forth at noonday, bandaged his eyes, and then declared that there was no sun shining in the heavens. I brought some of our nice native Christian girls to introduce to her, some of the workers in the schools and zenanas, and also some of the daughters of the bright Christian homes which now, happily, are multiplying in the land. They looked very neat and dainty in their pretty native dress, the *sari*, in different hues. I was much pleased afterwards when the lady remarked not only on their intelligence, but the modesty and general propriety of demeanour they evinced; which, indeed, is characteristic of Hindu ladies.

Among women of the higher castes in India, there is a wonderful amount of natural refinement, with a certain attractive gentleness and quiet self-restraint of manner. You feel this in visiting among them. I have gone into the most squalid and unpromising zenana, and yet found at once that I was among ladies. The poor things may be only half-clad, very sad and crushed-looking; all their surroundings (which often are little more than bare dirty walls) may be utterly sordid and mean, and yet they will receive you with all the quiet courtesy of gentlefolks. Of course, I know how easily all this can be marred, and how spoilt one of these women is if she becomes bold, or too suddenly adopts the free manners of the West. The peril lies in a too rapid transition from the restraints which Eastern customs enjoin, and a premature introduction into general society, which is public life to one who has lived her life previously in the seclusion of a Hindu home. Freedom must come, but let it come gradually—let it come last! First let *the soul* be set free! 'The soul must be educated,' as one of themselves truly says. When this takes place, when our Eastern sisters have received the truth, and the truth has made them free, then they will be free indeed; and to their own pleasant heritage of womanly decorum will be added the ornament of 'a meek and quiet spirit, which, in the sight of God, is of great price.' My new friend and I had much converse over such matters, which must be my excuse for the digression.

After tea, Mr. Cook gave us an address, which, as usual, was most stirring. In speaking of the difficulties with which missionaries have to contend, he made use of a happy illustration. He compared the work to the building of a lighthouse. He said there is so much important and preliminary labour to be done *first*, below the surface of the water—blasting of rocks, building of foundations, much buffeting with the waves—and all to be bravely endured and overcome. But when all this is accomplished, the majestic tower begins to rise. The worst is over; the difficulties are mastered; the grand purpose is achieved; the *light* appears! And, thank God, it will go on and shine for evermore.

All the strangers remarked on the beautiful exhibition of Christian union which the native Churches of India generally present. This is true. In these days of division, the brotherly love, and mutual trust, and common purpose often found existing among the Christians all over India cheer one's heart unspeakably. Long may this condition of things last!

Our beautiful Western Ghāts were as beautiful as ever as we ascended yesterday, and the railway line as striking as usual. Our train zigzagged its seemingly perilous path, first up the gentle green slopes, then, as it got higher, round precipitous crags, skirting deep gorges and stupendous precipices, pursuing its way slowly and steadily from ridge to ridge through the sinuosities of the chain, until at length we got to the top of the great mountain wall, and the huge panting engine drew up in the pretty station of Khandala. We had left the Konkan, with its wavy palm-trees, and rich tropical vegetation, and cultivated lands, and moist, warm air, lying far below on the margin by the sea, and had mounted to the brown plains and fresher air of the Deccan plateau.

I shall never forget how grand the scenery looked as we went down to Bombay a few weeks ago, soon after the rains had ceased. The face of the Ghāts was one blaze of beauty. There were waterfalls almost at every few yards: some like silver threads suspended over the cliffs, others great foaming torrents dashing down from the heights, while others were simply airy clouds of delicate spray, which, when the sun's rays caught them, gleamed exquisitely with all the hues of the prism. The whole mountain-sides were a mass of gorgeous living green. Woods and jungles, and ferns and wild flowers in endless variety and wanton profusion, clothed every slope and filled every valley, and ravine, and cleft; while the majestic mountains towered overhead in all their varied and fantastic formations—a glorious panorama. The scenery on this famous railway, the Bhore Ghāt Incline, is always grand; but in the monsoon all this beauty is added, and forms a picture which becomes engraven on the memory, and can never be effaced.

Late in the evening we reached our goal for this day—the dear old Mission House at Poona, where the warmest of welcomes always awaits us.

## CHAPTER II.

### POONA—SHOLAPORE.

*January 24th.*

WE had another exciting day, for the Cooks joined us in Poona, and were also the guests of Mr. and Mrs. Beaumont, in the Mission House. . . . .

In the evening, we all went in company to the *Hira-bāg,* to hear Mr. Cook's lecture. This is a large hall, standing by itself in some pretty grounds on the outskirts of the native city, beside a beautiful tank filled with water, on which some water-lilies float, and just under the temple-crowned, picturesque little sacred hill of Parbutty. It was from his palace on this hill that Bājirao, the last of the Peshwās, watched the famous battle of Kirkee, which decided the fate of the Maratha dynasty. The hall was densely packed with all manner of people come to hear the celebrated lecturer; and crowds stood about every door and window.

Now, as always in Poona, the striking part of the audience was the number of fine-looking, fine-featured Hindu gentlemen, the *élite* of native society, who filled the benches—remarkable-looking men, in white garb, strictly national, with huge red or white turbans, wonderfully fair in complèxion, with the keen, intellectual countenance of the Maratha Brahman.

These are Hindus of the Hindus—not half-Europeanised, like the Bengali Baboos,—though they are as thoroughly educated, and many of them first-rate speakers themselves. They are intensely national, and naturally so. Poona was the capital of the Maratha empire, and the Peshwās—the rulers—being themselves Brahmans, they were great patrons of their caste. The present inhabitants naturally look back with a wistful eye to the glories—real or imaginary—of the old days of Maratha supremacy; and whatever old national beliefs and customs they can possibly retain, they do retain. Politics seem to occupy their attention more than religion; and sometimes they, no doubt, practise the rites of Hinduism without believing in their efficacy. They are sometimes extremely severe in their criticism on the measures of Government; though most of them are far too high-minded and honourable to be consciously unjust.

Such an intelligent people are sure to advance. Education, Missionary influence, and other forces have done their work. *Destruction* of the old faith has come; but the *reconstruction* has yet to come. What is needed is a touch from the life-giving Spirit of the Living God, that the train which has been so diligently laid by all the influences at work may be fired by Divine power. Then we should see this fine, interesting people, with so many noble qualities, flocking to the feet of Christ. The pity is that Christianity comes to them as the religion of the conqueror. This circumstance, of course, increases the difficulty of the missionaries' task. But more faith and prayer and earnest work, more pleading with Him whose cause it is, would bring down that quickening power without which nothing that man can do will avail.

As I sat watching the thoughtful faces, and the effect of Mr. Cook's stirring words upon them, I could not help praying that some of those sharp arrows from above, so effectual in the Spirit's hand, would come direct to some of these men—such as was shot into the mind of Luther, when, with grand inspiration, he exclaimed: 'The just shall live by faith!' Thus would they become the best apostles and teachers of their countrymen; and the salvation of God would come to this people.

We had to leave before the meeting closed; we rushed to our train, secured a good second-class carriage to ourselves, spread our quilts on the hard benches, slept as well as we could under the circumstances, and before daybreak, shivering in the cold of the Deccan morning, we arrived at Sholapore. A special pleasure has awaited us here in being the guests of our dear old friends the Johnstones, Mr. Johnstone being now Assistant-Judge of this station. . . .

I need not describe Sholapore; it is well-trodden ground. I am not sure that it can be called a pretty station, though it is extensive and occupies a large, flat area. However, I can hardly judge; for what we ladies like best is to do nothing but sit together on long chairs, in the cool, shady, pillared verandah, chatting of old times, and of our homes and dear ones far away. The splendid baby-boy is in his swinging hammock beside us, while flocks of bright-winged, screeching, forward paroquets flit about the porch, making daring inroads on the ceiling. Sweet, silken doves are quietly building under the eaves, greeting each other and us with their plaintive coo-coo; and a gentle breeze begins to temper the mid-day heat, and make music in the trees which surround the house. . . . .

There is a flourishing branch Mission of the American Board in Sholapore, and the Rev. Mr. Gates and his wife are at the head of it. She has come of a missionary family, her father being our old friend the Rev. Mr. Hazen of Ahmednagar. I have had her on my knee when a baby. There are several of these missionary families who have done noble service in the foreign field; and many dark places of the earth would be still darker but for the energy and practical wisdom which the Americans bring to bear on all that they do. We British people, to whom India has been especially entrusted, ought to be grateful to our American friends for their zealous and successful work among the heathen.

One of the most interesting parts of Mr. Gates's Mission is the medical department. It is conducted by a native practitioner, who seems to manage it admirably. We visited him and his wife this morning, and saw their own neat little dwelling, as well as the dispensary, both under one roof, and literally smothered by a lovely mass of creeping convolvulus. The patients pay for their medicines; and it is remarkable that though there are three charitable dispensaries in the city, where medicines are free, yet the numbers who come to the Mission increased day by day. Let us hope that the medicine for their souls, which they also receive, may be part of the attraction! Mr. Gates thinks it is so, for many of the patients in their sorrow and suffering seem to hear the Word gladly.

Among those who came to-day was a native Christian from a village called Wātwad, a place about seventy-five miles north-east of Sholapore, in the Nizam's dominions. It seems that this village is the centre of an indigenous and most hopeful little Mission; and the story of the entrance of light into that dark region is so interesting that I think I must relate it.

Nearly seventeen years ago a *gosāvi*, or religious mendicant, named Mhasoba, was sent to prison by the well-known Meadows Taylor for cattle-stealing. While in prison he happily learnt to read. He had a friend, another *gosāvi*, who, after Mhasoba's release, came to him, telling him he had heard of some new, strange doctrines taught by white missionaries, and he wanted to find out what these doctrines were. 'You now can read,' he said; 'you can help me to find out what it all means.'

The two men consulted together, and decided that they would go and seek for the missionaries, who, they heard, were to be found at Sholapore. After a weary trudge of many days, to Sholapore they came.

The missionary who was labouring then at this station was Mr. Hazen, Mrs. Gates' father, who has now returned to America. He received the wayfarers most kindly, hearing their request, so similar to that of the Greeks to Philip: 'We would see Jesus.' He instructed them, gave them tracts and books, one of which was called *The True Way*, and pointed them to Him who *is* 'the Way, the Truth, and the Life.' They carried the books back to their village, where Mhasoba read them aloud to his fellow-inquirers, and the rest of the people. After much thought, and study, and earnest prayer, seeking the Lord with sincere hearts, if 'haply they might feel after Him and find Him,' they did find Him, as every real seeker does, and made up their minds that they would enter on this new way, and become Christians. But they did not quite know how; and it was years before they had an opportunity of being baptised.

At length, in the cold season of 1874, the Rev. Mr. Park, lately of the American Mission, Bombay, was itinerating in the district. Mhasoba heard of his arrival, and came twenty miles to see the missionary, and ask to be baptised. He had had no human instructor, only the little books, blessed by the teaching of the Holy Ghost; but Mr. Park found him prepared. Like the Ethiopian of old, he believed with all his heart; he had manifestly received the baptism of the Spirit, so Mr. Park administered the ordinance to him and his wife and children, and to two other men whom he had instructed.

After this, the missionaries visited the village occasionally—about once a year or so; but Mhasoba and the other converts have carried on the work themselves. He taught his daughter to read, and she now regularly teaches the other women to read, and sew, and sing. The work has spread to other villages, and now there are sixty adults and twenty-eight children baptised. These people receive no regular pecuniary help from the parent Mission in Sholapore. They work at their calling, whatever that may be, and give regularly—of their great poverty often—that Christ's cause may spread among their people. At the same time every convert seems to be an evangelist. Even the women, Mr. Gates says, go many miles to other villages, often carrying their infants in their arms, to tell other women the joyful news; and gladly are they welcomed everywhere. The people beg these Christians to come and teach them, and lead them also into the 'true way.' They have a schoolroom and a little church, which, strange to say, the heathen people in the village helped them to build. They got but very small contributions towards the buildings from the Mission funds.

These Christians are chiefly Mangs—a low caste; but physically they are fine men, and are often of manly, independent character.

After we had seen what our friends had to show us in the Mission, we went on to visit the fine old temple of Sideshwar, which occupies one side of a handsome large tank. We also saw the Fort, which covers an immense area. The walls and ramparts are in excellent preservation, and there is a wide moat all round, with some water in it, and some lovely water-lilies. A legend says that when this Fort was being built, the walls repeatedly tumbled down. This misfortune was, of course, attributed, not to any fault in the work, but to the malignity of a certain deity. So, in order to propitiate the angry god, and to cure this unsatisfactory state of matters, it was resolved to offer a human sacrifice. Accordingly a woman and a boy were buried alive in the foundations, after which the building proceeded without further accident, and the walls fell down no more. We were told that the Brahman family who had the honour of contributing the victims for the sacrifice, actually now receive a pension in consideration of this act of devotion and patriotism!

Dr. Mitchell preached twice on Sunday, the morning service being chiefly for the officials connected with the railway and their families, on each one of whom he afterwards called, meeting with the most cordial reception. Our country-people here are often thankful for the visit of a minister. In the railway community alone, in Sholapore, there are fifty-eight men and women who are Protestants, a few being East-Indian, but most are English. In the evening, the whole station gathered into the pretty little station church, and again we had a most refreshing service.

Dr. Mitchell has now proceeded along the line to hold services for other people who occupy isolated positions in out-of-the-way stations, and are often too much neglected as far as the ordinances of religion are concerned. It has been arranged that I shall rejoin him at Raichore, *en route* to Madras.

After a visit of unceasing enjoyment, having seen everything there is to see, and met everybody there is to meet in this most social abode, I prepared, with our excellent factotum, Joseph, to depart.

At two in the morning of the 26th, I turned our

friends' dwelling upside down by having to start, there being no train suitable at a less inconvenient hour; and my kindest of hosts insisted on escorting me. His influence with the powers of the railway procured me a carriage free, at least, of human company; for the rest, I spied a mighty cockroach on the cushion, glowering at me with malignant eyes at having his monopoly disturbed. He was soon dislodged, however, and I took possession, and knew little more until the dawn looked in at the windows, and woke me up to the noise and monotony, and dust and fatigue, and all the general discomfort of a long Indian railway journey. But presently, at our next halt, my prince of domestics appeared in his noiseless way at the door with a cup of tea in his hand; whence procured, I cannot tell, for Joseph is not a man of speech; 'deeds, not words,' being his motto. After this, I could look more at the bright side of things; especially as, by this time, dawn had turned to day; the sun shone joyously over the wide-spread plain, and was not yet too fiery for comfort.

The country in this part of the Deccan is not pretty. Now and then we passed towns with great gateways and the remains of fortifications, which, in the old troublous times of incessant turmoil and war, were needful for their protection. There were occasional villages also, surrounded by old mud-walls, to protect them from dacoits and marauders, and other unwelcome visitors,—now peacefully crumbling to ruin. On the outskirts of the towns there were generally a few trees to be seen; but, beyond these, our route was mostly over vast plains, brown, bare, burnt-up, and perfect solitudes, as far as human habitation went, having little and very imperfect cultivation. The stations, however, always prettily decorated with shrubs and flowers, were full of life and most amusing; and we had plenty of time to enjoy the sights they presented. Though this was the mail-train, we stopped very often, and halted very long; and, manifestly, time did not count for much.

At the station for Hyderabad, I noticed some unusually fine men, with grand, flowing beards, much latent fire in their handsome faces, and swords at their sides. They accompanied a Musulman grandee, who was seated on a remarkably beautiful black horse, with scarlet saddle-cloth, and trappings of gold and silver, whose gorgeous appearance altogether suggested Akbar, or Hyder Ali. One or two elephants, with glittering howdahs, stood in the background, tossing their fine trunks about; and these helped the illusion.

The poor women squat about the platforms, very helpless - looking, but in wonderfully picturesque groups, clothed in their Turkey-red 'cloths,' and surrounded by their little naked, brown children, and quantities of *gutries*, the inevitable bundle without which no Hindu can travel. One young creature, with dark Madrassee face, and her jet-black hair drawn to one side of her head in a huge knot, stalked past, with a bottle poised on her head, at the same time carrying an infant in her arms, and showing the utmost freedom and grace of movement. A water-chatty or basket is nothing after a bottle! How gracefully these women contrive to wear the *sari*, the long, scarf-like garment which is the usual dress of Hindu women. It is wound round the person, with the end carried over the head, after the modest fashion of most Eastern women. This garment may be coloured or white. Generally, the higher classes wear it of some colour, while servants and ayahs wear it white; but all with gay bordering round, and very elaborate ends. The prevailing colour in this region, I observe, is red in a variety of shades.

One certainly has excellent opportunities at the stations, as you pass along, of observing the marvellous variety there is, in this extraordinary country, of race, form, feature, colour, costume, head-gear, and everything. People congregate, from the most respectable of native gentry down to the wretched fakir smeared with paint and ashes, and the grinning little gipsy boys and girls, who turn somersaults and hold up their dirty little palms to the carriage windows for a pice. The interest is never-ending.

Early in the afternoon we crossed the broad bed of the Krishnā river. In the rains, this is a magnificent, sea-like stream, but now it was simply a wide expanse of sand, with a few small shallow streamlets flowing dully here and there.

Soon after this, we got to Raichore, where I spied my husband waiting on the platform. He had had one or two hearty meetings, and altogether enjoyed the little ministry in these 'regions beyond.' There are always sorrowing people, and sick, whose hearts are soft, where the furrows have gone deep, who are ready and thankful to receive the good and comforting seed of the Word into the prepared soil.

It is always a joy to minister to such; and he had been most hospitably entertained by the kindly people.

The heat is much greater here than in the regions from which we have come, and has not tended to cure my husband's fever, so it is with some anxiety we face the long night-journey before us. We changed into the carriages of the Madras Railway, and got into a tiny box of a second-class compartment, with very narrow and very hard benches; but we had it to ourselves. There was water in it, and every convenience, and it gave me occupation to battle with the thick, white, stifling dust, and keep ourselves tolerably clean.

I had noticed early in my journey that, in a compartment for women next to mine, a native lady was travelling alone, and often, when we stopped, I got out and spoke to her, sometimes going in to keep her company between two stations. She was extremely nice and intelligent, and talked Hindustani. Her husband, she told me, was in another compartment—hers being the zenana of the train. At Raichore, he introduced himself to Dr. Mitchell, and politely asked him to thank me for my attention to his wife. We found she was the daughter of Sir T. Madhavarao of Baroda, and he a Brahmin occupying a high official position in the native court of Travancore. We became great friends, and he proved to be a very clever, highly-educated man, speaking English with a purity of accent I have rarely heard from any but an Englishman. They had been at Baroda for the grand doings when the new Gaekwar was installed, and were now returning to Trevandrum. They begged us to come and see them when we ourselves should reach that place. In spite of the dreadful heat, and fatigue, and dust, we managed to get a little sleep, and about six next morning we swept into the station at Madras.

A PRIEST OF SIVA.

# CHAPTER III.

## MADRAS.

*February 1st.*

ANYONE who has undergone a hot dusty journey of twenty-six hours on hard benches in India, will comprehend how pleasant it was to feel that we had arrived; and I shall not easily forget our feeling of gratitude to Him who had so graciously 'preserved our going out and our coming in,' now, as in so many wanderings by sea and land. It was indeed a welcome sight, as we got out of our dusty little den, to spy our friend Mr. Rae, of the Free Church Mission, waiting for us; he and his wife having most hospitably claimed us as their guests. We were soon driven to the Mission Boarding School, which is their home at present, Mrs. Rae having lately undertaken the superintendence of it.

It is quite in accordance with the tradition of this good old school, that a missionary lady should be at its head. Many of our best missionaries have occupied the post, whose names deserve to be held in grateful and lasting remembrance, as having borne the heat and burden of the troublous day which saw female education started in Madras; and now it is delightful to find Mrs. Rae taking up the work heart and soul. She and hers have just removed from their pleasant, roomy house, with its grounds and garden, to the circumscribed quarters which the upper floor of this school offers. I need not add that our hostess is the author of *Morag* and some other delightful books.

She stood on the steps, as we drove up to the door, ready to welcome us, with her children at her side—fair little creatures, with curly hair, and dainty, airy attire, which looked cool in the heat of the too brilliant morning. They looked wonderingly at the strangers, but had none of the shyness most English children have. We were soon installed in our comfortable quarters, and, after a good bath and some tea, were ready for anything. The two bairnies, who soon made up their minds to be friendly, brought us out, each with a hand, to receive our first visitors. These were the two native clergymen, Mr. Rajahgopāl and Mr. Banboo, names well known to all who care for Missions. Principal Miller and Mr. Cooper, of the Christian College, speedily followed. We all breakfasted together, and ere long we had been welcomed by all the missionaries of our own Church, and many others besides.

I soon found my way downstairs among Mrs. Rae's large flock of schoolgirls and normal pupils, with their teacher, Mrs. Harris; and I was glad to find some old acquaintances among them whom I had seen on a former visit. One of the most important and interesting parts of Mrs. Rae's work is a Bible class for advanced students, which she conducts every day, Sundays and weekdays, from seven to eight in the morning. I delight in this hour, with its admirable instruction for the training of teachers and workers who are to go out by-and-by among the zenanas and day-schools.

Since the first hour of our arrival we have been as busy as possible; and it is hard to find leisure for one's pen. Our sightseeing has been almost entirely confined to schools and other operations of the kind, the single regret being that, as our time is so short, we cannot see all the work of all the Missions in this great centre as we should desire.

Madras differs in a good many points from the other cities of India we have seen. The European part is of immense extent, and has far more beauty to show than I remembered. The houses are large, two-storied, and exceedingly handsome. They are surrounded by extensive gardens and grounds, wonderfully green, and ornamented by clumps of fine trees, and shrubs, and evergreens, in all the luxuriance of beautiful tropical foliage. These residences, standing in their park-like enclosures, extend for miles chiefly along the shore, and there is a sense of delightful expansiveness everywhere as if space counted for nothing, which is extremely pleasant in so very hot a climate. This is altogether different from crowded Bombay, where every foot of ground is of value. If Washington is called the city of 'magnificent distances,' much more, I am sure, may Madras be so.

It is certainly strange for situation. It was an odd idea to plant a great city down on a long sea-shore without reference to bays or harbours, or even a reasonably safe approach by the natural way to it, the sea. On this coast the surf-wave is very dangerous: even in fine weather it rises several feet; and everyone knows what it means to land at Madras when the weather is at all tempestuous. I have found it quite exciting to watch the catamarans cut through the boiling surf on a stormy evening. They disappear entirely for a few moments, and you think it is all over with the poor fishermen-crew. But no; they hold on somehow to their frail-looking barks, and emerge presently none the worse, shaking themselves free from the white foam like so many water-dogs. The dark skins, happily, do not seem to attract the numerous sharks so readily as white ones would do in similar circumstances.

An unusually wide and beautifully-kept road stretches along the beach for miles. This is The Drive, where everyone comes of an evening for a breath of cool air from the sea, to bring some fresh life into the poor frame, weary and limp from the pitiless heat of the tropical day.

I am bound to admit that there are two drawbacks to the full enjoyment of a visit to Madras; the wearing heat, which is terribly trying even in the so-called 'cold weather,' and the unspeakable plague of mosquitoes, which seem to be of the most malignant, wicked type. They attack one with a fierce pertinacity I have seldom seen equalled; they buzz, sting, stab, until you are fairly driven frantic with the irritation to both nerves and skin.

One of the first objects which would attract your notice, if you should happen to cast anchor in the roadstead of Madras, would be the line of handsome

MADRAS SURF.

buildings which form the head-quarters of the old-established and well-known Free Church Mission. First in the line comes the Boarding School, corresponding in decoration and appearance with its next neighbour, the Christian College, which is a very handsome and extensive building. Next comes the Free Church, and, last, the Evangelistic Memorial Hall. These present an imposing front to the sea, and certainly give the Mission a striking and desirable visibility in the eyes of the natives. There is a new and handsome verandah added to this school, which is our favourite haunt. It is shady and cool, and bowery with numbers of pretty plants; for here, as everywhere in and about the house, the æsthetic tastes of its mistress are apparent.

From the verandah there is a glorious view of the sea. It stretches before us a vast expanse, bounded by the wide horizon, the waters of the darkest blue, generally restless and crested with white, and sometimes wildly tumultuous, rising, when there is anything of a storm, to grand sublimity, and looking the very type of power, as one magnificent billow after another comes rolling up with thundering din, and breaks on the rocky shore. But, usually, at this season 'old Ocean smiles'; and the dancing, sparkling blue below is responsive to the sunlit blue of the sky above. Then the scene is beautiful. Or when the golden light of evening floods both earth and sea, as now, while I write, and a tender peace steals over everything, even this restless, tossing tide. The heart then seems filled with corresponding peace, and all things within and without blend in harmony. Then it is as if one united 'sacrifice of praise' rose to Him who gave the beauty and the peace, and who is Himself 'the first good, first perfect, and first fair.'

> 'For the beauty of each hour
>   Of the day and of the night,
> Hill, and vale, and tree, and flower,
>   Sun and moon, and stars of light,
> Christ, our Lord, to Thee we raise
> This our sacrifice of praise.'

Why Madras has been called the 'benighted Presidency' is always a puzzle to me. At all events, it no longer deserves the epithet; for, I believe, there is no city in India where education and missionary enterprise have had more success. Female education especially has made most encouraging progress, and this is always a test of enlightenment and advance. We have spent one of the most interesting and delightful mornings I remember in seeing the Christian College, under the auspices of its able and excellent Principal, Dr. Miller. He took us all over it, from the lowest class-room for beginners to the highest section for the advanced students of the college.

This noble catholic institution has grown out of the Free Church Institute, which was founded by the Rev. J. Anderson in 1837. It is still maintained chiefly by the Free Church; but the Church Missionary and Wesleyan Societies also contribute to its support, and the professors are drawn from various Evangelical Churches. The story is still told how, at its commencement, the death-blow was given to all caste distinctions within its walls. The year after it was opened, the admirable John

Anderson admitted two very low-caste boys, with the immediate result that the whole of the two-hundred and fifty good-caste pupils took their departure. Great commotion followed. Pressure was brought to bear on the bold innovator to get him to eject the offending Pariahs; but he was firm as a rock. No; he went on with his two low-caste

A WATER-CARRIER.

pupils until the rest should come to their senses, which they gradually did. They thought better of it, and returned; and from that day to this the claims of caste have had no recognition in this college, though planted in the very heart of this caste-ridden Presidency.

Again, this uncompromising missionary told his pupils openly that his grand object and aim was to teach them Christ and His religion, and win their countrymen for Him; consequently, the chief feature of his teaching would be the Christian's book—the Bible, the Word of God. That was the chief feature in Mr. Anderson's time; and I am glad to say it is the chief feature still. The most interesting and stirring classes we saw were those for Bible knowledge; and, judging from the attention of the pupils, and the eager, earnest look with which they received the lesson, I should say that the Bible class is one of the most popular in the work of the day.

Unfortunately, the college is not yet in full working order, as the pupils are only gathering after the recess. The results of the University examinations have not yet been made known; consequently, it is not possible to reconstruct the classes. But the class-rooms are full, and the benches crowded; and still candidates for admission are flocking to the doors. Every boy puts himself into as small a space as possible, trying to make room for a friend; but, after all, many have to be refused. It was sad to see numbers of disappointed lads hanging about the corridors disconsolate when not another one could possibly be admitted. The school, already so large, could be increased to any extent if there was only more room. Indeed, the pursuit of knowledge presented itself in some of its droll aspects, especially in the rooms for beginners, where you find the very rawest material. I noticed one tall, lanky youth towering beside a very small boy with a high white cap on his head like that of a French cook, who stood next above him in the class. The wee fellow hardly came to the other's knee, but he was as keen as a needle, and preternaturally quick. He kept surreptitiously prompting his tall friend, who had evidently begun learning too late in life, though he was intensely earnest about it. It was touching to see the two, the little one trying to hide the deficiencies of the older, and looking all the time out of the corner of his quick eye to see whether Dr. Miller noticed, which, of course, he did, but said nothing; he only smiled at the small Ramasamy, and gave a playful pinch to his ear as we were going out.

The large classes filled with such motley material were most interesting, and rather picturesque. The head-gear was especially remarkable and varied, the huge white bunchy turban predominating. There were no bare heads with short-cropped hair, as in Bengal; every head had something on it in the shape of turban. The Madrassees are dark-complexioned—more so a good deal than the Marathas—with open, good-humoured expression, and more thoughtful in look than sharp or intellectual. I think it was all more novel and interesting in this transition state than if everything had been in shape as usual, and the students at their ordinary work. Poor fellows! I was very sorry for some of them, waiting to know the result of the University examinations. There was a look of expectancy on some of the faces, and of sore anxiety on others; some seemed full of despair, and others defiant. What was their fate to be? Who would 'pass'?

Who would be 'plucked'? These were the momentous questions which were pressing on every heart. One could not but sympathise,—so much depended upon it in their future, and yet it was difficult to suppress a smile at some of the countenances, so full of woe.

Their kind master understood them all. He addressed many by name (and the Madras names are so puzzling to a new ear), individualising each among the hundreds present; spoke words of cheer to some, of playful reproach to others, and of sympathy and kindness to all. I was amazed to see how he could keep all their different cases in his memory—like a doctor among his patients; but many a nice, good, honest face looked brighter after Dr. Miller had passed through and dropped a kind and stimulating word here and there. He has manifestly gained the entire confidence and affection of the lads. He is the moving spirit of the whole; but he is most ably seconded by an admirable staff of missionary professors and native teachers. We saw Mr. Paterson amid his philosophical and chemical apparatus, Mr. Rae at his delightful Bible class; and, indeed, all of them—each at his own particular and important work.

It is indeed a noble institution, numbering over 1,300, taking school and college together. It is acknowledged to be the most influential of all the educational institutions in South India, and in advance of all similar establishments in this city in attendance, popularity, and in the number of men it now passes. In University honours it stands first. But, what is of infinitely more importance, the whole influence, the genius of the place, is

Christianity. The flower of the youth of South India are here presented with Bible truth by men who are themselves deeply imbued with the spirit of truth; and thus this college is a centre whence Christian enlightenment is spreading, surely and steadily, not only in the city of Madras, but in all the Presidency.

A YOGI ENGAGED IN MEDITATION.

## CHAPTER IV.

### MADRAS—FEMALE WORK.

We have had two or three good mornings' work in seeing the Girls' Schools connected with our own Mission. I am sorry we have had time for hardly any others. One day, our friend Mr. Rajahgopāl called for us, and took us over those in which he has special interest, and another day Mr. and Mrs. Bauboo conducted us in like manner over a number which they have ably superintended for many years. These were all day-schools, admirably conducted, and both attractive and interesting.

Female education has made very considerable progress in Madras. It has had a chequered history, like similar efforts in the other Presidencies. There was a fight, of course, at the commencement—a hard struggle with seemingly insuperable difficulties—ups and downs, hopes and fears; but with determination, energy, perseverance, and unfailing faith, the cause has been fought by every missionary who successively settled in the country. The early Danish missionaries tried to establish schools for girls; and every society which came after them followed their example, and did its best. Some brave and devoted women, whose names are still remembered with veneration, succeeded, after many self-denying efforts, in establishing orphanages and a few small day-schools. But their experience was the same as that of all the early workers in the same cause; they could only manage to reach the very lowest of the people. A few orphans were gathered in, and some poor children of the lowest castes; and this was so far a happy commencement, and answered its own important end: but the great Hindu community remained utterly untouched. It was reserved for three Scottish missionaries—a singular triumvirate of much-honoured men, Messrs. Anderson, Johnstone, and Braidwood—to succeed, and establish what we may really call female education in this part of India. They had successfully introduced high-class English education for the men; and now, with immense difficulty, by very slow degrees, and by God's blessing and help, they accomplished the same for the women.

It was in 1843 that Mrs. Braidwood managed to get in the thin end of the wedge, by gathering a few good-caste girls into what is still called the 'Madras Girls' Day School.' Graphic pictures are often given on the spot of the way she toiled and struggled, and how the gentlemen aided by bringing their influence to bear on the young husbands and brothers who were being taught in the Institution, or English School. Indeed, without the co-operation of these educated young men, the work could never have been done. She added the inducement of liberal presents, both in money and dress, and so the end was achieved, and she had the joy of seeing a few gathered in to receive the merest elements of education; of course in their mother-tongue.

Mrs. Anderson joined the Mission soon after, and threw herself heart and soul into the grand work. It is delightful to think that this excellent lady is still in the field, and with plenty of freshness and vigour. She is now watching over her spiritual children and children's children in the native Church; and she is a mother in Israel to the whole community. It was a great pleasure indeed to meet her again.

So the great question was practically settled. Female education, once fairly started, went steadily on. The prejudice of ages began to give way; and no one can doubt that the movement thus commenced will eventually work a great social and religious revolution in the condition of the people.

But in 1847 a check was experienced from the very success of the work. Five of the pupils became Christians, and were baptised. This created a panic, and the school was emptied for a time. The five girls took refuge in the Mission house; but a home was needed for them, and for others who, through God's blessing on the scriptural teaching, might happily follow their example. This resulted in the formation of the Boarding School, which was thus begun as an asylum and school for Christian girls, and has ever since been as a nursery for Christ in the Mission. The Day School—the first, as I said, for caste-girls ever opened in the city—soon recovered from the shock it had received by reason of the baptisms. It was soon as full as ever. Other schools were opened in other parts, and now there are *twelve* such day-schools in connection with the Free Church, having an aggregate attendance of over 1,400. Altogether, counting also the pupils in the zenanas, those in poor and ragged schools, those in the Boarding School for Christian Girls, and the students in the Normal School, we have the large number of 1,800 females under Christian instruction.

Other agencies, also, are at work, such as zenana-teaching, Sunday-schools, and Bible-women's work. The people generally are eager for education; the women want it for themselves, and the men want it for their wives and daughters. Thus, the little seed planted with so many tears, but with patience and faith and prayer, forty years ago, has grown into a goodly tree, which—who can doubt?—will one day fill the land. One thing which has struck us in visiting the schools is, that the buildings and class-rooms are so suitable and good. I confess I covet similar ones for other places not so highly favoured.

Mr. Rajahgopāl's new building for his Chetty school is specially handsome—a cool, convenient, spacious house, with verandahs, stone floors, green blinds, benches, and plenty of bright pictures on the walls, including one of Her Majesty the Queen. I only wish the friends of the cause at home could see the winsome little creatures who fill the rooms—so dainty and bedizened, so intelligent, too, and bright, —answering the questions put to them with eager readiness, their wonderful dark eyes fixed on your face all the time in a way, to me, quite bewitching. Their knowledge of Bible history would have done credit to any Sunday-school in Scotland. They questioned each other, too, in an amusing way; and to hear them sing such hymns as 'Jesus loves me,' and their own sweet Tamil lyrics, was a delight not to be forgotten.

The Chetties are a very good caste, though lower than Brahmans, and are the merchants of Madras. Like other good castes, they keep entirely to themselves, and do not intermarry with any other.

They still manifest much opposition to the Gospel, and do not quite like the Christian teaching for their girls. So they have set up some opposition schools, in which the education is gratis, while we charge fees. Still, mission work among them goes steadily on, making progress both among the children, and the women in their homes. Some most encouraging incidents showing this were related to me by Mr. Rajahgopāl; but I am afraid it would not be prudent to tell them here. The Chetties are a very rich community, and the amount of beautiful jewels they heap on their children is wonderful to see.

Mr. Rajahgopāl has a capital Ragged-school, which was one of the most interesting we saw. He has some two hundred and fifty poor little boys and girls, all of them waifs or orphans, many of whom are fed and clothed, and all have more or less education given them. It is very nice to see them occupying delightful premises lent to Mr. Rajahgopāl by Government, with excellent schoolrooms, a large compound, in which there is plenty of room to play, and fine fresh air. An industrial department added would be a great boon, with trades for the boys, and some simple, paying industry for the girls.

But what, I think, delighted me most in all that we saw was Mr. Bauboo's Normal School, which is one most important part of his work. I cannot tell the interest with which I looked at the forty pupils and talked to them—all well-educated, intelligent, Christian young women, pleasant and bright in manner, and cultivated in appearance. It was most delightful to think of the possibilities for the future they presented in increase of schools and other work for women; for these students are pledged to become teachers, and as soon as they are ready they are drafted into work of some sort. From the Boarding School, also, and Dr. Elder's schools, and Mr. Rajahgopāl's, pupils have passed the Government Teachers' examinations; and it is one of the most hopeful features of the work that most of the teachers in the day-schools are well-trained native Christian women.

A great quantity of pretty needlework was displayed in every school, and the children and their mothers like it, and are proud of their achievements in the way of rugs, cushions, slippers, and smoking-caps. They are also fond of their little hymns, and sing them with might and main both in school and in their homes.

Of course, Bible-teaching is the chief feature in every kind of school; but all the instruction is first-rate. There is a Government Inspectress to see that the work is thorough, and up to the prescribed standards; and grants in aid are provided by Government. In one point, I am sorry to say, Madras is just as much behind as other places—girls are not allowed to remain in school after they are married;

and early marriage is, unhappily, as much the rule now as it has been for ages. You hardly see a pupil in the classes over thirteen, and most of the children are under ten. Zenana-visiting, then, is as important here as elsewhere, in order that the girls, after they are betrothed, may be followed to their homes, and their education—only commenced really in school—may be carried on and completed. There is this happy difference between the women of Madras and their sisters in Bengal—they are not so much shut up—their houses are not so like prisons. I fancy that the Mohammadan conquest did not influence the South so much as other parts of India, and consequently did not revolutionise society by introducing Mohammadan customs—pre-eminently those affecting the treatment of women. But in character the women are all much alike. They ask the same foolish questions here about your children and husband, and your motives for coming to India, and especially why you visit them. It seems hard for them to believe that the only reason is to try and do them good.

It ought to be confessed that zenana-visiting is often trying and disappointing. Thus, on a little tour to-day, accompanying Miss Oxley, of the Church of England Zenana Society, we visited in the house of a Persian gentleman, whose ladies kept us waiting, and then appeared in fine English clothes, put on, I suppose, in honour of our visit. The dresses were made in the very height of Paris fashion, of rose-coloured and pale blue silk! But with their rich olive complexion, and generally Oriental style, they did not look quite so ridiculous as you would suppose. They would talk of nothing but clothes, and wanted to examine every article we had on. This is the sort of thing which tries the zenana visitor. However, there was a strong redeeming point in two bright, intelligent young girls, very fair and pretty, who are Miss Oxley's pupils, and full of interest in what they read, and desire to learn. They seemed rather ashamed of their gay, talkative elder relatives.

Let us, then, sympathise with our dear zenana missionaries, and help them with our prayers, thanking God always because these sad homes have been penetrated, and because *we know* that there are not a few within their walls who have learned to know and love Christ through the loving labours of the missionaries. These are of Christ's 'hidden ones,' and, though not known to the world, they are known to Him. Ah! they sometimes ask questions very different from those I have alluded to. They gaze at you with those large, liquid eyes, which look as if the fountain of their tears was very close, and ask, 'Why are we so different from you? Could *we* not enjoy the world, and be *free* like you?' They are, indeed, more to be pitied now than ever. Why? Because a glimmering of light has penetrated the darkness of these homes; *they see their bonds.* Formerly they did not know they were bound. Now they do; and they have a suspicion that a better fate might be theirs. The fair world outside they too might enjoy; there is a position they might attain to—a Father above who might be theirs as well as ours. 'You are like that dove,' said one young woman to me, pointing to a bird on the wing. 'You are like that bird soaring to heaven: we are like that same bird caught, its wings clipped, and shut up in a cage too narrow to hold it.' A common-place illustration, but how touching and true!

Mrs. Rae and I had nearly experienced one of those little misadventures this morning to which one is prone in a 'city of magnificent distances,' as I said Madras is. We set out at eleven in a 'bandy.' Let me explain that a bandy is the cab of Madras, a narrow, oblong box set on four little wheels, with high, hard seats, a well to contain your feet, and venetian windows, which will neither let down nor go up. It rattles loudly, and is drawn by a lean and hungry-looking horse, which is made to go spasmodically by the long handle of the whip continually applied to his flanks. The half-clad, keen-witted driver is perched aloft on the roof.

We drove for many miles through fiery heat and blinding glare and dust, to call on a lady I particularly wanted to see. When we drew up at length below the porch of a splendid mansion, a small box was handed to us by 'the boy' at the door, a scarlet-robed, white-bearded official, with a belt across his breast. The box had a slit in the top, like a child's missionary box, and the words 'Not at home' faced us in big, portentous letters.

In answer to our remonstrances, the civil 'boy' assured us that Madam was out. We deposited our cards in the slit, and, hot and grumbling, told the weary driver to turn his weary beast again to the road. We were hardly at the gate, however, when the man came shouting after us. Madam, after all, *was* at home, and would like to see us. Most pleasant it was to exchange the hot, dusty bandy for the cool shady pretty drawing-room, and have the talk we wanted, with the agreeable, lady-like woman, who welcomed us with great cordiality and warmth.

On our return, my husband joined us, and we looked in at the Government Normal School, superintended by Miss Rajahgopāl, where Europeans and East Indians chiefly are trained. We were specially pleased with the preparatory school in connection with it, in which there is a charming Infant department, conducted on the Kindergarten system. Here we saw groups of happy little bright creatures, busy playing at learning. They dance, and sing, and march, and learn their lessons under the guise of fun. This is all carried on by the Normal pupils, who are thus taught to teach after the best, and brightest, and most sensible plan.

It is curious how much more English is talked in Madras than either in Bombay or Calcutta. You hear it everywhere. Not only do the servants address you in tolerably good English, but the poor bandy-men, and even the coolies on the street, seem to know a smattering. It is often an odd jumble as to idiom, but not the monstrosity that 'pidgin English' is in China. This prevalence of our own language is a great comfort to strangers like ourselves, to whom the unknown tongues of the South are a perplexity and a drawback. For once, we have the sorrow of being unable to speak to the people of India in their own tongue. Hindustani is a sort of *lingua franca,* which carries one almost anywhere else; but it is of little use in Madras.

Tamil is the chief language of the people here; but there are four or five Southern tongues which are as closely allied to each other as the languages of Southern Europe. These belong to the Dravidian dialects, which, of course, differ entirely from Marathi or Hindi, or any which come mainly from the Sanscrit, though my husband says Sanscrit words are freely introduced into them. Of these languages Tamil seems to be the most cultivated, though it sounds to the ear harsh and unpleasant, the words running into each other in a sort of rippling stream, instead of distinct utterance. Tamil has a literature of no small antiquity. There is, for example, a great ethical poem in it called 'Kural,' the work of Tiruvallavar, who is as great a man among the Tamil people, as much revered—one might almost say worshipped—as the poet Tukārám is among the Marathas. In regard to *race,* the Hindu element is comparatively small in the populations of the South. The Hindu *religion,* on the contrary, has penetrated to a large extent; though, on the other hand, it has itself been powerfully affected by the demonology of the Dravidian races.

Soon after the sun rose this morning, we drove over to the Free Church Mission House, where Mr. and Mrs. Stevenson reside, and spent the cool early hours in wandering over the beautiful garden and compound with Mr. Stevenson, who is the Secretary of the Mission. We afterwards breakfasted with the family, and met some pleasant friends. Here we had the pleasure of making Miss Cross's acquaintance, a lady who came out to *see* Mission work in the schools and among the women, and has had her heart so stirred by its needs and its absorbing interest that she has stayed to take part in it. Would that many more of our good Christian ladies at home, who are without any great object to fill their lives, would come and do likewise! She goes daily to the girls' schools with Mr. or Mrs. Bauboo, and is already attracting the children to her and doing good service among them.

In the afternoon, Mrs. Rae drove me to the European Orphan Asylum—a large, commodious building standing in extensive, park-like grounds, with lovely greensward and a wealth of splendid trees. It was the day of the annual fête and prize-giving, and it was a great pleasure to see the little white boys and girls, children of our own country-people, so well-cared for and so happy. A band was playing in the centre of the garden; and plenty of flags floated gaily everywhere; merry-go-rounds and games were in full swing; Christmas-trees stood on open green spots, loaded with pretty presents; the relatives of the children, and many visitors, were roaming about, or regaling themselves with tea or ices under the trees; while the rich soft lights of the tropical evening streamed through the high-arching boughs, glinted across the sward, and sent a golden gleam over the whole scene. We also roamed about, talked to many friends, had some tea, and greatly enjoyed the cool evening air, and pretty, gay, cheery scene.

*February 2nd.*

Another of these little school fêtes has taken place, and I had a very special and delightful interest in it. It was the annual exhibition of the high-caste girls' day-schools connected with our own Mission; and, through the kindness of Mr. Stevenson, the Secretary, and Mr. Bauboo, the Superintendent, I had the honour of being invited to give away the prizes. I need not say what a pleasure this was to me. The pretty fête was held in the school in Black Town, which was originally founded by Mrs. Braidwood; and when the eventful day came, Mr. and Mrs. Rae drove us to the place. It is a large good house, standing in a garden which is full of green loveliness from the kind gifts of a native gentleman, who is a lover of flowers, and happily also, a lover of children. I think it was the same friend who presented a little fountain to the school, which was now playing, throwing sparkling jets of water over a mass of lovely ferns in pots, prettily grouped about the base. Flags were flying, picturesque crowds were standing about as the carriage drove up, and the whole place looked festal.

As we entered the large upper hall where the distribution was to take place, the scene was singularly striking and pretty. The upper end of the room was filled with visitors; and I observed many native gentlemen present, with the dark, strong, good Madrassee face, surmounted by a huge turban. Facing the door, there was a lovely erection, a sort of canopy supported by tiny columns, which were all wreathed over with exquisite fronds of delicate and rare ferns. It looked a fairy bower, entirely fashioned as it was of the long, graceful, feathery fronds of freshest green, and was really the prettiest decoration of the kind I have ever seen. Below the canopy was a table loaded with the beautiful prizes, and chairs for those who were to have the honour of being the principal actors in the day's proceedings.

But the grand attraction was at the lower end of the hall, which was filled with a glittering and most fascinating crowd of small creatures, bespangled and bejewelled to an extraordinary degree. The young women of the Normal Class, the Christian teachers, and the bigger girls, all in their pretty, simple costumes, were ranged behind, and made a most effective background; while the throng of little ones, packed closely in front, looked one gorgeous mass of jewels, and flowers, and fine clothes. You could hardly see the sweet little brown faces for the fringes of gold and silver which hung across the foreheads, and the flowers which decked almost every head; while the armlets and anklets, and bracelets and necklaces, and nose-rings and toe-rings and ear-rings, and all the amazing things they wore, would make a list far too long to number. Poor little things, some could hardly walk for the weight of their finery when they came up to get their prizes.

These were very handsome indeed, and the curious thing was that they were all gifts from non-Christian Hindu gentlemen, friends of the Bauboos, and I may well add, friends of the schools. The prizes included three lovely gold medals, and one or two of silver. The medals had been struck in Scotland, one side bearing an inscription and the name of the successful competitor, and on the reverse, a representation of the Burning Bush, with the usual legend round it: *Nec tamen consumebatur!*

The proceedings were what are customary on such occasions. The singing was frequent, and specially beautiful. An encouraging and very interesting report was read by the superintendent, Mr. Bauboo; addresses were given by Dr. Mitchell and Mr. Stevenson, while I confess to have been very much in my element bestowing the beautiful boxes and books and toys on the happy children, and fastening the medals round their necks, with ribbon as true-blue as the decorations themselves!

When all was over, a dear little mite of a child came toddling up to me for a doll. She was a most quaint little figure, arrayed in a stiff, white muslin skirt, bordered with gold, which reached to her pretty little feet. But it was gathered in so full beneath her broad waistband of silver, that when I took her on my lap the whole thing stood out like a frill. So we placed her standing on a chair, and, with her little hands clasped together, she said a hymn in the prettiest way. It was quite touching to hear her; and then she repeated, 'Suffer little children to come unto Me,' in Tamil. This was the child of heathen parents! If we could only have pulled the finery off, she would have looked like a little bronze cherub.

In his report, Mr. Bauboo had told us of the examinations which had been conducted previously; and quoted some very laudatory remarks from the reports of the different examiners. Altogether, the condition of the schools, as to numbers and attendance, the amount of fees paid, and the attainments of the scholars, seemed to be highly satisfactory to their excellent superintendents, to the parents—that is, the fathers, for of course the mothers were not present,—to the missionaries, and to us all.

There are two flourishing Sabbath-schools in connection with these caste-girls' schools; and though the attendance is not compulsory, yet many of the pupils do attend. Of course, the instruction is entirely religious; and more than this, these little Hindu children bring voluntary offerings to put into the missionary box. Mrs. Bauboo told me that from these offerings they had last year given contributions to the Tract Society, to Dr. Elder's Medical Mission, and a good sum (I forget how much) to support a Bible-woman, who was to work in connection with the Mission in the *Pettah* where the schools are. Is not this a most cheering and uncommon fact in connection with a school composed entirely of heathen children? There are also two hundred and fifty of these volunteer Sunday scholars who would not lose the lesson on any account. On one occasion, when their teacher could not venture to go at the hour, because of a tremendous thunderstorm, on arriving somewhat late, she found several little creatures assembled notwithstanding the nature of the weather. The eldest had given out a hymn, and they were singing it when she came in. The dear little creatures! It would have been sweet to hear that hymn.

# CHAPTER V.

## CHINGLEPUT.

*February 4th.*

We are sitting in a large, cool, airy chamber, opening off a shady verandah, in the midst of profound and most restful quiet; truly a great contrast to the racket and roar, and heat and bustle of the great city.

Chingleput is one of the branch stations of our Mission in Madras; there are others also quite as interesting; but, alas! our time only allows of a visit to this one. The missionaries are Mr. and Mrs. Andrew, who were sent forth from Glasgow some two or three years ago; and we have come to-day that we may have the joy of spending to-morrow with them, and seeing their Sabbath work. On the previous Sabbath, Dr. Mitchell had preached in Madras,—in the Free Church, in the Tamil Church, and also in the church connected with Dr. Elder's important medical work, giving sundry lectures besides during the week.

We started about seven. It was one of those warm, cloudy mornings so frequent, seemingly, here, when it is hard even to breathe, there being nothing bright or elastic in the heavy air.

Near Madras, the country is generally flat, though green, with some fine wood. There is a distant background of mountains, however, with one or two low, isolated hills in the neighbourhood of the city. One of these is St. Thomas's Mount, so called from the tradition, preserved especially among the Syrian Christians, of St. Thomas's visit to this place. There is an old church, I believe, on the summit, which is held in reverence still among the Syrians and Portuguese. As you approach Chingleput, the character of the scenery changes, though it is only two hours by train from Madras; there are some low, undulating hills, green and picturesque, and it seems to be a beautiful little place.

Mr. Andrew met us, and we drove hither in a bandy clothed in a thick white quilted cover, which was most kindly sent to fetch us by the Station Judge. These white draperies give the carriages rather a droll look; but they are a famous protection to the occupants from the fierce rays of the tyrant sun. The horses also are often decorated; in their case with *sola topees*, or sun hats, a most benevolent arrangement, though having a particularly odd effect. We drove through a long, clean bazaar, called the Brahman Street, for in this caste-ridden Presidency no one of lower caste may live in the quarter sacred to these 'gods on earth,' as the Brahmans call themselves. Brahmanical influence is exceedingly strong here; and caste rules with a rod of iron. The Brahmans try to keep every post in their own hands; and the Sudras and lower castes do not get a chance if they can help it. It is still true, in many places, that a Pariah must not only not touch the sacred person of a Brahman, but he must not come within such range that there can be the possibility of his shadow falling on the holy man, or on the path he treads! I have often seen a low-caste man get out of the way, go up a bank, and even get behind a hedge, until a Brahman has gone on his way. Such is the fearful tyranny which this extraordinary law of caste still exercises over this fair land, with all its ancient boasted civilisation and its modern education and enlightenment! Nowhere, I believe, is caste feeling stronger than in the South; nowhere does it bind the people more inexorably in its cruel fetters, which nothing can break but the God-sent religion of Jesus Christ, which makes all men brethren.

Christianity is making way, but least among these proud Brahmans, to whom the preaching of its doctrines is as yet 'foolishness.' I do not think we have seen in other parts of India that the Brahmans live entirely in streets by themselves, aloof from all the rest of the population.

Passing from the native town, we turned into this pretty compound, where there are some fine trees, underneath which the grass is almost as green as on an English lawn. We stopped at the long, low bungalow with its deep verandah, which is prettily embellished with creepers, and plants and flowers in pots. It was indeed a restful moment when Mrs. Andrew showed me into this large, cool room, where the quiet is perfect. A sweet peace, as of the Sabbath, reigns, which is very delightful after the toiling and moiling, and all the interest and pleasure which have been crushed into the past busy week. For, besides our own special calling—seeing schools and all manner of Mission work, we have enjoyed an extraordinary amount of the hospitality for which

Madras is proverbial. We have been at some most pleasant entertainments, and have met many delightful people, including all the missionaries, I think,—who were invited by Dr. Miller to meet us at different times. . . . .

Now there is not a sound but the song of birds, or the chirrup of the merry little squirrels as they gambol beneath the eaves, or the caw of the ever-present son of the soil, the crow, or an occasional cry from poor little Jacko, a tiny monkey, who sits on a perch outside, whom I at once propitiated by an offering of plantains. It is all very rural and sweet, and much cooler than Madras. The single note of a small, scarlet-breasted bird, called by the natives in the Maratha country *sālunki*, now fills the still air, and is delicious in its plaintive sweetness. My husband tells me this dear little bird is mentioned by the great Marathi poet, Tukarām, in lines something like this:

> When the sweet sālunki
> Her clear note outpoureth,
> God gives, as she soareth,
> All the rapture.

After breakfast, the servants, and some other people, came trooping in to prayers, which Mr. Andrew conducted in Tamil. They sat cross-legged on the floor, having first reverently removed their turbans. Mr. and Mrs. Andrew just now are having some hours' hard work at the language, which they are studying with great diligence and success.

In the afternoon, Mrs. Andrew took me out in her little pony-carriage (the gift of her father), to show me the place where their lot is cast as ambassadors for Christ among the heathen. The native town is exceptionally clean and tidy, and tolerably prosperous-looking. The different castes seem to inhabit different streets. We saw only the outside of the Mission buildings now, and then went the Five-mile Round, which is a beautiful drive over undulating downs, by a succession of low hills, at once rocky and green. Some rise in short ranges, while some are isolated, with little smiling valleys between. The scenery altogether, with its green undulations and picturesque knolls and valleys, and tiny round hill-tops, put me a good deal in mind of Japan. There is plenty of water visible ; the country is well cultivated and irrigated, and the tiny rice-fields looked very pretty, filled with the tender green of the young plant. The sun was near his setting, flooding the beautiful scene with a glow of amber light.

We got back to the Institution, or English School, just in time for a lecture which Dr. Mitchell gave on Japan and China. There was an excellent audience, composed entirely of men, excepting two or three English ladies who were present. Mr. Hope, the judge, was in the chair ; who afterwards, with his pleasant wife, drove us all home to their house to dinner, and we spent a most agreeable evening.

Next day, being the Sabbath, was filled with services, beginning in the early morning with a large Sunday-school of over one hundred and twenty pupils, all heathen, and many of them grown lads. Dr. Mitchell gave them an address on the story of Nicodemus, and afterwards put questions which were readily answered, showing considerable Scripture knowledge. Tamil services followed, both in the forenoon and afternoon, the congregations being composed of Tamil Christians. Dr. Mitchell preached through an interpreter ; and a busy and delightful day was finished by his conducting the usual English service in the evening, which Mr. Andrew holds for the benefit of the English residents, there being no chaplain in the place.

What busy lives our missionaries lead! This Sunday at Chingleput, so filled with work, is a type of many Sundays we have spent in the Mission stations which it has been our great privilege in our wanderings to visit. Both on Sundays and weekdays an amount of hard, anxious, harassing work has to be got through which would astonish those who neither know nor care, and which ought to call forth deep consideration and sympathy toward the missionaries personally, as well as earnest prayer that they may be strengthened in body and mind, and upheld in this work, which seems to me so exceptionally arduous.

Next morning we were again early astir. Life begins betimes in India; at least, with those who care to utilise the cool, fresh, delicious morning hours. The gentlemen, accompanied by two evangelists, 'went forth to sow.' They went boldly to the Brahmans' quarter first, and were at least civilly received. My husband found a priest who knew Marathi, with whom he had much deeply interesting conversation, and left some little books with him. The evangelists everywhere always begin with singing, which at once attracts a gathering.

The people are very fond of hymns and lyrics, and gather in crowds to listen. The preaching follows, and, happily, here there does not seem to be much active opposition. Many seem now to hear gladly. But the difficulty everywhere is the same: the people lack the earnestness, or moral courage, which would lead them to profess what in their hearts they believe to be true.

After breakfast, we visited the Schools, both for girls and boys. In the Institution, we had a most lively time as Dr. Mitchell put the classes—filled with crowds of fine, intelligent, eager lads—through their facings,—a process they seemed greatly to enjoy. The building, which is spacious and airy, and all on one floor, was erected to commemorate an excellent man, who once was Judge in the station, Mr. Morehead, and who had always taken the most cordial interest in Missions. By his influence and personal efforts, he did much to promote the good cause in Chingleput; and, after his death, this excellent Institution was built as a lasting and useful monument to his memory.

As usual, I was greatly interested with the groups of dainty little creatures that filled the long, low, cool class-rooms in the Girls' School. There were over a hundred pupils present, all children of good-caste parents, and were under the charge of one of the nicest native Christian ladies I have met. This was Mrs. Zynul-abidene (I am always afraid to trust myself with Madras names). Mrs. Anderson, of Madras, called her 'My dear Barbara,' and I like best to remember her thus. She is the head-mistress; and it is easy to see that she does her work among the little ones quite *con amore.* She is the daughter of one of Mr. Anderson's converts, and the wife of another. It is touching to meet the traces and fruits of the labours of the first Scotch missionaries, Messrs. Anderson, Johnstone, and Braidwood, everywhere here. If you find an exceptionally interesting, mellowed old Christian, he is sure to say: 'I was baptised by Mr. Anderson.'

In the afternoon, we took leave of our kind friends and returned to Madras, by the slowest train, I think, it has been my misfortune to travel by. I am sure we could have walked a little faster.

But our day was not finished; we arrived just in time for a meeting of the Missionary Conference, which was held in the Raes' drawing-room. They had most kindly conceived the idea of accelerating the usual meeting by a week, that we might be present. There was an immense gathering of missionaries, with many other friends. Among them was a young German lady we had met before, who is now engaged in zenana work. She cheered us much by saying that words we had spoken to her in Nice years ago had led her, by God's blessing, to devote her life to the women of India. How grateful I felt!

The meeting proved intensely interesting. After Mr. Rae had introduced my husband, and he had spoken a little, he was well questioned regarding the Mission fields he had visited, especially China and Japan. Then his turn came to question, and in reply many most important facts and opinions were brought out regarding Southern India, and the condition of the work in this region. These were very valuable from such men as Dr. Scudder and Mr. Noyes, two of the oldest and most experienced of the American missionaries, Mr. Sell of the C.M.S., Dr. Chamberlain, Dr. Elder, Mr. Rajahgopāl, Mr. Satyanādhan, and many others.

Particularly cheering was the testimony which every speaker bore to the decided *rise* there is in the condition of the converts, in position, standing, intelligence, and also in the still more important matter of moral and religious character. Unfortunately, caste is not yet wholly rooted out from some of the native Christian communities. There still seems to be a tendency to keep up caste distinctions socially; and the converts belonging to different castes, though to the same Mission, sometimes will not intermarry; though, I believe, there is something to be said in excuse of this reluctance. The Roman Catholic Missions also proved an interesting subject of discussion. All seemed to agree that, though making way somewhat among the heathen, they are decidedly not gaining from the Protestant Missions. The reverse, indeed, seems to be the case. But about this we shall learn more as we proceed southward.

Our friend Mr. Fordyce of Simla, journeying in fulfilment of his mission to carry Gospel ordinances to our countrymen scattered through India who are destitute of such, made a rapid march to meet us; and my husband and he conferred all day concerning the interests of the important Society at home which Mr. Fordyce represents. Then the outcoming mail-steamer arrived—always an exciting event—bringing one or two visitors for the hours it remained.

I paid some final visits among the zenanas, saying many good-byes; the girls of the Boarding School clustered round me for a parting word; some of the native Christian ladies came for the same purpose; a good many of the most advanced pupils from the College came over, some from Mr. Rae's Bible class—interesting, earnest young men, who seem near the Kingdom; all our missionaries and professors came: and our hearts were deeply stirred, sorrowing most that many of these kind faces we cannot hope to see any more on earth.

So our memorable visit came to a close. As we had talked all day, we had to work all night,—to pack, to write letters, and be ready; for by six o'clock next morning we had bidden farewell to our kind host and hostess and their sweet children, and were *en route* for the further South.

# CHAPTER VI.

## THE EARLY MISSIONS TO INDIA.

ALTHOUGH my object in writing this little account of our missionary journey through part of South India is to tell simply what we saw with our own eyes, not what I have merely read, or other people have seen and observed,—yet a few words on the past history of these most interesting Mission fields may not be unwelcome, to make what follows more comprehensible. A heart which beats at all in sympathy with the great cause of the spread of Christ's Kingdom in the world, will surely beat a little faster at the very mention of such centres as Tanjore, Palamcotta, Madura, Nagercoil, and many others, which have stood out so conspicuously in the history of Missions. These are places where the everlasting Gospel has had some of its most striking truimphs, where a large harvest of souls has been gathered out of the darkest heathenism into the light and blessedness of Christianity.

It is now nearly two centuries since the eyes of Protestant Christendom began to turn with interest to the work, which was even then making a sure commencement in the southern part of the great Indian continent. The wide world of heathendom still lay in profound darkness. But, happily, there was a Danish settlement on this coast, at the South, where missionaries were welcomed and allowed to settle; and so, while the rest of India was still unvisited by the messengers of peace, the Madras Presidency had begun to hear the glad tidings of salvation. It is well to remember that Missions began in the South of India much sooner than in the North. In Western India their commencement was in 1813—a full century later than in Madras.

The first Protestant Mission in India was planted in Tranquebar, and to Denmark belongs the honour of having equipped and sent it forth. Not only so; the enterprise owed its origin to King Frederick IV., who commissioned the devoted Professor Franke, of Halle, at the suggestion of his court-preacher, Dr. Lütkens, to find missionaries to go to the heathen field in India. The result was the sending forth of the very noble Ziegenbalg and his associate Plutschau, and the founding of the Tranquebar Mission. This was as far back as 1706—a memorable year in the history of Protestant Missions in dark, heathen India.

Is it not both touching and suggestive to go back to that small beginning, and think of all it meant? The little water-spring, the tiny rill, was to swell into a goodly river of the water of life. It is surely a grand spectacle, these two men setting sail from the distant West, with their marvellous message for India—the message of Divine love—the hope of her future, the charter of her salvation!

When these humble missionaries set foot upon the strand, the day-star had risen on this Eastern world, and the angels had begun to sing over it their joyous song. I wonder what the scoffing Brahmans would have thought, or the proud Musulman! They little knew that, with these two simple, unknown men, there had landed on their shores forces, moral and spiritual, which would yet rouse and conquer even this land, so slow to change, which had slept so profound a sleep during the ages, content with its dreams and philosophies and old-world systems of faith. And it is changing, thank God! Emancipation, freedom, enlightenment, and all the blessings which accompany that glorious religion which God gave to the world, and the world so much needs, are partly come, and certainly coming; not so quickly perhaps as they came in the West, or as our impatient hearts would desire; but as surely as Ziegenbalg and Plutschau, and their noble successors from many lands and churches, came and preached the everlasting Gospel to this people, so surely will it go on to its victorious end, and win all India for Christ. These, and other missionary heroes, deserve to be held in honourable remembrance quite as much as Clive and the other heroes who won India for Britain.

Tranquebar in 1706, as I said, was a Danish settlement; and as the missionaries had come out under the protection of the king, the local Government, of course, had to receive and assist them. They obtained permission to build their first church, which was erected on a site by the sea-shore, near the native town. Schools soon followed, and Government ordered that all the Protestant inhabitants should send their slaves to be instructed, as well as that the children should be sent to school. Meanwhile, the two men studied the Tamil language diligently, and were soon able to preach in it. Thus the work began. The next missionary who arrived to join the first two was an able man named Gründler. Then afterwards came Dr. Schultze; and from time to time many other excellent coadjutors joined the Mission band, until, after a few years, there were as many as eight men labouring at once in the field.

On the 5th of September, 1707, though the work was still so new—hardly more than a year old—God had so blessed the labours of the first two men that they began to gather in their sheaves, and the first converts were baptised. There were nine adults baptised together; and these formed the nucleus of the now large and flourishing Tamil Church of Southern India.

But we must not forget, that though this venerable Mission was established by Denmark, it may be said to have been connected from the beginning with both Germany and England. The first missionaries were Germans; and funds were occasionally sent them from Germany. Then, from 1709, our own country took the liveliest interest in the enterprise, the Society for Promoting Christian Knowledge beginning from this time to contribute steadily to its support. It also sent the Mission a printing press and a printer. Early in his career, Ziegenbalg visited his own country and also England, in behalf of his Mission. He preached in the Savoy and Royal Chapels, and received generous donations, which were a great help in the work. The funds from Denmark did not always arrive with punctuality; and, in times of need, the Society for

Promoting Christian Knowledge still further increased its grants. Thus the struggling, hard-worked people at Tranquebar were effectually helped and remembered.

Another English Society, which worked hand-in-hand with the Society for Promoting Christian Knowledge, sent them gifts, both of books and money. This was the Society for the Propagation of the Gospel; and by-and-by, when the former wished to confine its operations more to its own proper sphere, the more directly missionary part of its work was handed over to the Society for the Propagation of the Gospel. This transference was accomplished in 1828; and from that time this Society became still more closely connected with the Tranquebar Mission.

The first fifty years saw much hard and earnest work accomplished. Ziegenbalg returned from his visit to Europe in behalf of his Mission to his loved field, but did not live many years after. Much indeed had been done; the tiny grain of mustard-seed had already begun to shoot out great branches. Schools had been established, churches built, native pastors ordained, a printing press set up, tracts had been written and widely circulated, and the Bible, both the Old and the New Testaments, had been translated into Tamil, and also into Telugu. The blessing of God had manifestly rested on the Mission; and when these fifty years were accomplished and its jubilee had come, the converts numbered eleven thousand. Literally, 'the little one had become a thousand, and the small one a strong nation.'

Thus it was that the pure Gospel of Christ first visited poor India: and the lamp of truth then lit in Tranquebar has never since become darkness. In estimating the good these early Missions accomplished, ought we quite to forget the effect their success must have had in stimulating the Mission cause over the world generally? The stirring tidings which now and then found their way across the sea, of men being turned from devil-worship and dark idolatries to serve the living and true God, must have carried reproach to many a faint as well as careless heart, though encouragement and hope to others who had begun to feel they had a responsibility in this matter. I like to think what the effect on the Churches must have been—so little awake as yet to the grand duty of making Christ known among the nations. Strange it was, when so many centuries had come and gone since the Lord Jesus had given the glorious command that 'repentance and remission of sins should be preached to all nations' in His name! But the awakening was near. Not very long after this time the Spirit of God moved on the face of society at home, and there was aroused in the Christian world a new interest and concern regarding the condition of the heathen world. Carey went to India in 1793; and the missionary ranks have never lacked able recruits since then, nor money to support them and their work, nor the prayers of Christ's people for their success.

This awakening, though it came gradually at first, was contemporaneous with others relating to matters in our own land, when humanity and philanthropy began to do their work. At this time the condition of our prisons, and asylums, and slaves began to be thought about, and the poor to be considered. Grand institutions like the Religious Tract Society, and the glorious Bible Society, and others, were formed. In a word, the highest interests of men began to be considered by their fellows, both as regards this world and the next. Surely that little light kindled so wonderfully in South India was as a beacon-light of hope to the world! And now, thank God! in the present happy days, not India only, but China, Africa, the Islands of the Sea, nearly 'all nations,' have that glorious message declared to them, which was left so graciously as a legacy to His Church by the Lord Himself.

The way in which the truth spread from Tranquebar into the neighbouring province of Tanjore is very interesting. Tanjore was then under a native Rāj, and the missionaries were not at first allowed to preach the new doctrines within its borders. In God's wonderful providence, however, a native officer, named Rājnaiken, who had been brought up a Roman Catholic, had the loan given him of a copy of the Gospels in Tamil. He was so moved and interested with what he found in the wonderful book, that he began to copy the whole on palmyra leaves. Soon after, hearing that there were missionaries only fifty miles away, he sought them, received instruction, and eventually joined their Church. Much opposition was made by the Jesuits, and also by his family. The latter, however, influenced and instructed by him, were in

SCHWARTZ.

time one and all converted, and admitted into the Church. But sore persecution followed. At one time Rājnaiken was so savagely beaten that he was left for dead on the ground. Then his father was cruelly murdered, and his brother half killed from the barbarous treatment he received. But the devoted converts firmly and bravely held on their way. God marvellously preserved Rājnaiken; and he worked faithfully and efficiently as a missionary among his own people for full forty years.

With the entrance of the truth into Tanjore, the name of another missionary hero is inseparably connected. This was the celebrated and devoted Schwartz. He founded a Mission in Trichinopoly, but afterwards removed to Tanjore, where he settled finally. I never shall forget the thrill with which I entered the first chapel built by him in the city of Tanjore—alas! silent now and unused—and looked at the primitive pulpit where he had preached, and the flag-stone on the floor under which he was buried (though now, I believe, his tomb is elsewhere), and the simple inscription, in Latin, which the venerable building bears: 'This house of prayer was built A.D. 1779.' [1]

But I anticipate. Let me now proceed with the narrative of our journey, telling, as so strictly enjoined by many at home to do, what we have seen among these interesting Missions. It would indeed be selfish to keep all the pleasure and instruction we have so richly gathered to ourselves.

[1] I do not attempt any account of Roman Catholic Missions. These began two centuries before the time of Ziegenbalg.

## CHAPTER VII.

### TANJORE.

It was another still, stifling morning when we started to join the early mail-train for Tanjore. The atmosphere felt like a Turkish bath; and our weary selves were more fit to go to bed than to sit for the next twenty hours in the unlovely compartment which opened for our reception.

After careful consultation with our friends, we had arranged to proceed down the east coast as far as the railway would take us, then enter the beautiful little kingdom of Travancore, traversing it to the Cape, and seeing its famed Mission work, chiefly among the Shanars, or devil-worshippers; then return northward by the famous Backwater of the Malabar coast, visiting Cottyam, Cochin, etc., *en route;* and so on to the Blue Hills, the famed Nielgherries.

One of the odd things about this primitive railway is, that the first-class fare costs three times as much as that of second class! So there is an object in systematically choosing these boxed-up, cushionless carriages, with their hard, narrow benches. It is certainly pleasanter to travel on a shady day like this, than when the fierce, furious sun is streaming mercilessly in at curtainless windows; and a bright little touch of beauty and sweetness was added to our dingy surroundings by the kind hands of some native friends who came to see us off. Along with some pomegranates and other fruit, which we found most cooling and delicious, they brought us two magnificent bouquets, and great was the pleasure the lovely, fragrant flowers afforded us all the weary day. By a little occasional watering when we halted, they remained fresh to the end; and I wondered sometimes if these kind people knew, or ever imagined, that in this little act of graceful attention they had really given a 'cup of cold water,' which oft refreshed us during the long, dusty travel.

One of the many fallacies current at home concerning things Indian is, that roses have here no perfume. On the contrary, some vases full of beautiful roses, which stand beside me now, as I write, are sending forth the most delicate and delicious odour, and are quite as sweet-scented as if they had had the advantage of growing in our own favoured isle. It is true, however, that some Indian flowers have no scent at all; while others, especially those of flowering shrubs, are often too heavily-scented to be pleasant.

One of the kind friends who stood beside us until the train moved off was a youth of whom we had seen a good deal in Madras, and with whom Dr. Mitchell has had much cheering intercourse. He has come under that wonderful personal influence which Dr. Miller and his colleagues exercise so largely over young men. He has also enjoyed the training which Mr. Rae gives in his admirable Bible class, and he certainly is, in one sense, a believer.

But to many such young men one might put Paul's question: 'Have ye received the Holy Ghost since ye believed?' One cannot help hoping that he has. There is something so peculiarly attractive about him. He stood there, in his snow-white starched coat, and bunchy, loose turban, his open, honest face beaming with a light which surely came from true light and peace within. We said some earnest words to him, and the tears stood in his eyes, and we cannot but hope for him. God grant that he may not neglect or stifle his convictions, as so many have done! His was the last face we saw as he followed our moving train down the platform and salaamed his adieus.

It is curious how popular the Bible class is among the heathen pupils; that is, if it is well and brightly taught. This young man said that, in the Christian College, it is the favourite class; and, indeed, it is easy for visitors to see that this is the case, from the intense and thoughtful interest depicted on every face as the teacher goes on opening up and questioning the students on the sacred theme. All this precious seed which is being so largely sown in the rich soil of these young hearts will surely fulfil its end, and bring forth fruit in the saving of souls, and to the glory of God.

Until we leave Madras a good way behind, the country is flat and monotonous, but wonderfully green; and near the stations, especially where there are English cantonments, the clumps and plantations of fine, shady trees are most refreshing to the eye. Huge hedges of spiky cactus abound, instead of the prickly pear of the Deccan, and some palm trees here and there soon begin to dot the plains; but they look stunted and scraggy, especially to eyes accustomed to the stately growth which these picturesque children of the tropics attain in the low-lying, humid Konkan. A good deal of water lay in the rice—or paddy—fields, which accounted for the general aspect of green freshness and fertility, though the large river-beds were generally dry, or had only a tiny stream trickling through the broad, sandy bottom.

The country, as a rule, is well peopled and well cultivated, and there were many quiet, pastoral scenes I noticed as we passed, which were full of interest and had their own beauty. The rice crops were in every stage of progress,—some being cut and harvested; some about attaining to the golden tint of ripeness; while other tiny fields, in which the young plants had just been bedded out, looked full of a lovely, delicate green, standing out of the water with which they had been flooded. Every rice-field is surrounded by a small, low embankment, which is also a tiny watercourse, as the plant loves plenty of moisture, and does not flourish without it. Does not this remind one of the Spirit-taught heart? It, too, can only flourish and be green when abundantly watered with heavenly dews by Him who is Himself 'as the dew unto Israel.' As I watched the cultivator open a little sluice in the watercourse, and let in a gentle stream, which wandered over the rice-bed until every tiny leaf held up its head, revived and full of fresh beauty, giving promise of the ripe, yellow grain to come, the expression, 'They shall revive as the corn,' seemed to gain new significance and beauty. And then the thought naturally followed, and turned to a prayer, that the Good Husbandman would yet turn this parched land of heathenism into water-springs of truth, and fill it with the beauties of holiness and fruits of righteousness. Oh! there is need. Nothing strikes you more, as you pass along, than the indications of idolatry which everywhere abound. At every village, under every green tree, at the road-side, everywhere, are idol shrines, or 'Swami houses,' or grotesque, ugly images, smeared over with flaming red paint; while in every town, of any size, the tall *Gōpuram*, or pyramidal top of some pagoda, rears itself, often most picturesquely, over the beautiful trees which generally surround it.

Early in the day we stopped for a little at Punrooty, a pretty, green, well-wooded station; and also, thanks be to God, an oasis in this wilderness of heathenism. The Mission at this place is conducted by Miss Reade. She is the daughter of a Madras civilian who was long in this district. To any who are unacquainted with this most interesting work, I would recommend a little book, entitled 'Punrooty,' by Miss Lowe, which tells the story of Miss Reade's Mission far better than I could, even if we had seen it. It was a great disappointment not to see it; but time pressed, and Miss Reade was absent in Europe, her health having completely failed under her manifold labours. Her large Orphanage for girls, gathered during the famine, is, however, in full operation, and the Mission is carried on by efficient workers. A friend, who knows her well, writes to me thus: 'Miss Reade itinerates much in all the district, giving addresses both in Tamil and Hindoostanee. She feels more called to this work than any other; just sowing the seed is her one great aim and desire. She is often asked to go again and again to the villages where she has already been and made the Gospel known; and just at the time of her illness, last November, many were coming to her desiring to know how they were to give up their idols and become Christians.'

Thus, through this excellent lady's instrumentality, many in this region who sat in darkness are coming to see a great light. Will not some at home, who have the means and the time, and could be spared, come out and follow Miss Reade's example?

We have long and frequent halts, though this is the mail-train. My husband gets out and talks to the people who throng the stations, for we desire to make this a missionary tour in every sense. All are glad, too, to accept tracts and books; but it is a new and not very agreeable experience to us to have to pass through any part of India and not be able to speak to the people in their own tongue. A French lady, of Pondicherry, who is our only fellow-traveller, comes to our aid when we have any wants to make known, though she knows only French and Tamil; but it is wonderful how wide-spread some knowledge of English is, even in these regions beyond: and, of course, the station-masters and officials are educated men and talk English perfectly. We found one or two intelligent young Madrasees employed by Government, or on the railway, who had been students at our College in Madras. Our French friend, who was quite as dark-complexioned as any native, became very confidential on the subject of her own history, and that of Pondicherry, still a French settlement, where she had spent her life. She described it as *bien triste;* she thought Paris might be a more cheerful place of abode, and certainly Madras was,—but cordially invited us to come and see for ourselves. If we had only had the time, I should like to have seen the old place —not certainly for its present attractions, but for its interesting past.

We had intended, on reaching Tanjore, to put up at the Travellers' Bungalow—that refuge for the pilgrim and stranger which a paternal Government provides; but as we passed through one of the stations *en route*, a telegram was put into my husband's hand, from some kind benefactor there, inviting us to be his guests during our stay. This was totally unexpected, as we had no acquaintance in the place that we knew of. We could not even decipher the name the message bore, only we knew that our Heavenly Father was 'mindful of us,' and goodness and mercy were following us continually. During the day, we found out our unknown friend was Mr. Buick, the Collector of Tanjore; so when our train drew slowly into the station, some-time after midnight, there, sure enough, were a couple of belted, scarlet-coated peons, with the Collector-Sahib's badge across their breasts, ready to take charge of us and our belongings. We soon found ourselves in charming quarters. There was a blaze of cheery, welcoming light; servants with hot chocolate and other good things were ready; and ere long our aching heads and weary bones were reposing deliciously in this large, airy, quiet chamber. We knew nothing more until the early sunlight shining in through the *jilmils*, or venetian blinds, showed us our fresh surroundings. My husband was soon without; and over the high screen which divided us from the drawing-room, I heard a lady's cheery voice bidding him heartily welcome, and telling him he was an old friend.

Some years ago, during the revival in Ireland, we were the guests of the well-known Rev. J. H. Moore, now of Elmwood, Belfast, but then of Connor, where, if I mistake not, the revival movement began. Mr. Moore showed us much of that great work, and he and his wife—also a former friend—were most hospitable and kind. Our hostess is their daughter, and she remembers us and our visit, though then little more than a child. How grateful I felt as I listened to her pleasant greeting, to which her husband's was soon added!

We could now, indeed, see Tanjore under the best possible auspices. Their kindness was simply unwearied and unbounded, as well as the pains they took to let us see and understand everything in this old city, so wonderfully interesting in many aspects.

The first thing we did after breakfast was to go to the flat roof-top of Mr. Buick's house, as the highest point at command, to get a general view of the main features of the place. This always helps one afterwards in taking in details more correctly. The great plain of Tanjore lay spread out at our feet, bounded on all sides by the horizon, except where a range of far-off, dreamy hills, faintly discernible in the distance, seemed to mingle with the clouds. The plain is beautifully wooded in some parts and well cultivated; that is, it seems one vast paddy or rice-field, except where thick jungle prevails. The roads seem well lined with trees, while the houses stand in the midst of clumps and topes; but the foliage is dusty and brown. The native town lies a good deal within the walls of the Fort, where the fine old palace is the chief feature, with its towers and gateway, and lofty, grim old walls. But the most conspicuous and striking object in the scene, which one cannot help looking down upon with wondering admiration, is the Grand Pagoda, one of the sights of Tanjore. It is a huge, pyramidal structure, standing in a great court, with a lofty gateway, and surrounded by a high wall. It is considered one of the finest temples of the kind in all India, and our friends promised us a nearer inspection by and-by.

We denizens of the Maratha country ought to have felt here we were breathing familiar air, for this great province was long under the sovereignty of the Marathas. It seems to have become subject to the Chieftain Shāhji in the year 1661. This was the father of the great Shivaji, who founded the Maratha empire. The fine old Rajah Sarfoji, who was the devoted friend of the missionary Schwartz, was one of this line of Tanjore princes. The last Rajah, who died in 1855, unfortunately had no male issue; so, according to the policy which then ruled in English councils, the sovereignty lapsed to the Honourable East India Company. I fancy this annexation policy has not quite so many

COURT IN THE RAJAH'S PALACE, TANJORE.

supporters as it once had; but, meanwhile, it is not bad for Tanjore that it is under the benign rule of Britain.

Though this last Rajah had no son, he left two daughters: one of these has since died, and the other, who is called the Princess, is now the recognised representative of royalty in all that remains of the native court. There are plenty of Rānis, or queens, in the palace, but they are of no account: they are only the widows of the late Rajah; and there is not a son among them, alas! Had even one of them been the happy mother of a son, what a change the circumstance would have caused! The nobody would have become a person of consequence at once. As it is, the Princess is the Great Lady, and her husband, Sakharām Saheb—quite a Maratha name—is called the Prince Consort.

But what we wanted to see first, was something of the Missions in this famous old Mission field, where the light began to shine when so much of the rest of the land was still dark. Dr. Claudius Buchanan had called Tanjore the garden of the Gospel; we wondered if it still deserved the high designation. A carriage from the palace was most kindly put at our disposal, to go where we liked; so we soon found our way to the German Mission House, where we made the acquaintance of Mr. and Mrs. Pamperien, the missionary and his wife in charge of the Leipzig Mission.

There are two Missions in operation in the city now: this one in connection with the Leipzig Lutheran Society, and the other belonging to the Society for the Propagation of the Gospel—the well-known S. P. G. which, as I related in the last chapter, early began to work in South India. Both Missions, I believe, have their head-quarters at Tranquebar, and both claim to be the successors of the first old Danish Mission. Each Society seems to have had congregations, lands, and buildings handed over to it either by the missionaries or by the Royal Mission College at Copenhagen, and thus they divide the honour of the succession between them ; though we must not forget that the Germans were the *first* to start Protestant Missions in India. After all, the true successors of the grand old pioneers are surely those on whom their mantle has fallen, to whom has been transmitted most of the courageous, devoted spirit which animated them. I confess I wish very much that another Society or Church—and that a purely Evangelical one—would go in and share the work in this exceedingly important and still most needy centre. I am sure there is ample room.

We were delighted with the tall, pleasant German pastor and his young wife, who gave us a most cordial welcome, and took us all over their full, busy Mission compound. There are day-schools and orphanages both for boys and girls, all located round the centre Mission bungalow, and thus are directly under the missionary's eye. The church also stands conspicuous at one side of the spacious enclosure. It is a fine, large, white building, airy and roomy inside, with some pretty coloured-glass windows, and memorial slabs on the walls. The floor is comfortably matted, but has no pews or seats of any kind ; the people sit on the floor, the men on one side, and the women on the other, as in China ; and thus it holds a larger congregation. Some of the native Christians, hearing of our arrival, gathered about the church door, and gave us the most kindly, warm greeting. We had some very nice talk with them, especially with two elder men, who are catechists, or rather pastors, and assist Mr. Pamperien chiefly in the village and district work. The furthest station occupied by the Mission is thirty-six miles off. Mr. Pamperien told us that ten thousand converts have been added to the Missions of their Society in India during the last four or five years. This indeed was cheering news.

We spent a long, pleasant morning in the midst of this active Mission circle, and then drove to the Fort to see the English School and College connected with the Society for the Propagation of the Gospel. There are only two missionaries of this Society at present in Tanjore, Messrs. Kay and Blake. Having sent in our cards, the latter, whose work seems chiefly to be in the College, came down, and received us very courteously. Being one of those gentlemen who now-a-days walk in long robes — more numerous in India than once was the case—he was habited from head to foot in a very long white coat, confined at the waist by a knotted cord of thick black silk twist. There are three knots—those, I am told, of obedience, poverty, and celibacy. We found afterwards, however, that one of these missionary gentlemen was about to cut the knot of celibacy, and tie one of matrimony instead, which I thought was a most sensible exchange.

Mr. Blake was extremely kind, and took us all through the quaint, queer, white-washed native building, where every room and corner seemed turned into class-rooms. These were filled with some three to four hundred lads, who looked bright and intelligent. The Madrasees have, as a rule, honest, good-humoured countenances, broader of feature and darker in complexion than the Marathas; more open, perhaps, in expression, but not, I think, so intellectual. They wear large soft turbans, which suit an Oriental face, instead of the bare heads of the young Bengalis, who only wear turbans in full dress, and have their thick black hair cropped and dressed like English lads.

I asked some of Mr. Blake's pupils why they were so anxious to acquire an English education. 'Oh!' said they, very honestly, 'because we want to get Government employment.' A knowledge of English is the ladder by which they hope to mount to this grand prize which lies at the top. Poor fellows! It is quite natural; and though education for its own sake is not yet always the attraction it ought to be, may we not hope that many taught in Christian schools, who have the additional advantage of a thorough training in Bible knowledge, may find a better prize even than they dream of at the top—namely, the salvation of their immortal souls?

Mr. Blake is very enthusiastic about his school, and works hard, generally spending the whole day in it. In the terrible heat of these crowded rooms this is no small self-denial and toil. My husband found a good many Marathas among the pupils, and many Brahmans, and had much interesting talk.

This was all we saw of the S. P. G. Missions or missionaries, except, indeed, a very nice girls' school taught by Mrs. Gahan and her daughter, also accommodated in the Fort. There were sixty-three bright-looking girls present, bigger and older too, than are usually to be found in day-schools of this sort. Mrs. Gahan also visits in the zenanas, and teaches in the palace. The Princess is one of her pupils, and a very intelligent pupil she is. I have just seen a grateful letter from her to my friend Mrs. Buick, written in rather a school-girl hand, but well expressed in good English, thanking her for some kindness done to her, and saying how grateful she is to 'the good Collector,' as she calls Mr. Buick.

Early yesterday afternoon, our friends took us a round of sight-seeing. We drove to the Fort in state, the Collector being the embodiment of authority as the representative of the English Government, and we were received at the entrance by the guard, who beat a salute in honour of the visitors. The *Sirkele* of the palace, or Prime Minister, was waiting with a grand retinue of smaller officials, red-coated peons, and all manner of attendants, and conducted us over the palace. It is a dreary old pile, full of the indications and remains of fallen greatness. It was altogether very pathetic—there is such an extraordinary mingling of ruin and decay, with relics of old court pageantry and pomp, and tawdry finery, and barbaric splendour. In the same way, some of the rooms are exceedingly handsome, while the labyrinthine passages which lead to them are narrow and squalid, and some of the walls and courts, though fine in design, are tumble-down or unfinished. We first visited the Museum, an *omnium gatherum* of old State property—weapons, saddles, and rich saddle-cloths of gold, splendid shawls, quaint turbans which had graced the heads of the old Rajahs, old chairs of state, and many other relics, too numerous to name, while whole centuries of story seemed to fill the place. We next saw the old Durbar-room, or Hall of Audience, where the gilt canopy stands, under which is the *Gadi*, or throne. The walls are decorated with some portraits, very well painted, of one of the Rajahs with a Dewan, or minister, on each side of him. On the same side of the quadrangle is the library, full of dusty old tomes,—a very valuable collection, I believe, where my husband was much in his element over some curious old Sanscrit and Marathi manuscripts. We then crossed a spacious court, in which multitudes of tame pigeons were being fed, to another and more modern Durbar-hall, used by the later Maratha Rajahs, which is an exceedingly handsome room of stately proportions, with a highly-polished floor, and some fine pillars. In this hall is the beautiful statue, in white marble, of the father of the last Rajah, which stands on a magnificent slab of black marble or porphyry, I am not sure which. Here, also, is a curious old swinging cot, suspended from the roof, at which I looked with much interest, as I found it was the same described by Schwartz in an account of his interview with the Rajah on the occasion of his first visit to Tanjore. This was long before he finally settled here. I find this account in a letter to Professor Franke, given in an interesting old book by Pastor Fenger, and translated from the Danish. The letter is so quaint that I may quote one or two passages. It is dated 3rd June, 1769. He says: 'After the English had concluded a peace with Hyder Ali, I went to Tanjore . . . . I preached three times every day, and had many conferences with the heathen. The king sent word that he wished to speak to me. On the 30th of April, after I had preached to the Tamil congregation on Prayer, I was summoned to the Fort. From eleven o'clock in the morning till five I was at the Castle, talking to all sorts of people till I was quite tired. A Brahman asked me how we could overcome our fleshly lusts. I pointed out the Saviour of the world to him. . . . To others I preached on the deep-seated corruption of man. . . . When I arrived at the palace, there were many hundred writers, accountants, and servants, who were very friendly, and wished that I might preach in such a way that injustice and godless manners might be annihilated. Till five o'clock I remained in a place where the king sometimes shows himself in public. Then I was led through many dark passages to the king, who sat in a four-cornered space, on a bed made fast at the roof, so that he could rock himself. His servants were ranged at his feet on both sides. Opposite to him, at a distance of ten or twelve feet, a chair was placed for me.' Then follows a long account of his conversation with the king, who asked many intelligent questions, such as, 'Why do some Europeans refuse to worship images, while others, like the French and Portuguese, worship them?' He also asked, 'How man can attain to a knowledge of God?' Schwartz records his answers. He preached the Gospel freely to the king and the assembled Court, and thus concludes: 'Here I was interrupted, for pastry was brought in, of which I was required to partake. I ate a little, and said that we Christians, when we enjoy bodily comforts, or meat or drink, thank God for them. At the king's request, I then said a prayer. He wished also to hear a hymn, as he had heard it was our custom to sing. I had the hymn "Mein Gott, das Herze bring' ich dir," translated [into Tamil] by our brother Fabricius with me, of which I sang the three first verses. . . . The king expressed himself much pleased, and said he had never heard such things before. I answered that I wished him all good things and blessings from my heart, and then took my leave.'

When Schwartz afterwards had to leave Tanjore, this heathen king sent him a message, saying, 'Remember, you are my Padre.'

It was a disappointment to us that the Princess was not at home. She and her Consort were away at Baroda, at the grand doings on the Gaekwar's accession. We saw her state reception rooms, however, which are very handsome, and full of modern adornments, such as carpets, mirrors, chandeliers, etc. There are some pictures also, of the Queen, Lord Lytton, and others, and some good French prints. At the upper end, there is a raised daïs, with great chairs beneath a canopy, where Her Royal Highness receives her lady-guests, a transparent curtain being drawn across, which propriety requires should divide her from the party of the other sex gathered in the apartment below. Here her Consort presides for her.

We finished our interesting investigations in the palace by a visit to the old Rānis, the widows of the last Rajah. Having threaded some more dark passages and courts, still led by the *Sirkele*—a most intelligent, pleasant man, who speaks English perfectly—we ascended a steep, short stair leading to their apartments, where we were received with great courtesy by a weak-looking young man, the adopted son of one of the Rānis. There was little of the grandeur of a palace visible. We were ushered into an apartment, handsome as to proportions, but faded and forlorn, with a tattered curtain of yellow satin drawn along the whole length of the room. As we entered we saw many little stirrings at the foot of this curtain, and curious eyes peeping forth to catch a sight of the strangers. Mrs. Buick and I went within the curtain, and were at once surrounded by a number of women of different ages. The principal wife is a grey-haired, withered old woman; but many of those we saw must have been perfect children when the old man died. He left seventeen widows, twelve of whom are still alive. I cannot say they looked interesting, but one could not help one's heart going out to them in pity, with a longing desire to give them something which might brighten their cheerless, empty lives. They were greatly pleased when I spoke to them in Marathi; though I don't think they really knew much of the language. My husband, too, talked to them a good deal from outside the purdah. He says they spoke to him in a harsh form of Marathi;

but the language they talk among themselves is Tamil. They wore no jewels, being widows; but a relative, a pretty, bright young girl just lately married, came in literally smothered in jewels and finery, and formed a great contrast to the faded women who filled the room. They spoke of their wrongs, and seemed discontented and unhappy; but we did not comprehend much of what they said. How I longed to tell them of the Friend of the friendless, the Judge of the widow! But they did not seem to care much to be taught, and I came away from the visit feeling rather depressed.

The Temple, or Pagoda, at Tanjore is a magnificent structure, and we saw as much of it and its wonderful surroundings as any European is allowed to see, for no unclean foreign foot may tread the sacred interior. The appearance of a colossal *Nandi*, or sacred bull, in black basalt, erected in the court in front of the principal shrine, showed at once that the Temple is dedicated to the god Shiva—*Nandi* being the bull on which Shiva rides. The basalt was well oiled all over, and so, looked like bronze. This figure, the natives say, was first a calf size, then a cow's, and now it is as big as an elephant; but the foreigners came, and the growth was stopped, or who knows but in time it might have grown up to heaven itself! The Brahmans say also that the tower of this temple 'throws no shadow.' As it was evening when we saw it, and no sun shining at the time, we could not test the truth of this last assertion.

TEMPLE OF SUBRAHMANYA, TANJORE.

There are inscriptions all round the base, which have been translated by the learned civilian, Dr. Burnell. The court is handsome and very spacious, with cloisters all round, in which are small symbols of Shiva. There is a second temple in the enclosure, dedicated to Subrahmanya, the son of Shiva, which is also of the usual elaborate construction, and has a beautiful *gōparam* or tower. In a chamber connected with the pagoda, there is a series of portraits, life size, of the Royal Family of Tanjore, from the great Shivaji and his father Shahji, down to the last Rajah. The chief pagoda is surmounted by a very fine monolith of granite, which is said to weigh eighty tons. All these temples belong to the senior Rāni at the palace, who pays the *pujāris*, or priests, feeds the Brahmans, and keeps up the place.

I observe that the people here generally wear very conspicuous idolatrous marks. These are either on the forehead, or breast, or neck, and are usually made with daubs of white paint put on in long lines. They are very pronounced in their religiousness, greatly caste-ridden, and under the sway and dread of the Brahmans to a very great extent.

But certainly the interest of our stay in Tanjore culminated in our visit to the venerable church of the illustrious Schwartz. Altogether one seemed to live more in the past as to Missions than the present, in a place so full of memories as this; except, indeed, when one longed that the present might more fully realise the expectations awakened by the past.

It is not that there is so much to see or tell about

in the touching old chapel, though we felt it to be so infinitely more interesting than any simply classic ground could ever be:

'Above all Greek, above all Roman fame.'

It is an unpretending, plain, barn-like building, with no ecclesiastical pretensions at all—a bare stone floor, white-washed walls, no seats of any sort, only a small, primitive pulpit at one end, in which we stood, with a thrill in our hearts, for it is the same in which Schwartz so often preached. The church is not now used; it is empty, deserted, silent! Why? I often asked; for it seems in tolerable preservation, or might be, if ordinary care were taken to preserve it. One would like to see an edifice like this cared for, which has received the consecration it has enjoyed, and filled daily for God's worship. Surely it is the truest and highest consecration which comes from the faithful teachings of men like those who here 'preached boldly in the Lord,' and gathered out a people for Him from the heathen round.

But another interest attaches to the church besides its hallowed memories. The celebrated monument by Flaxman, erected to the memory of Schwartz by the Rajah Sarfoji, is placed in the wall inside at the end of the *building*. It is a very beautiful bas-relief in white marble, representing the dying missionary, his countenance full of a bright, beaming calm, and hope, and holy peace, taking leave of the king, who stands beside the couch weeping, and grasping the hand of his 'father and friend,' as he always called him.

A few of Schwartz's pupils stand about, and some of the king's ministers behind. It is a most lovely work of art, and tells its touching and strange story exquisitely. The inscription is in English.

The king himself wrote to the Society at home with which Schwartz was connected, to order the monument, using these remarkable words: 'I have asked your missionaries . . . . to procure a marble monument, which may be erected in their church in my principal city and residence, to keep up the remembrance of the departed revered Father Schwartz, and to testify to the extreme respect with which I regard the character of that great and good man, and the gratitude I owe him as my father and friend, and the protector and guardian of my youth.' He adds, at the close of his letter, 'Oh! gentlemen, that you were but able to send missionaries here who should resemble the departed Schwartz!' Shall we not echo this sentiment, and turn it into a prayer to Him who is able now as then to send forth such labourers into His vineyard?

Another monument was erected to Schwartz by the Honourable East India Company. It stands in the Fort Church, in Madras.

This King Sarfoji, who so loved Schwartz, and was his beloved pupil, is not the same referred to by him in his letter to Franke, describing his first visit to Tanjore. It was not for some years after that interview, that he finally settled in the place.

The brief history is this. In 1749, Schwartz was ordained at Copenhagen, sailed from London, and arrived at Cuddalore the following year, and at once joined the Mission circle at Tranquebar. 'By the end of the same year,' says Fenger, 'he preached his first sermon in Tamil.' He himself tells that the text of his first sermon was, 'Nevertheless at Thy word I will let down the net; and when they had done this they enclosed a great multitude of fishes.' He adds: 'God has wrought in me humility and a child-like confidence in His word by this text.' It became the key-note of his whole simple and devoted missionary life. He worked for ten years in Tranquebar, then went to Trichinopoly where he founded a branch of the Mission; and finally, in 1778, he settled in Tanjore. By the following year this church was built, as the simple inscription tells. He also erected other buildings, such as schools, and a mission-house, and gathered a large congregation together, training some of the more able from among his converts to be pastors, evangelists, and teachers. He laboured for twenty years in Tanjore, and is said to have baptised over two thousand persons, many of whom were of high caste. He died on the 13th February, 1798, in the seventy-second year of his age, after forty-seven years of actual service in the Mission field. His brother missionary, Mr. Gericke, who was present when he died, with his beloved pupil and adopted son and successor, John C. Kohlhoff, tells, that 'he died in the arms of his faithful and grateful native assistants,' and speaks of the general and profound grief his death awakened: 'the weeping and sobbing of the people in the two Christian villages was most touching. We could hear it all the night through. It is not we only,' he adds, 'who have lost a father, but the whole country.' Gericke also tells that the Tanjore Mission, and the institutions belonging to it, had been left his heirs. This was consistent with the practice of his life; his liberality was extraordinary, and whatever means he received he spent not on himself, but on his beloved Mission.

In his character there was a wonderful combination of simplicity and power, and every one who writes of him agrees as to the great influence he possessed with the natives. He had also great weight with the English Government. It is matter of history how useful he was in the embassy to Hyder Ali, with which the Madras Government entrusted him. 'Let them send the Christian,' said the great warrior; 'he will not deceive me.' And we have already seen how successful he was in the educating and training of the young king. Of his appearance and habits his friend Sir William Chambers gives the following interesting description: 'Picture to yourself a well-grown man, above middle height, holding himself naturally, yet erect, of rather dark yet healthy complexion, with black curly hair, and a powerful, manly glance, expressing unaffected modesty, uprightness, and benevolence, and then you have an idea of the impression the first sight of Schwartz makes on a stranger. A plateful of rice, with some vegetable curry, formed the daily meal to which he sat down with a cheerful countenance, and a piece of native cloth dyed black formed the material for his dress for a year. Thus, raised above all earthly cares, his whole attention is turned towards spreading the Gospel.'

But I must not go on, though the theme is a

tempting one, and it is not needful to dilate on the grandeur of his character or work: is not his praise in all the Churches? But one thing seems clear—it was not so much his intellect, or his undoubted sagacity and prudence, which gave him the command he possessed over men, especially over the natives, as it was the singular simplicity of aim which characterised his life, his unselfishness also, and the evident absence of all covetousness in regard to money, spending as he did all he had on God's work. Then, above all, there was the manifest reality of his religion, and the sincerity of his personal godliness. These things showed the power of God in him, and *these* told on the natives, and formed the secret of his influence and success as a missionary. I may be allowed to quote a single sentence from Bishop Caldwell, showing the estimation in which Schwartz is held by one so eminently fitted to judge as the Bishop. 'Schwartz undoubtedly deserves to be placed in the first rank of Indian missionaries. It is true that he cannot be described as a man of genius, like Francis Xavier . . . . but he was not inferior to the great Jesuit missionaries, or to any missionaries of any Church or Society that ever lived, in simplicity and godly sincerity, in piety and devotedness, in wisdom, philanthropy, and zeal.'

A few glimmering rays of light had broken on the midnight darkness of the Tanjore province in the early days of the Danish Mission through the labours of Rājnaiken, whose story I have told; but the daybreak came with Schwartz. Darkness was on the face of the deep; but the Spirit of God moved upon the face of the waters. After a time, when he and his immediate successors had passed away, the light perhaps grew dim; but now, in these days of modern effort, and fresh awakening to the great interests of the heathen world, let us hope and pray that it may soon grow bright again, and wax brighter and brighter until the perfect day of truth and righteousness shall have come over the whole province.

## CHAPTER VIII.

### DINDIGAL—ITS MEDICAL MISSION.

OUR next halt is to be Dindigal, where there is a flourishing branch of the American Mission, which has worked in the province of Madura for the last fifty years.

We had a most comfortable start, after a substantial breakfast, when a whole company of kind people assembled on the platform to see us off. Our carriage was stuffed with good things by our very kindest of hostesses; even dark blinds for the glaring windows were not forgotten.

It was a curious thing, as we sped over this vast Tanjore plain, smiling now in green tranquillity, to think of the times, not so very far past, when it was scoured by troops of fierce Maratha horse; 'hordes of imperial robbers,' Sir Thomas Munro called them, doubtless with too much justice, in those troublous times; though I don't think we should forget their gallantry and patriotism. Many are the legends which still survive of the doughty deeds done by these wild warriors. It is certainly a pleasant change now, when nothing is to be seen but peaceful, waving crops, and the staid population, and quiet, rural scenes. I have been wondering whether they would rather go back to the stirring days of native Rāj, when might was right—fancying, perhaps, as distance lends enchantment to the view in various senses, that in these old times they were better off. Those who know seem to think that the people of the South are contented and happy—perhaps exceptionally so—and acknowledge the benefit there is to their country in the beneficent rule of the Kaiser-i-Hind. Indeed, I am quite sure that our beloved Queen has just as good and loyal subjects in India as in any part of her dominions. There is one thing the people do heartily appreciate—that now they can live in security, without dread of dacoity, or robbery, which used to be so rife; or, perhaps, torture and death. They can even travel now with their families from one end of the land to the other, carrying their money-bags and jewels with them, no one daring to make them afraid.

We had hoped to pay a visit to Trichinopoly, or Trichy, as it is popularly called; but we find that cholera is raging in all the district, and our kind friends at Tanjore would not hear of our venturing into the infected city; we, therefore, reluctantly passed it by, prudently contenting ourselves with what could be seen during the hour our train halted at the station.

Trichinopoly is famed for more than its lovely silver filigree-work, or its cigars and tobacco! Here the good Bishop Heber lies buried,—and we should have liked much to visit his tomb; and here Schwartz laboured most successfully. There are Missions of the present day also, full of interest; but we had to bow to the inevitable, and turn away. This is the head-quarters of the Roman Catholic

Missions of the South; and I am told that here they are particularly flourishing.

We managed to get an excellent though distant view of the famous 'Rock'; but it was a great disappointment not to be able to explore its wonderful chambers, which are said to be so curious and intricate, and its extensive fortifications. Fine flights of steps ascend to its summit, from which there must be a beautiful prospect of mountain and plain, cities and temples. The country immediately round, though generally flat, is dotted here and there with curious, isolated rocks, and is cultivated and well wooded. The *casuarina*, or *babul* tree, abounds, and the crops, besides the staple rice, include sugar-cane, tobacco, and cotton.

Some time after we had passed Trichinopoly we got into a region of hills, some of picturesque formation, and pretty with grass, broken jungle, and rock. This was a most pleasant change from the flat monotony of the scantily-peopled plains. Some quaint bee-hive huts, with thatched roofs, shaped like extinguishers, lay nestling in brown groups about the base of the hills; and the simple people seemed busy in their little fields. There are great plantations of the castor-oil plant, and the ditches are filled with quantities of gigantic feathery grasses, which are exceedingly beautiful. We had certainly plenty of time to examine everything, as our lazy train dragged its slow length along, at the rate of barely twenty miles an hour. As it grew cool in the evening, and the shadows were deepening beneath the trees, we drew near our journey's end. Suddenly a little detention occurred, and, to our great distress, we found we had run over a poor cow, which had strayed on the line; but, happily, through God's goodness, no further mischief resulted from the accident.

As soon as we entered the station, a vigorous man, of middle-age, with a ringing voice and hearty manner, came straight to our carriage, and welcomed us to Dindigal. This was Dr. Chester, the well-known and much-respected head of the Medical branch of the Madura Mission. He has laboured in Dindigal, which is his head-quarters, and in all the district round about, for full twenty years, and has done a noble work, which grows more important every day. We were soon in his 'trap,' being driven by the energetic doctor, with whom we were at home in a moment, toward the cantonment, while the golden light of the setting sun came glinting across the green esplanade and through the leafy screen which the beautiful arching trees made along the road. The great orb was descending in stately grandeur to his royal chamber for the night, behind a glorious rampart of encircling hills; and I thought we had not seen so pretty a station on this side of India.

We were received in the bowery porch of the comfortable Mission bungalow by Mrs. Chester, who gave us as kindly a welcome as her husband had done. The venerable missionary, Mr. Chandler, was beside her: he had driven in his bullock-coach from his distant station on purpose to meet us, and carry us back with him if he could. But, alas! this great pleasure cannot be ours at present; our limited time and the quickly advancing heat warn us to go on our way as quickly as possible, for there is much to do, and see, before we reach our resting-place for the hot months. But the disappointment is great; for we have long known this excellent man by name.

The Chandlers are a missionary race. Like the Gulicks of Japan, and other American families, fathers and children have all cast in their lot with the same grand cause, and are missionaries in different parts of the heathen field. This fine old man, who stood in the doorway as we arrived, and greeted us with so much feeling, has grown grey in the service of his Mission. He was one of the first who came to Madura. Soon after we arrived, his son came in from his station, which lies quite in a different direction from his father's; and we spent a delightful evening, chiefly in hearing of the progress of the Lord's work in this successful and long-established Mission. It was commenced by the American Board of Commissioners for Foreign Missions, in 1834, and the progress in all departments, with the results in churches and schools, and Christian families, naturally fills the hearts of the missionaries, as well as those of the Board at home, with encouragement and thankfulness.

There are ten stations in all, with at least one American missionary to each; the parish attached to every station being somewhere about eight hundred square miles! The population of the whole Madura Province is nearly two millions, and all these people, more or less, have been brought under the sound and influence of the Gospel. Each missionary is expected to work his eight hundred square miles, which, of course, would be an impossibility, but for the admirable staff of native assistants attached to each station, who have been carefully trained as pastors, evangelists, catechists, Bible-women, and teachers.

This whole district is rich agriculturally, and possesses a great deal of material prosperity. The people, as a rule, are well off, and well-dressed; and among the coffee-planters of the Lower Pulney Hills not a few are natives. Money, too, seems wonderfully abundant; and the people do not seem to mind how much they spend on their festivals and weddings, or in building themselves better houses, and especially in erecting and endowing new temples and Swami-shrines. But they also take a pride in having their children educated, and are quite willing to pay substantial school-fees.

This flourishing district, of such immense extent, then, has been taken possession of for Christ by these energetic Americans, and the banner of the Gospel floats over it from end to end. The people, generally, do not offer much opposition when preaching is going on; and they are not altogether unfavourable to the spread of Christianity in their country. Still, the complaint is the same as you hear expressed everywhere,—that the indifference displayed is often most disappointing: they care for none of these things; they acquiesce, agree that it is all true, and go away and forget all about it. And yet much has been accomplished. In connection with the ten stations, there are thirty-four native Christian congregations, most of them ministered to by native pastors, with a membership, besides adherents, of 2,827. These converts are drawn from all castes, but chiefly from the Vellālas, or cultivators. Several of the churches are self-sustaining, paying their own pastor; and the district is covered with a network of schools, taught by Christian teachers, both male and female. All that is needed is a rich effusion of the Holy Spirit of God, the watering with the dew from heaven; then would all this good seed, so diligently sowed, spring up, and 'the glory of Lebanon' be given to this whole Province.

As I said, Dindigal is the head-quarters of the Medical part of the Mission, as Madura city is of other departments; and Dr. Chester, a thoroughly educated medical man, and also an ordained clergyman, is the missionary who superintends it.

This morning we were astir betimes, and after the early cup of tea, which only dwellers in the tropics know how to appreciate, we joined our host outside, and off we started to make the round of the station and the Mission premises. What a joyous morning it was!—fresh, cheery, and exhilarating. The birds were in full chorus, and the sun came striding up from behind the hills into the pearly sky with a gladsomeness that was quite infectious, the bright beams dancing down among the big dewdrops in the grass, making them sparkle like so many brilliants. It was deliciously cool: this plateau stands high, and the temperature was down to 58°.

In situation Dindigal is exceedingly pretty. The plain, which is green and well wooded, is a wide amphitheatre, almost entirely surrounded by fine ranges of mountains, the chief being the Sira-mālis and Lower Pulneys. But the most striking object, and one which at once attracts attention, is the curious Dindigal Rock, which stands quite by itself near the native city. It is a great solid mass of granite, I think—bare, and brown, and isolated, and you wonder if this curious natural fortress is really Nature's own workmanship. Man has certainly taken advantage of it, and utilised it for his own purposes. The face of the Rock is strongly fortified, and its firm old walls and ramparts look as if they could still resist many a martial shock.

In ancient days this fort was an important strategical position, and was often the scene of tough encounters between the Marathas and the people of Mysore. In 1755, Hyder Ali garrisoned it, and afterwards it was greatly strengthened by Tippoo-Sultan, from whom finally, in 1792, the British took it. The summit is crowned by some temples, with their tall pagoda-towers, and altogether it is a most picturesque and striking feature in the scene. At the base, a bit of green esplanade stretches, very like a village common at home.

We drove through the native town, which has wide streets, wonderfully clean, where the different castes live in separate quarters. The Brahman street looked particularly tidy, with neat little houses and a stone bench built-in in front, where the men were sitting, wrapped in their 'cloths,' sunning themselves.

Dr. Chester's work is very interesting and varied. He is obliged to exercise the functions of an ordinary missionary, preaching, itinerating, etc., and dispensing the Sacraments in places connected with his district where there is no ordained native helper. But the chief interest lies in his medical work, the organisation of which seems perfect. He took us over his dispensary, which stands in a large compound, with its well-stocked drug-store, its waiting-rooms and surgery, to which are attached an apothecary, a good staff of dressers, and other assistants. We then saw his Rest House, where there is accommodation for people of four different castes while waiting for treatment; and then his Cottage Hospitals with native Christian nurses in attendance. He favours the plan of Cottage Hospitals and has several small bungalows as wards, affording accommodation also for a few convalescent patients. In the department specially set apart for women, Dr. Chester introduced us to a very intelligent, pleasing woman—a native Christian, who is the head matron of the Lying-in Hospital. She is thoroughly trained, and holds a diploma from the Government Medical School in Madras, and is quite capable of herself conducting difficult and dangerous cases. There are two other such native Christian nurses, who are employed in district hospitals. Finally, the Doctor introduced us to his medical school, in which there are thirty students, occupying three class-rooms; and bright, intelligent, young fellows they looked. Most are Christians: there are a few Hindus; but I noticed only one who had an idolatrous mark on his forehead. The students are admitted after a competitive examination. The course of study is for three years; and the young men who pass out, after thorough testing examinations, are appointed as hospital-assistants to stations generally connected with the Mission. Who can tell the good which may result when these fully-trained young men go forth among the people, and new branch dispensaries are set up and additional hospitals established? Their medical skill will open every heathen door to them; and more than this, many a heathen heart will be opened, and people will be led to the Physician of souls. I hope the time will come when a medical department will be connected with every Mission. Surely none should be considered complete until a dispensary stands side by side with the schoolroom and the church.

Dr. Chester has already ten branch dispensaries in different parts of the district, all of which he personally superintends, and their number is increased as students are prepared to take charge of them. The number of cases treated in the whole Mission in the past year was over forty-six thousand!

We next paid a visit to the church, and were introduced to the native pastor, Mr. Coltan, a superior, earnest man, with whom we had much cheering intercourse. He told us of his schools, especially of his large Sunday school, which is attended by heathen and Mohammedan, as well as Christian children, all of whom alike are taught a great deal of Scripture by heart. Some of these heathen children intelligently refuse to worship the idol when there is any festival in their village. This pastor is supported entirely by his congregation.

I noticed that all the buildings were substantial, clean, airy, and well-ventilated, but exceedingly plain and suited to the occupants. There is no needless expenditure anywhere; and Dr. Chester, though he does not refuse his services when called in as a medical man, never accepts a fee.

Before leaving Dindigal, we paid a visit to the Training School of the Christian Vernacular Education Society, of which Mr. Evans is Principal. There seems to be rather a deficiency of accommodation, which this important and useful Society ought to increase. My husband put the lads thoroughly through their facings. He had been requested by the Society at home to see their seminaries in India as far as possible, and he was greatly pleased with this one at Dindigal. Mr. Evans evidently labours for and with his pupils, a good many of whom are native Christians. Some of the Missions send their young men here to be trained; after which they return to their stations as teachers. The students gave us specimens of their power of teaching, which was very amusing, as they tried to puzzle each other, and then criticised the questioner, and a famous heckling they gave the poor fellow, who stood like a man in a pillory. This system must make them very sharp. They also sang some hymns and lyrics both in Tamil and English.

This Christian Vernacular Education Society does indeed a most important work in India—its master-spirit being our friend Dr. Murdoch, whose indefatigable labours as secretary have mainly helped to make the Society the valuable institution it is. It dates back to 1857, when it was established directly after the Mutiny. It trains teachers, supports primary schools, sends forth colporteurs, who sell many thousand copies of the Scriptures and other publications during the year; while Dr. Murdoch scatters his admirable series of school-books broadcast over the land, and is always producing something new and fresh in other useful books. The Society has three great training institutions, one at Ahmednuggur, one in the Punjaub, and this one in Dindigal.

Altogether we had a busy day in the hands of our energetic host, including a visit to Mrs. Chester's Boarding School, full of bright Christian girls. We felt to the full how stimulating it is to come in contact with men of large views and undaunted spirit, full of practical wisdom, too, like these missionaries, who seem to know no difficulty. This is one of the things Dr. Chester says:—'Be sure you are right, then go ahead. This will make any Mission plan a success, while croakers and drones go to their graves, still fearing to put their fingers to it. It is the *go-ahead* as well as the *be sure you are right* which is needed in India in every part of the Mission work!'

I commend these words to the careful consideration of all who have to do with Mission work at home as well as on the foreign field.

After an early dinner, we were again *en route*, accompanied by the younger Mr. Chandler, who was returning to his home, and by the time the sun was sinking towards the western hills we had taken our places in the train corresponding to that which we had quitted twenty-four hours before. We had a sunset of singular beauty, and the mountain ranges looked inexpressibly grand in their dark blue outline beneath a sky full of the most exquisite and gorgeous colour. A broad line of deep blood-red lay along at the horizon, shading off upward into glowing amber and then to the most delicate lemon-tints and aqua-marine, until all colour was lost in the darkening upper sky, where by-and-by the cheery stars came twinkling out one by one. Below, the dark walls of giant mountains with their picturesque, castellated tops looked most striking and beautiful; one or two forest fires were blazing half-way down the mountain slopes, having a most weird effect; nearer, there were the greens and browns of the jungle, growing sombre in the fading light, with a solitary, sentinel-like palm here and there rearing its majestic head to the heavens. The long grey shadows were fast deepening in the hollows; and as the colour faded, and the darkness grew, a pensive desolateness seemed to settle on the scene, which soon brought the mind into sympathy with itself.

Mr. Chandler pointed out the Higher Pulneys as we came in sight of them in the darkening distance, where the coffee and cinchona are largely cultivated. There is a delightful sanatorium somewhere on the summits, which the American Board, with its usual consideration, has provided for its missionaries. In the height of the hot season, each Mission family can escape to these charming hills, and have two months of coolness and rest. This sanatorium was established when wild elephants and tigers were still the chief inhabitants. But now many other residents are attracted from the plains by the pleasanter climate of the mountains during the hottest portion of the year. When we came to his station Mr. Chandler left us, driving away into the darkness to his dwelling, lying twelve miles off in some valley behind the giant wall of hills. How I wished we could have gone with him, to see his wife, and work, and Mission home! But it could not be.

A long sweep round the base of the Sira-mālis concluded our two-and-a-half hours' journey, and we glided into the station at Madura. Late as it was, the Rev. Mr. Rendall, head of this branch of the Mission, awaited us, and drove me off in his tiny pony-carriage with his frisky little steed. My husband followed more humbly in a bullock-bandy, with our belongings, including the useful Joseph. After a good two miles' drive, chiefly through an extensive native city, with very wide and very dark streets, we passed a handsome white church, which Mr. Rendall pointed out as his own, then turned into a large compound, and stopped under the well-lighted, hospitable-looking porch of the Mission House. Here Miss Rendall was waiting to receive us, and the welcome tea was ready spread in the room within.

Mr. Rendall is a widower, and he and his daughter live and work together. He has laboured in this Mission since 1834. These short sojourns in the homes of the missionaries make one of the most delightful and enjoyable parts of our tour, and certainly will furnish some of its pleasantest memories.

# CHAPTER IX.

## MADURA AND ITS MISSIONS.

THE day after our arrival in Madura was Sunday. My husband had happily arranged that we should have a Sabbath in this important centre, that we might see the Sabbath work; for this is the head-quarters of the great American Madura Mission, generally called by its own Board—the American Board of Commissioners for Foreign Missions—'the model Mission.'

I was too tired, after our grand field-day at Dindigal, to be quite in time to accompany the rest of the party to the early morning service in the native church; but by-and-by, hearing a lady's voice outside inquiring for me, I hurried out, and found Mrs. Capron—a lady I was glad indeed to meet. Her name is a familiar one in connection with women's work in India. Her husband was one of the early Madura missionaries; but he died, and instead of abandoning the field, she only saw a new call, in her less occupied life, to devote herself more entirely to God's work among her poor heathen sisters. She sent her children home to America to be educated, and has ever since laboured in Madura, and with wonderful success. Her work is very varied: she teaches in the zenanas, conducts a dispensary in connection with

Dr. Chester, has several day-schools, and receives many women in her own house.

She and I soon became friends, and we sallied forth together. She led me through the spacious compound, which has within its wide enclosure the complete paraphernalia of a Mission. Beside the Mission House stands the bungalow occupied by Mrs. Capron and her assistant lady-missionary; then come the dispensary, the dressers' premises, and other houses. On the opposite side are Miss Rendall's Day and Boarding Schools, including a handsome and commodious building just erected to provide class-rooms for her higher school. It makes a capital public hall also for all manner of purposes, and is called the Otis Hall, because it was built by a grant from a munificent legacy of a million dollars left by a Mr. Otis to the American Board at Boston, to aid them in their great missionary undertakings. I saw more of these delightful schools afterwards.

Meanwhile Mrs. Capron and I hurried to the Tamil service, and entered the large church we had passed the evening before when driving in. It was closely packed throughout by a good, respectable congregation of well-dressed men and women, seated separately. Miss Rendall's sixty-six Christian schoolgirls occupied one section, seated closely packed on the floor; she herself had been presiding at the organ, and my husband was preaching with great animation in English, being interpreted by a fine-looking, oldish man, whom we found afterwards to be Pastor Cornelius. Responses were used, and the service was a good deal liturgical, though the prayers were not read. The music was excellent, the hymns being partly English and partly Tamil lyrics, with native tunes.

After all was over, the pleasant-looking people crowded round us, and we had much talk and shaking of hands. Some of the fine young men we saw conduct the weekly prayer-meeting by turns, and spend the Sunday afternoons in going out among the villages and districts, preaching the Word and holding prayer-meetings. Some of the young women meet in the girls' school every week, and have prayer together; and there seems to be generally a vitality of faith and love among these Christians, and a good deal of spiritual life, which is refreshing to see.

A strange prophecy had gone forth somehow that the Lord's Second Advent was to take place in the end of 1881, and there was a wide-spread expectancy and excitement all over South India. Some people left off work, and said and did other foolish things; but the movement had this effect, that the heathen were roused as well as the Christians, and many began to inquire, and to read and study the Christian's Bible to find out what it had to say on the point. The missionaries hope that, though the excitement has passed away, the interest in the Bible continues, and will yet lead some to Christ.

After breakfast, Dr. Mitchell went to the Sunday school in connection with Mr. Rendall's English City School, and again gave an address. He says there were a good many Brahman lads present, who were as sharp as needles, but did not cavil nearly as much as a similar class in Maharashtra would have done. I spent most of the morning with Mrs. Capron, hearing about her work, in the special sanctum where she receives private visits from her 'dear women,' as she calls them. I sat at her feet, and learnt much from her. She is a grave, earnest, middle-aged woman, her whole face and manner being expressive of calm, subdued power and purpose. Her work is systematically and beautifully arranged; not only her own, but that of the six Bible-women she employs. She could not do half she does but for her great power of organisation and perfect system. Five hundred women in her zenanas are now learning to read the Bible; and the extraordinary number of *over fifteen thousand* have had the Bible *read to them*, by herself and her Bible-women, during the past year. Surely this sowing *of* the seed broadcast *must* soon produce its fruit in souls saved and brought to the feet of Christ.

Besides this zenana visitation, she has four day-schools, some of which I had the pleasure of visiting, and in one helped to give away some little gifts as prizes, which greatly delighted the bonny little brown bairnies, who gathered in great numbers in the upper schoolroom, where they were distributed. Her pupils, old and young, all seem to be very fond of her and to trust her perfectly. She has an additional hold of them through her medical knowledge, and the dispensing of medicine, which takes place every morning. How she manages it all I cannot tell.

One of the most interesting parts of her work consists in the visits the women pay to her; for here, happily, the women are not so secluded as in some other parts, and may venture forth from their zenanas. She told me many anecdotes of these visits, which show most encouraging progress and inquiry among the people. One dying woman, in a heathen home, said to her the other day, 'I am thinking so much of the thief on the cross beside Jesus. He said to him, "*To-day* you will be with Me in heaven." Oh, do you think He will say this to me on this my last dying day?' Another woman, when reproached by her priest for giving up idolatry, retorted: 'Which of our gods have suffered anything for us? Look what the Christians' Christ has suffered for them!' She had read Luke's Gospel with Mrs. Capron. Another intelligent woman, not a Christian, but one whom she had instructed for some time, having no children and plenty of leisure, interested herself in the daughters of a neighbour's family. She got them to come to her house, bought books for them, and taught them to read. When they were sufficiently advanced to read the Bible, she persuaded them to become pupils of the Mem-Sahib, and handed them over to Mrs. Capron.

Another of her pupils, who had been obliged to go to a neighbouring city, returned after a time, and said to her: 'There I found the water good, and the air good, but *here* I receive the living water, and it is good to come back.' The morning I was sitting with her she received a most touching letter from one of her pupils, a heathen woman, telling her of the death of the husband of a friend. She expresses great grief, for now her friend is a widow (and we all know what that means); 'but,' she adds, 'she knows Christ as her refuge; He will comfort her.' Is not this remarkable language for one not a professed Christian to use? But she must be a Christian in heart; probably one of His hidden ones, of whom there are many, I believe, to be found in the homes of India. Another woman won her unbelieving husband to Christ by inducing him, when very ill, to listen to Mrs. Capron as she knelt down and offered up earnest prayer for him, by what seemed to be his dying bed.

In her schools and houses Mrs. Capron has two hundred subscribers for a Sunday-school magazine. Her chief work, and that of her Bible-women, always is teaching, expounding, and reading to the women the Word of God. Every other kind of instruction has a secondary place. She gives them text-cards also, from which they learn verses by heart. And this bears its own fruit. She is by no means alone in this work for women. It is diligently prosecuted by all the missionaries' wives in the various districts, and a large staff of Bible-women and zenana teachers. The converting power of God's own simple Word, carried home by the Holy Spirit, is often seen in a striking and unexpected way among the people, even in remote villages. This is partly from her work, and that of other ladies in other places, and partly from the constant labours of the preachers and evangelists. Cases are discovered by the missionaries in which idolatry has been abandoned, and the almost 'unknown God' worshipped instead, simply from having been listeners to Bible-reading at some time or other. Some are so afraid of the influence of this wonderful

Book, that they frankly say they cannot continue to listen. They say, too, that since the famine the gods themselves are afraid their power is departing, and have gone off to the jungles and mountains.

There is constant itineracy going on throughout the Province, and there is much encouragement in preaching the Word. Mr. Rendall says over 300,000 people are having the Gospel preached to them. Much use is made of singing, and the people are greatly attracted by it, especially when lyrics are used. Dr. Sutton of Orissa, says: 'The people here are fast singing away their prejudices.' So may it be said of the Madura district. The lyrics are sung to native tunes—or rather, are chanted, with a monotonous refrain, which is highly pleasing to native taste.

One could not help being struck with the completeness and thorough nature of the work in every department of this Mission. The schools for both boys and girls are admirable, and the buildings and arrangements the same. I have already referred to Miss Rendall's institution. Her Boarding School is altogether for the daughters of native Christians and the agents of the Mission; and every missionary lady has her own Boarding School at her own station. Thus the children of the native Christians are all well-trained and educated—a most important matter; and good Christian workers are also trained and sent out to villages and districts as teachers, Bible-women, etc., according to their ability or fitness. Miss Rendall teaches up to the middle standard, and receives a large grant from Government. Fourteen different castes are represented in her day-schools, but caste is not observed in any way in the Mission. All Church members sit promiscuously at the Lord's table; but the different castes do not care to intermarry. Some missionaries think it is as well for social reasons that they should not do so at present.

And yet, prosperous as this Mission is, here, as elsewhere, the cry is, how much more might be done, if funds were forthcoming! Alas! everywhere devoted missionaries seem crushed by the word 'retrench.' 'We cannot send means we have not got,' say the Boards. It is true, they cannot. Then let me say to Christian friends who love the work, and who can give the means, that *now* missionaries are heart-stricken in presence of a work they might do, but cannot even touch, having resolutely to shut their ears to the cry, 'Come over and help us,' because they have not the means. They are like generals in front of an enemy's position, which they feel they could carry if only men and means, the sinews of war, were sufficiently placed at their disposal. Oh! that Christian and philanthropic people in Britain and America would but lay this to heart!

Madura was, and is, the seat of one of the chief Roman Catholic Missions in India. The fame of Xavier has naturally eclipsed that of all other Romish Missionaries; but it would be wrong to forget the labours of such men as Roberto de Nobili and Beschi. The former, a nephew of the celebrated Cardinal Bellarmine, laboured from 1606. The natives called him *Tatwabodhak-Swami*, or the 'philosophical teacher.' The moral character of some of the proceedings of the Jesuit missionaries has been vehemently assailed by Romanists as well as Protestants; but it is unnecessary to enter on this painful subject here. There is a handsome modern Roman Catholic church close by, which my husband has seen. It contains a good many pictures, including two or three portraits of Xavier. The priests do not preach in public or in the streets; their services are all conducted in their churches; but processions are numerous, when images are carried about through the city.

Since this delightful visit to Madura was paid, our dear friend who then so kindly entertained us has been called to his rest. The Rev. Mr. Rendall died toward the end of 1883. When we saw him he seemed in vigorous health, and one could not but hope that many days of faithful work for his beloved Mission were still before him. But the Master has seen fit to order it otherwise, and to summon His servant home. His loss is deeply and increasingly felt by his associates, and he is most truly mourned by the whole native Christian community.

In a memorial address by Dr. Chester, of Dindigal, he says of this admirable missionary: 'Love was the secret of Mr. Rendall's power as a Christian and as a missionary. A more unselfish man never lived. . . . His whole wish was to see the kingdom of the Heavenly Master come, and come speedily, in India and in the Madura district. Every meeting he attended, the work of every committee of which he was a member, every letter he wrote, every sermon he preached, and every address he made, proved this.'

# CHAPTER X.

## MADURA AND ITS TEMPLES.

BESIDES the Missions, there is much to interest in this curious old place. Madura was once the capital of a great and powerful kingdom, having a stirring history, like most of its neighbours; and it is still a remarkable and extensive city. It abounds in temples, palaces, fine old tanks, towers and cupolas, and other striking architectural monuments. These amply testify to the greatness of its past, as well as add much to the picturesqueness of its present. It has also a good deal of natural beauty. The modern city covers an immense area, and has unusually wide streets, with low, white-washed houses generally ornamented with stripes and patches of colour, especially in the Brahmans' streets, and stone benches built on to the houses, where you can often catch a quaint and pleasing picture from the life of the people. The streets are wonderfully clean and tidy, and tolerably free from those peculiar odours—not certainly those of 'Araby the blest'—which usually assail one in Indian cities. There are open spaces here and there, full of greenness and sunshine; long wide avenues fringed with beautiful trees; great groves of the palmyra palm; large, park-like compounds, where the Europeans reside; and, in the midst of all, paddy-fields curiously intermingling with the streets and buildings, so that the whole place looks framed in richest green; while the lofty gōparams, or pagoda towers of the temples, rise majestically, and with most picturesque effect, over the whole.

It must have been a splendid city in the days of the famous Tirumalai Naik, who reigned in the seventeenth century, and who did much for the strengthening and beautifying of his capital. Even now it is the finest city of South India. The oldest parts date from the time of the Pandyan kings, before the Christian era. Curious traditions are still told regarding its rise. One is, that a rich merchant once lost his way in the dense forests which then filled this part of the country. In his wanderings, he came on an old temple, dedicated to the god Shiva. Here he was directed by the deity to intimate to the Pandyan king that it was his will and pleasure that a city should be built on this holy spot. The king obeyed, founded the city and temple, whereupon a shower of 'sweet dew' (or manna) fell from heaven, and covered the ground: so the city was named Madura, or *Sweet*.

A flourishing period in the history of this kingdom seems to have been about the first or second century after Christ, when the famous Rishi, or Sage, Agastya, lived. He is said to have been the introducer of Brahmanical civilisation into South India. His exploit in leading a colony of Brahmans southward, is mentioned in the Sanscrit poem, the *Ramayan;* but the date—indeed, everything about this holy and enlightened personage, said to have been the offspring of two gods—is most uncertain, if not mythical. A learned author calls him 'the fabled civiliser of the South.'

TANK AND TEMPLE AT MADURA.

Very early this morning, while it was still cool, our kind host, accompanied by one or two of his native assistants, took us out to see the far-famed pagoda—the finest temple, I suppose, in all India. Certainly none of those we have seen, even in the holiest cities of the Hindus in other parts of India, at all approach this one in grandeur and extent, and also in the value of its endowments and its jewels. But how shall I describe this extraordinary place in all its curious and endless ramifications? What seems to remain in the mind of the wonderful things which go to make up this gorgeous temple, is a confused and bewildering recollection of halls, and corridors, and labyrinthine passages; cloisters, and crypts, and shrines, with all their puzzling native names; grotesque deities, griffins, and quaint hybrid creatures, carved in stone and wood; gilding, and painting, and carving, and pictures; and new, strange architecture one had never seen before; while the notes, hurriedly taken on the spot, only seem at the first look, to make 'confusion worse confounded.'

This great fabric covers twenty acres of ground, and is surrounded by a lofty brick wall, forming a perfect square, and ornamented by red and white stripes, the holy colour of the Hindus. It is dedicated to the god Shiva, and his wife, *Minākshi,* or 'the fish-eyed goddess;' probably, my husband says, an aboriginal deity, who has been identified with *Durga* of Bengal, and *Parvati* of Western India, the wives of Shiva. As you approach the mighty fane, what you are first struck with are the grand gōparams, or towers, which are pyramidal in structure, and are peculiar to this Dravidian style of architecture. These are very lofty and massive; in shape a truncated cone, gorgeously carved, and coloured, and ornamented, the summit being crowned with a fan-shaped erection like the hood of a snake. The entire cone is covered, row on row, and tier on tier, with elaborately carved Hindu deities. Many millions of the gods of the Hindu Pantheon are thus sculptured on the exteriors of these pagoda towers. I forget how many towers there are connected with this temple; but they rise over the gateways, ornament the four corners of the walls, crown the inferior shrines; and, from one point near the sacred tank, I counted thirteen visible at once, two or more of which were covered with gold, and gleamed with dazzling brightness in the sunlight.

We entered the main edifice by a huge, massive, carved gateway of teakwood, guarded on either side by the most fantastic mythological figures, sculptured in stone. Opposite the gateway are four lofty pillars, or shafts, forty-five feet high, and sunk fifteen feet below the surface of the ground, most beautifully carved, and each composed of a single stone. Entering, we found ourselves in a handsome court, called the *Mandapam*, a sort of arcade, with a stone roof supported by rows of fine pillars, ending in a raised daïs, or throne, the canopy of which is supported by lovely spiral columns of highly-polished black basalt. This outer court is used as a place of merchandise, putting one in mind of the Gospel narrative of those who bought and sold in the Temple, who were cast out by Christ. Many people were seated cross-legged on their mats beneath the arches, with all manner of wares spread out around them, and evidently doing an active business.

From this we entered another hall of grand proportions, within which is the chief sanctuary, or Holy of Holies, the shrine which contains the

*Sokalinga*, or sacred symbol of the god Shiva. Into this shrine no one is allowed to penetrate but the Brahman priest. It stands beneath a golden cupola, two huge, furious-looking creatures keeping fantastic watch on either side of the entrance; within, lights glimmer in the darkness, and opposite stands a gigantic *Nandi*, or sacred bull, on which Shiva usually rides, also in black basalt, under a canopy supported by four slender columns most exquisitely carved. This figure is surrounded by tall, graceful candelabra in gold; and in front is a golden altar. The elaborateness of the workmanship everywhere is extraordinary, and the lavish expenditure which must be practised in order to keep it all in preservation and repair, is equally surprising.

From this we wandered over corridors and cloisters of immense extent, all filled with curious things in pictures and carvings, absurd figures in every fantastic attitude; with elephants and bulls, peacocks with expanded tails, and other creatures, all made of pure gold, ready for carrying forth in grand procession at festival times. A fellow-tourist who joined our party exclaimed: 'What grand loot for the Russians when they come!' 'Yes, *when they come*,' we replied. The jewels belonging to this temple, with which the gods and goddesses are decked on great occasions, are of extraordinary beauty and value.

In passing through one long aisle we disturbed a numerous colony of bats, the rush of their flapping wings making the most dismal sounds in the arched roof. The whole place, too, was filled with the horrid din of tomtoms, and the shrill noise of pipes, reverberating through the weird gloom of the passages, and giving one quite an uncanny feeling. At one place we came on a reservoir, filled with abominable things unutterable. All the libations poured out and on to the gods—of holy water, oil, ghee, curd, milk, paint, etc.—flow in one loathsome stream into this reservoir, where it remains stagnant and poisonous. Horrible to tell, this disgusting mixture is actually drunk; partaken of by devotees and their dupes, because it is said to cleanse away all sin. There is no crime, however dreadful or unnatural, that this potion cannot cleanse; no sin so unpardonable but that, if this is imbibed, the offender shall be forgiven!

Is there any depth of error or degradation too low for the human mind to descend to? Would that these miserable people could have their eyes opened to see the true fountain which has been opened for sin and uncleanness, and learn to avail themselves of its real pardoning and purifying power!

Before we passed from the temple, a great man arrived in grand procession to worship. He had brought some holy water from Mother Gunga to offer to the god, and, being a rich merchant of the Chetty caste, he rode on an elephant gaudily caparisoned in gold and silver trappings. The huge beast strode right though the cloisters, making the people fly to right and left, flapped his great ears, and tossed his trunk, grunting and snorting, as if he did not half like his mission. The great man was accompanied by a numerous and picturesque following, carrying red umbrellas, little brown and red flags, tails of the Yak cow, etc. As we walked through the Hall of the Thousand Pillars we were accosted by some holy men smeared all over with ashes, having hardly any other covering, who did not at all seem to relish our intrusion; but Mr. Rendall everywhere was received and treated with perfect respect.

There was once a famous school of poets in connection with the temple, and we saw the cloister where they used to have their sittings. Strange stories and legends of these Tamil *littérateurs* were told us; but I have not space to relate them. Finally, we visited the famous sacred Tank of the Golden Lotus. It is a sheet of dirty green water, with stone steps descending to it, the banks being also faced with stone. A broad, terraced, paved walk goes completely round, beneath a handsome colonnade of beautiful pillars carved in relief, while the whole is encircled by a high wall. Men were busily employed all along this wall, standing on scaffoldings, restoring old frescoes and pictures in the gayest colouring. These chiefly represented fights between the Brahmans and Jains—a quasi-Buddhist sect—wherein the latter always seemed to come worst off, and to be cruelly maltreated; as no doubt they were in fact, when the Hindus succeeded in almost banishing them and their faith from Madura, where once they were paramount.

It is not easy to find out the exact date when this temple was founded; but the building seems to have been begun before the Christian era, and is, indeed, of all ages, having been added to at different dates. Whatever its origin and age, however, its

ENTRANCE TO GREAT HALL, MADURA.

fame is chiefly bound up with that of Tirumalai Naik, who added to the original structure some of its finest halls and shrines.

The palace also, which we next visited, is associated with this great ruler. He built it and lived in it when it was in all its glory. Now, even in comparative ruin, it is a magnificent building; its style of architecture, which is quite different from that of the pagoda, being a mixture of Hindu and Saracenic. Government is now having it extensively and carefully restored, and its spacious halls are to be utilised for public offices. As you enter, there is a splendid quadrangular court, with side aisles, which have roofs elaborately carved in relief with mythological subjects, and supported by double rows of massive granite pillars, coated with finely-polished chunam. From one end of this handsome court, a broad flight of steps leads to the main hall, which is quite as grand in its proportions as the court. It is surmounted by a beautiful domed roof, very lofty, and skirted by open galleries, and has the same sort of pillars as ornament the outer court and other chambers. In one of the chambers there are some graceful columns in black basalt. Altogether, within and without, it is a most imposing structure.

In the afternoon we had tea with Mrs. Hutchins, the wife of the Judge, and saw, in the compound, the finest and biggest banyan tree, I fancy, that exists. They say it is larger even than the wonderful old tree in the Botanic Gardens in Calcutta. Quite an army of graceful slender stems descend from the great canopy of upper branches, and are most beautifully trained and cared for by Mr. Hutchins. A real army might encamp beneath the shadow of this magnificent specimen of the monarch of Indian woods, so wide an area does it cover. Of course, one could not look at the majestic tree without recalling Milton's description:

> 'The fig-tree, not that kind for fruit renowned;
> But such as at this day, to Indians known,
> In Malabar or Deccan spreads her arms.'

Miss Rendall then drove us round and round a magnificent tank, a great sheet of water enclosed by walls of solid masonry, also a monument of the enlightened ruler I have already often referred to, Tirumalai Naik. At festival times, this whole immense square, in the centre of which a temple stands, is lit up with thousands upon thousands of tiny oil-lamps, which must have the loveliest effect, like the glimmering and gleaming of myriad fire-flies. On such occasions all the grand golden things of the temple are brought forth by the priests, and borne aloft in gorgeous procession, amid the plaudits and acclamations of the enthusiastic populace.

On the last morning of our stay, we had a most inspiriting little expedition to Pasumalai, where there is a branch Mission, and an excellent institution for the training and education of native Christian lads and boys. It is under the charge of Mr. and Mrs. Washburn and Mr. and Mrs. Burnell. Mr. Washburn sent his 'rockaway' for us, a pleasant sort of conveyance, like a noddy with the front away, with which we became acquainted first in Quebec. It was drawn by a tiny Pegu pony, the briskest little creature you can imagine. The drive

AUDIENCE CHAMBER IN THE PALACE, MADURA.

in the fresh, cool, morning air was most enjoyable. It was a shady road, fringed with beautiful trees, the neem, tamarind, banyan, peepul, and plenty of palms; the paddy-fields filled with richest green, mingled with brown knolls, isolated rocks, tanks, and clumps of wood, while blue, mist-veiled hills bounded the distant view. The bright little pony danced along almost too quickly, with his picturesque driver astride in front of us, in red turban, and blue coat all edged and slashed with red. Presently a church tower rose above some trees lying in the shelter of a bare, brown hill, and we turned into a large compound filled with buildings of every size and shape. We breakfasted with our friends in one of the pretty Mission bungalows, the very picture of New England neatness, the parlours being laid with cool, clean matting, and having the American rocking-chair about everywhere. A dish we find at every breakfast-table in these regions is a kind of mulligatawny, which is eaten with rice, and comes in place of the cracked wheat and oatmeal which precede the substantials in America.

After breakfast and prayers we went out to see the Institution. The number of buildings shows its extensive character. It includes a High School, an Industrial Department, where trades are taught, a College, and also a Theological Department for the training of aspirants to the ministry, as well as catechists and evangelists. One hundred and eight students were enrolled last year. An interesting feature is, that the pupils gather to it from such distances. They come from towns and villages and

Mission stations extending over an area of six thousand miles; and half of these are the sons of pastors and catechists; others are converts from their own conviction, who have been cast adrift by their friends, and who here find a home and sympathy, and good training for future work. All pay fees, except poor boys, who get scholarships. We spent an hour or two most happily among these nice lads. My husband questioned and addressed all the different departments, and found many in the theological classes earnest, thoughtful young men. This department exercises a most salutary influence on the school-boys; they have meetings for prayer, and go out on itinerating work when opportunity offers. Seeing a row of small, cell-like chambers, I asked their use. I found they were prayer-rooms, where the pupils may retire for private reading and prayer—a most needful arrangement in India, where the houses are so open that it is a hard matter to find a closet to which you can retire and shut your door about you, and 'pray to your Father who is in secret.'

Thus the Mission provides for the proper training and upbringing of the children of its converts, the next generation of Christians; surely a matter of the very greatest importance, to which every Mission should wisely attend.

## CHAPTER XI.

### TINNEVELLY—PALAMCOTTA.

We have now come to our last day of railway travelling. We waved our adieux to our kind entertainers and to beautiful Madura, and are now journeying in a south-easterly direction toward the great district of Tinnevelly. The country is flat, except for some dim, blue, hazy hill-ranges in the far distance; and though the soil is rather sandy, it is generally well cultivated and covered with crops; not in little patches like a patch-work quilt, which is the aspect cultivation too often presents in India, but in big fields worthy the name. The paddy-fields, where rice is grown, abound the most, but bajri, jowari, millet, and cotton in great quantities are also largely cultivated; coffee, too, wherever there are hills or higher ground.

The province is rich agriculturally, and the scenery rural in its character. It might remind one of our own midland counties, but for the great groves of the palmyra palm, which now became the chief feature in the landscape, and are certainly not English. This marvellous tree, which everywhere in South India is the real staff of life to the people, covers many hundred square miles; and though its lofty top is not so beautiful as the cocoa palm, with its crown of long, graceful fronds, yet it is most picturesque and stately, and gives a thoroughly Oriental and varied aspect to the scene.

The district is interesting, too, to the lover of antiquarian research, from the curious remains which are to be found of pre-historic races, in weapons, implements, pottery, etc. It is also the scene of the early Dravidian civilisation. But I confess that, to me, the chief interest lies in its being the scene of some of the most successful missionary enterprises the world has ever seen.

As we journey onward, we find it becomes hotter and hotter, and the train slower and slower. Our patience and endurance are indeed sorely taxed. Tuticorin is a considerable town further south, and the terminus of the railway. We earnestly wished and hoped to go there, to visit our old friends, the learned and revered Bishop Caldwell, of the Society for the Propagation of the Gospel, and his wife, who now have the head-quarters of their Mission in Tuticorin. But this pleasure is not to be ours at present, and it is a very great disappointment to us both.

When it began to grow dark, though hardly yet cool, after what had seemed an interminable day, we changed into a short branch line for Tinnevelly. At the station, we found a young native Christian waiting with a servant and note from Bishop Sargent, who was expecting us. There was also the bishop's large, comfortable bandy, something like a small omnibus, drawn by a pair of huge white bullocks, into which we thankfully got. We left the native city behind, called Tinnevelly, like the province of which it is the capital, and turned toward the English cantonment Palamcotta, and were soon welcomed by the venerable Bishop and his most gentle wife. A long-cherished dream was realised : we were at Palamcotta.

Bishop Sargent looks a much younger man than I expected: his manner is youthful and vivacious; his silvery white hair is brushed back off his fine, lofty forehead; his face is clean shaved, and fresh, with a bright, pleasant expression; his movements are rapid, and he looks still full of vigour and force. One may well hope that God will yet, for a good many years, spare this excellent missionary-bishop to carry on the glorious work for Christ he has been conducting for now nearly half a century. Mrs. Sargent is in extremely feeble health; but though she cannot walk without help, yet she is literally from morn till night engaged in Mission work. It is her meat and drink, her very life. I do not think I ever saw a more touching picture than this infirm, venerable lady, sitting on her low chair in her verandah, surrounded by a group of school-girls, or a company of poor, desolate-looking widows, in whom she always takes special interest, while with feeble but earnest voice she instructs them, or reads to them, and tells them of the Saviour, always finishing off with prayer. I never go to her rooms any time of the day but I find her thus engaged, and she always brightens up with such a look of love and interest when her 'dear girls' come about her.

The house has nothing palatial about it. It is by no means a bishop's palace. It is simply a comfortable large bungalow, having no upstairs; the rooms are lofty, and opening off each other, with a wide pillared verandah stretching along the front, and a pretty bowery porch. The furnishings and fittings, with all the surroundings, are simplicity itself; there is every needful comfort, but nothing more. It is a true missionary home: the work is all in all; everything is subordinate to this; it is the one idea of the place and people. This was the house in which the excellent missionary Rhenius lived, a well-known name among the many associated with the history of Tinnevelly Missions. Joseph Wolfe rightly called him 'the great Rhenius.'

Soon after we arrived, dinner was announced, during which the Bishop talked in the most entertaining way, giving information, and relating incidents and anecdotes with immense animation. We quite forgot our fatigue and weary journey. Then, before we left the table, a troop of native servants filed in, sat down cross-legged on the floor, removed their turbans, and the Bishop conducted worship in Tamil.

The Tinnevelly district as a Mission field is divided between the Church Missionary Society and the Society for the Propagation of the Gospel, the greater portion belonging to the former. Dr. Sargent is Suffragan Bishop for the Church Missionary Society Missions, and Bishop Caldwell the same in connection with the Society for the Propagation of the Gospel.

The venerable Schwartz—'the most memorable name in the history of Protestant Missions in South India,' as Bishop Caldwell says—was connected with these Missions, as well as with those of Tranquebar, Trichinopoly, and Tanjore. He visited Tinnevelly in 1771, also in 1782, and again in 1785. He baptised the first convert, a Brahman woman, named Clarinda. On the occasion of this baptism, Schwartz wrote: 'Oh, let us pray for more faithful labourers. May God send such, for Christ's sake. May He send such *in troops!*' Surely this prayer has since been signally answered. After a few years, Clarinda and two other Christians went the long journey to Tanjore to see Schwartz, and to beg that a missionary might be settled in their district. The consequence was that successive catechists were sent. Sathianāden especially—a native missionary, educated by himself—did admirable work, and laboured long in the district; and under him the native Church made steady progress. Chiefly from the efforts made by Clarinda, the first Christian church was built; and so began the Protestant Mission Churches of Tinnevelly, now so flourishing.

The Christian community in connection with Bishop Sargent at present numbers fifty-five thousand. Under Bishop Caldwell of the Society for the Propagation of the Gospel, there are forty-five thousand more; so that the wonderful and delightful fact remains to cheer the hearts of the friends of Missions, that, out of a population of about two millions, one hundred thousand are Protestant Christians. The number has quadrupled itself in twenty years. Let all who talk of missions as a failure be told this weighty fact.

I can hardly attempt to speak of Roman Catholic Missions. It was on the Tinnevelly coast that

Francis Xavier, in 1542, after staying a short time in Goa, commenced his labours. The Jesuits, after being repressed as a society for some time, again received charge of the Tinnevelly Missions in 1837. Their converts still increase in number; although, as far as I can learn, not so rapidly as those of the Protestants; and they are very diligent with schools, orphanages, and such kinds of Mission work.

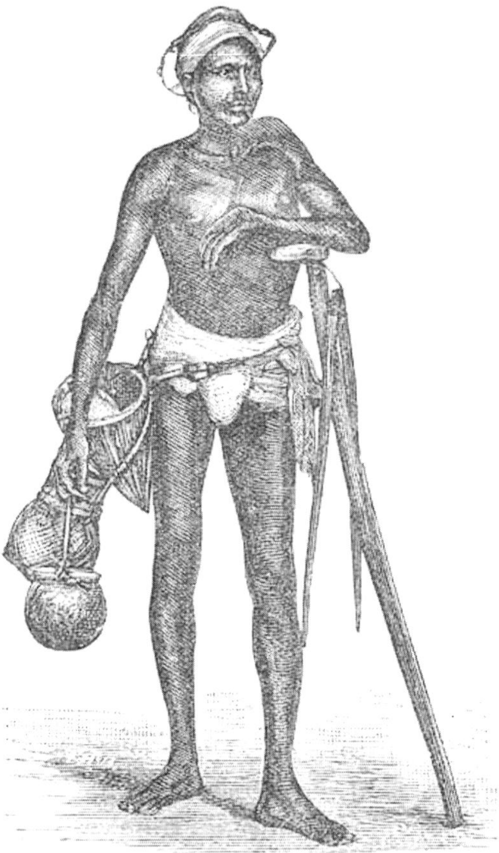

A PALMYRA CLIMBER.

Most of the Bishop's converts—quite two-thirds, I think—are drawn from the Shanars, who, as I said, are worshippers of devils. They are a low caste, but claim to be the original inhabitants of this part of the country, and have never been much influenced by Hindus or Hinduism. The Shanars live chiefly by the palmyra palm, and are the palmyra climbers; that is, it is they who mount these branchless trees, sometimes to the height of eighty or ninety feet, to remove the sap or juice, which has been drawn off in a small earthen pot at the top. This beverage is much used by the people, and is very refreshing, though it becomes intoxicating if left to ferment. It is also made into sugar, and is used in other ways. From many villages in the heart of these palmyra groves, where formerly only the horrible and degrading rites of devil-worship were practised, you now hear the voice of prayer ascending to the God and Father of all.

The people usually have good faces, with marked features, very dark skin, and bright, good-tempered expressions. The men and women both wear the hair long, and generally tied in a knot behind. Among the women the barbaric, and I must say, very ugly, decoration of the torn ear is universal; which we saw, I think, for the first time in Madura. The lobe is perforated, or rather torn, and the aperture hung with rings of brass, lead, iron, or anything heavy, so that it is weighed down and elongated until it sometimes reaches half-way to the shoulder. The longer it is, the more elegant and the more admired. The operation begins in childhood, and is really a cruel one, and as unreasonable as the bound foot among the women of China; but the fashion is inexorable for all well-to-do women. It is considered quite a disgrace if the ear is *torn open* in the process, so that it cannot hold the ornaments. The women are so proud of this decoration that you see it constantly in the schools, and often even among the Christian women; and the missionaries find it difficult to induce the mothers to leave it off in the upbringing of their children. Mrs. Lewis, of the Zenana Mission here, told me of a little blind girl in one of her houses, out of whose ear she had taken metal rings which weighed two and a half ounces.

Life begins early in India, and we were up betimes, —now waiting in the verandah to go out with the Bishop. The heat is stifling, though it is hardly yet six o'clock, and of the exhausting, soaking, steamy sort. Not a breath stirs, everything is still; but by-and-by the welcome breeze will come, and it will be cooler. The whole scene is full of peace, and so pretty. It is a large, park-like compound. The sun begins to mount into the sky, but the bright beams are shaded with banks of white, vapoury clouds; the lovely green of the paddy-fields which lie away beyond the compound is sweet and tender, and looks refreshed by the dews of night. You are almost cheated into the belief that you are looking at an English park. The trees stand about the house in leafy grandeur, throwing long shadows on the grass. The branches are only stirred by the brisk, funny little squirrels, who bound about at their merry gambols, and the long-tailed, white *bulbul*, which I thought at first must be a bird of paradise, as the sun gleamed on the long, beautiful feathers, while it flitted among the leaves. The ubiquitous crow, too, of course is here, with his usual swagger and trim black coat, and breaks the sweet silence with his impertinent caw. The sward is wonderfully green, but will not remain long so now, as the fierce sun grows daily more fierce, and will scorch it up. There are many substantial buildings about, which, I suppose, are schools and boarding-houses; and above all, a little to the right, also within the compound, stands the handsome Mission church, gleaming white among the trees, with a graceful spire towering over everything. As I write, the church-bell begins to chime forth its invitation to morning prayer, and a troop of school girls in bright garments marches past to attend the service. An ideal scene! full of encouragement and holy joy to the Christian heart; for it tells of work earnest and fruitful, of hopes fulfilled and promises made good; and one cannot but look onward to the glorious future—perhaps, not so very far off—when the nations shall be gathered in, and the whole earth filled with the glory of God.

The Bishop came for us, and we soon followed to church. Mr. Jesudās (the name means Servant of Jesus), the native pastor, was just beginning the service. The Bishop and Dr. Mitchell sat within the Communion rails, while the pews were filled with the pupils from the Boys' Seminary, the Boarding School girls, the teachers, and all the people of the compound. It is a very large church, holding more than a thousand people, and at the Sabbath services it is always crowded. The Bishop has had the joy of seeing 'the little one' literally 'become a thousand' in his time; for when he came to Palamcotta there were only about forty members in connection with this church. The service was very simple and the music excellent, though there was no instrument of any kind used.

The music was rendered entirely by the young people of the schools.

But it is not only in the numbers of the converts that the progress is remarkable. In his *Lectures on the Tinnevelly Missions* Bishop Caldwell speaks very strongly regarding the improvement in the character and standing of the native Christians. They are rapidly rising in many respects. At the last examination of the Madras University, the Christians, in proportion to their numbers, obtained a higher place even than the Brahmins, who are confessedly an intellectual race. The Missions educate their people thoroughly, and so, though of the low Shanar caste originally, they are fast outstripping the Hindus in position and standing. It is true of the whole native Christian community that it is steadily growing in influence and importance; and I am told that this is specially the case among the Protestants. 'The very look of the people is changed,' as Bishop Sargent truly remarked.

He spoke also rejoicingly of their increased liberality. A few years ago they gave very little in support even of their own churches and schools. They expected the Mission to maintain the pastors and schoolmasters, to build their churches, and do everything for them. But now all this has entirely changed. Last year the native Christians here, connected with the Church Missionary Society, contributed 32,000 rupees towards the work of the Mission; and school-fees are now universally paid, even in the Boarding Schools.

The Bishop also spoke most hopefully regarding the experiment which is being made in this district by the Church Missionary Society of withdrawing European missionaries as much as possible, and replacing them by native agents. The European missionaries now in the field are employed as educationists, while the charge of congregations, evangelistic work, and itineracy are all carried on by ordained pastors and catechists. Consequently, the native ministry has been largely increased. There are now sixty-four ordained native clergymen, though, when Dr. Sargent came to Tinnevelly, there was only one. There are also a good many honorary catechists, men who support themselves and do a great and good work, preaching to the heathen as well as among the Churches. It was delightful to hear the Bishop talk. He told us also of the native councils, which have been successfully introduced. There is a Congregational Council, consisting of the pastor and three or four persons chosen by the congregation; a Financial Council, and lastly, a General Council, which meets once a year, and reviews the proceedings of the inferior courts.

Thus the native Churches are moving steadily onward, and are being trained to self-government and self-support; while the good Bishop—always the father of his people, the shepherd of the flock—superintends, and presides, and watches over the whole.

After service, Mr. Jesudās, the pastor, and Mrs. Lewis, from the Zenana Home, breakfasted with us, and then the fifty pupils from Mrs. Sargent's Girls' Boarding School filed in to prayers, and stood in a ring round the drawing-room. The Bishop and my husband asked many questions of the girls, especially in Scripture, which were answered with readiness and understanding; and some questions were pretty hard. I never saw brighter or more intelligent scholars anywhere. They were of all sizes and ages, neatly dressed alike in a pretty costume of buff and scarlet, with pleasant, intelligent, and, in some cases, refined faces. They are all the Christian daughters of Christian parents. There are no orphanages here. The system is to board the orphans in respectable Christian households, where they are cared for and trained at a comparatively small outlay. But all look on boarding-schools, where the children can remain apart from heathen influences, as most important. On this point Bishop Caldwell says 'that day-schools will not suffice; for one or two generations, at least, we must rely on Boarding Schools.'

What delighted me very much was the singing, so softly sweet, so beautifully harmonised. The voices were so much sweeter and better modulated than is usually the case in India, that I was surprised. Besides several of Sankey's best hymns, and some plaintive Tamil lyrics, they sang some beautiful pieces from the *Messiah* with feeling and taste. The truth is, the Bishop himself takes much pains with the musical department in all the schools, and this is the reason there are so few harsh tones or jarring notes.

In the afternoon the lads came in from the boys' school at the other side of the compound, and stood round the drawing-room as the girls had done, and answered and sang just as well. Some of them accompanied themselves with the violin. The Bishop has lately had fourteen violins sent out as gifts to the best musicians, which are much appreciated, and at play-hours are in constant use. These lads are also the children of Christian parents, or Christians on their own profession of faith. Many of them are supported by friends in Australia. And so the important matter of the right upbringing of the youth—the next generation of Christians, on whom so much will depend—is thus carefully attended to in this thoroughly-equipped and excellent Mission.

In the cool of the evening there was a pretty little demonstration on the lawn. The Bishop had all the schools, girls and boys, marshalled forth, bearing the flags and banners, with pretty devices, which had assisted at the grand reception this Mission had given to the Prince of Wales on his visit to India. The young folks marched about, played games, sang songs, when the precious fiddles did ample duty, and altogether enjoyed the fun and frolic. And I think that we enjoyed it quite as much as they did, for it was pleasant to see that these school-children could play well as well as work well, and that 'Jack was not a dull boy.' It was delightful, too, to see how thoroughly the good Bishop enters into their sports, and how much at home with him the young folks are. He is full of mechanical ingenuity, too. We found him superintending the construction of a water-wheel in the compound to-day, on some new principle of his own; and there is a gigantic globe in the hall, fashioned by his own hands. He pointed out a fine spreading banyan tree to us, standing over the wall in what is now a paddy-field, but formerly was part of the compound. The curious and beautiful tree, truly the king of the Indian forest, had dropped some roots from the upper branches, as its manner is, and flung them over the wall, so that 'daughters grew about the mother-tree,' and the daughter was now bigger than the mother. The tree seemed determined to take possession anew of the Mission grounds. 'See,' said the Bishop, 'it won't be separated from us.' 'True,' added my husband; 'and look, is not that increasing army of strong young stems, all separately springing from the glorious roof-tree, like the youthful Church of India, of which we have been speaking? Above, in Christ our head, they are one; but they multiply and spread, each a new, strong tree, taking possession of the land.' The good Bishop's face quite kindled at the thought.

We have spent a day with our friends, Mr. and Mrs. Kember, of the Theological Training College of the Mission; and another with Mr. and Mrs. Harcourt, who, since the departure of the Rev. Mr. Lush, have had the charge and management of the well-known Sarah Tucker Institution. This is for the training of schoolmistresses and the higher classes of native Christian girls. I cannot tell the interest with which we have gone over these first-rate institutions, nor how grateful we feel to our kind friends for the infinite trouble and pains they have taken to show us the classes, and all the arrangements, outside and in. I must be allowed to say, over and over, that nothing strikes one more in some of these delightful Missions we have now the privilege of visiting, than the perfect organisation there is: every department is made perfect in its way; nothing is spared which can make the work more real, and thorough, and successful.

The compounds belonging to both the Training Institutions are not far from the Bishop's, and are very spacious. They are beautified, too, with clumps and lines of banyan, mango, tamarind, neem, and other fine trees; ample playgrounds there are, and tennis-courts, hedgerows, and good sward, which is still wonderfully green. In Mr. Kember's, besides the Mission House, there are groups of low bungalows used as class-rooms, mess-rooms, dormitories, and small rooms for 'studies,' all of the same type—plain, substantial, white-washed buildings, airy and clean. This Institution is entirely for the training of workers—pastors, evangelists, catechists, and schoolmasters. All who enter understand that they are thenceforward to be agents of the Mission, to go where they may be sent. There were eight men whom we saw, and had much talk with, in Mr. Kember's own Theological Class, who are soon to be ordained to the office of the ministry.

This solemn service took place about a month after our visit. It was held in the large Mission Church, which was filled to overflowing. 'It was a most striking scene,' a friend writes, 'when the eight candidates, the native clergy, forty-seven in number, the European missionaries, and the venerable Bishop passed in procession up the central aisle. After the sermon, and before the imposition of hands, there was an impressive season of silent prayer; and when the candidates had been set apart, the Holy Communion followed, and concluded the deeply interesting and impressive service.'

Another interesting half-hour we spent with Mr. David Solomon, the head-master, in his class of catechists, who told us a good deal about the progress of the work among the heathen, and their attitude towards Christianity. They say the Shanars are much stirred up at present in behalf of their own system, and frightened because of the triumphs the Gospel is making. 'The Gospel is strong,' they say, 'and will conquer us if we do not conquer it;' so they are furbishing up every old heathenish rite and are much on their guard. They acknowledge, however, that they are not so much in terror of the devils since Christianity came; 'the missionaries have frightened them,' they say, 'and they have retreated to the forests and jungles.' Surely this Shanar worship is the most degrading of all heathen systems, for the objects of their worship are not devilish deities only, but devils simply and literally. It is a system of terrorism: they worship these malevolent beings from dread; and it is surely a great matter if this dread is lessened, and this sad and degrading bondage begins to be broken.

Fifteen catechists have gone forth from Mr. Solomon's class this year, and three more are ready to go, and most of them are converted Shanars. While we were at Mr. Kember's, fifty new pupils from a distant district arrived, who were at once drafted into the departments suited to them.

The Sarah Tucker Institution was built by Bishop Sargent and the Rev. Mr. Spratt, in 1862. Miss Tucker never was in India herself, but her brother was one of the secretaries of the Church Missionary Society, I think, in Madras; and she took so deep and active an interest in the women of India that she worked constantly for them, and, though a great invalid, accomplished much in raising funds and otherwise helping on the cause. At her death, this most useful and much-needed Institution was erected as a memorial of her. It is rather an imposing structure, standing in the same compound with Mr. Harcourt's house, with massive pillars supporting the portico, and a wide verandah running along the entire front. It accommodates one hundred and twenty girls, who board and live in the premises, and are trained to teach in normal classes. They are then sent out to take charge of branch affiliated schools, of which there are now forty-two, all taught by Christian teachers, and attended by many children of the highest caste. We were greatly pleased with the way in which some of the young women communicated instruction to their pupils—in a bright, quick, animated way which at once secured the attention of the nice little girls. We were delighted here, too, with the singing, which was led by Mrs. Harcourt, who manages this department entirely herself, and with quite as pleasing results as we had noticed among Mrs. Sargent's flock. Indeed, Palamcotta quite carries the palm in the matter of music over all the Missions we have seen. The girls do a great deal of lovely embroidery, which Mrs. Harcourt is very glad to take orders for, disposing of it for the benefit of the Institution.

A lady has lately been sent out by the Church Missionary Zenana Society to assist Mrs. Harcourt, of whom we have seen a good deal. This is Miss

Askwith, who is already a favourite with the missionaries and pupils, and takes her own good share of the work, including the acquisition of that dreadfully hard Tamil tongue.

I must also refer to another part of the work which had especial attraction for me, that was the Zenana Mission conducted by Mrs. Lewis and Miss McDonald. We lunched in the pleasant, bright Zenana Home with these ladies, and Miss Ling, who has just lately joined them. Mrs. Thomas is a name every one always remembers in connection with woman's work in South India. I was glad to find that she is still working in a station about thirty miles off, which rejoices in the name of Mengnanapuram. Almost every Christian woman one meets with here seems to have been under her tuition or influence in some way or other; and she still has a boarding-school in which there are eighty-six girls.

After lunch Mrs. Lewis and I started for the native city—a hot, dusty, disagreeable drive of three miles, in a peculiarly slow, shaky, bullock-coach. The wilful beasts absolutely declined to go out of a walk. Palamcotta is the place where the English reside, and the head-quarters of the administration, while Tinnevelly, a biggish place, situated on the banks of the Tambrapani, is the chief native town of the district. Bishop Caldwell says that, until the English rule began in 1802, Tinnevelly had probably never had two successive years of peace. But the days of misrule have happily passed away. There are some handsome temples, with the usual gōparams; but there is nothing striking in the town.

Zenana work has had the same happy effect among the people of the Madras Presidency as in other parts of India. Bishop Sargent thinks that the visits of European ladies to their wives have done more to secure a friendly feeling toward the English among the men than anything else has done. He says in a paper read before the Bangalore Missionary Conference of 1879: 'No proclamation from the highest in power could so impress the minds of high-caste native women in regard to the kind feeling which English people bear towards them, as does the frequent contact of these zenana ladies with them for the Gospel's sake. I am convinced that, since this work has commenced, a more favourable opinion, within a limited sphere, must now be entertained of us than ever was before.'

Mrs. Lewis took me to some of the houses in which she teaches; and I noticed that the zenana apartments were better furnished, and the women better off and brighter-looking than the women of the same class are in Bengal and the North-west. They are, of course, as ignorant and superstitious, and as much in need of being taught; but those I saw have not an imprisoned look; they can look out and go out, and their apartments are not shut off from the rest of the house and the rest of the world, as those where the poor women of Calcutta live their joyless, hopeless, objectless lives.

The most interesting visit we paid was to a gentle-looking, very poor woman who had once sent urgently for Mrs. Lewis, when her son was dying. When her friend arrived, she exclaimed: 'Do send me that Jesus. I want to see Him. He will cure my boy.' When told she must pray to Him, she said: 'How shall I speak to Him? I don't know what words to use.' Mrs. Lewis taught her a short, simple prayer, which she repeated. Her boy recovered. Now, though unbaptised, she seems a sincere believer in that Jesus she so earnestly asked, like the Greeks, to see.

During our drive, both going and coming, I was amused with the number of men and boys who pursued us, keeping alongside the bandy, entreating Mrs. Lewis for books. They all seemed to know her and her large bag, in which the precious books were carried. They were quite willing to pay for them; and when the supply was exhausted, the disappointment was great, while some of the lads stipulated that they should be remembered first next time.

On our return, in the cool of the evening, I found two huge, curious machines standing in the compound, with some meek-looking bullocks tied under the trees. These were the vehicles in which we were to proceed on our travels—for we had done with railways for the present,—one for ourselves and one for our servant and baggage. I surveyed them with considerable foreboding, seeing we were to spend the night in them. They were the common carts of the country, very narrow, very long, and very high, with arched roof covered with matting, giving the interior a vault-like look. There was a hard, wooden bottom, and tremendously high wheels, rough and strong. My husband had taken the precaution of having a good bed of clean straw laid in the bottom. Joseph was deftly and silently

BULLOCK CARTS.

stowing away bundles and packages and portmanteaus in one of the cave-like dens, the cheeriest of the party, while in the other were heaped quilts, and cushions, and rugs, and shawls, the bullocks looking on, evidently in a very dejected frame of mind, knowing the work that was before them, while their drivers were calmly asleep on the sward beside them. Soon all was ready for the start. We had already taken leave of the Bishop, who had started on some pastoral work which awaited him in a distant part of his diocese. A little later, we dined with Mrs. Sargent, then had prayer together, and took leave of the gentle lady, hoping to meet again shortly on the Nielgherry Hills. When everybody else went to bed, we climbed into our lair, made ourselves as snug as we could on the straw, and set out into the darkness.

## CHAPTER XII.

### TRAVANCORE—NAGERCOIL.

LOOKING onward, in a south-westerly direction, as you journey from Tinnevelly toward Cape Comorin, you see a range of purple mountains stretching across the plain in broken, and picturesque, and most striking masses. Beyond this grand natural rampart lies the beautiful little kingdom of Travancore—an independent State, having a Maharajah, or king, of its own—toward which our faces were now turned. This country is often called the Garden of South India; which it undoubtedly is, being full of loveliness, in smiling valleys and verdant rice-fields, waters, rocks, trees, hills—often green to their summits,—extensive palmyra forests, and a marvellous wealth of tropical vegetation, while its shores are washed by the great blue Southern Sea.

It has other attractions, however, which transcend even these; for Travancore is becoming, also, a garden of the Lord. Once, with all its natural beauty, it was a wilderness of moral and spiritual darkness too deep to be told: Brahmanism, demon-worship, caste, slavery, and every sort of oppression, held undisputed sway. But now these things are changing, and the wilderness begins to 'blossom like the rose.' There are green spots now. There are the homes of the missionaries, and the Christian churches, which, through their labours, blest by God's Spirit, are filled with men and women gathered out of this heathenism. There are places where for long ages devil-worshippers practised their abominable and degrading rites, that are now Christian hamlets, whence praise and prayer ascend from loving hearts to the loving Father in heaven, and where the temples and altar-stones for this wretched worship have been changed for churches, and schools, and Christian homes. Superstition, of course, still reigns over much of the region; but a great deal has been done. The Gospel has taken root marvellously, bringing forth golden fruit for Christ's kingdom; and the story of its introduction among the Shanars of Tinnevelly and Travancore cannot be told too often, if only it stimulates the faith and zeal of God's people to go on to renewed thanksgiving and fresh effort.

We had a toiling night of it after we got clear of the station roads and cantonment civilisation. We lay on our straw bed beneath the low-arched roof of our novel conveyance—I coiled up at the head, and my husband, a sort of guard, across the foot. It was fortunate he had got us so well padded in, for the roads—so called by courtesy—were only tracks in the deep sand, and full of formidable ruts and holes. One moment a wheel would dash down into a deep rut, while the other had mounted over a piece of rock; and many a time we thought it was all over with us; but we struggled and scrambled on, the meek, patient bullocks, quite accustomed to the yoke and to the road, creeping cautiously along, while the drivers sat on their benches placidly asleep. I believe they slept all night, except when, after a worse lurch than usual, the Saheb would pour forth a volley of shouts upon them. To talk was of no use, as they did not understand a word we said. They would then wake up, use the stick zealously on the unoffending beasts, jerk the tails, admonish them in Tamil, and then go off to sleep again.

At dawn we found ourselves in a picturesque region of rocks and hills, intermingled with the rich green of the rice-fields, and always great clumps of the stately palmyra palm. The mountains lay near us now, in long, undulating lines and ridges or lofty summits, with fantastic, jagged peaks, unspeakably grand. Soon the valley narrowed, and our route lay between ridges of rock and low hills, with an occasional small temple of the rudest description; also rest-houses, and the curious white altar-stones used in demon-worship, standing here and there along the road beneath the trees. We encountered many wayfarers, who stood and stared at us in wonderment as we passed. They were most strange, wild-looking people, with shaggy, unkempt, turbanless heads, lines and patches of white paint all over their breasts, and no clothing to speak of—only a dirty rag across their loins.

A group gathered round us, eying all we did with stupid but good-humoured astonishment, when we scrambled down from the cart, and bivouacked under the thick shade of a grand banyan-tree, while Joseph made us a cup of tea. It was delicious to rest a while, and breathe the sweet, cool air, and let our poor bones get into their usual places after the process of dislocation they had been subjected to all night. Meanwhile a few sticks were gathered, a bottle of water was emptied into a tiny kettle, which was sat on to boil, and 'the cup which cheers' seemed more to cheer,—more fragrant and refreshing than ever it had done before. The poor gaping people looked on awestruck. Their speech was utterly incomprehensible, and we were very sorry we could only smile our good-will, with accompanying signs; for a talk with them, as we should have had in Western or Northern India, was, alas! impossible in this the extreme South.

The scenery became more and more beautiful as we neared the goal—Nagercoil. The giant ghāts rose before us like a wall, as if to bar further progress; but at length, rounding a spur, we came to a gap or pass—a small opening in the great rampart, so remarkable that it might have led to a lair of Rob Roy's—and by this natural portal we entered the kingdom of Travancore. After we had passed through this, we soon came on the signs of a denser population. There were a few scattered houses. Then came more houses and streets; we found we had entered the town; and soon the glad moment arrived when our queer cavalcade drew up before the door of our friend the Rev. Mr. Duthie's Mission House. He, and his wife, and daughter and son, all ran out to bid us welcome, and help us to alight, 'a heap of dust and broken bones,' as my husband said.

We were meeting now for the first time in our lives; but Mr. Duthie had frequently written to us during our progress hither; and no one has been more cordial or helpful to us in forming our plans.

Indeed, the Nagercoil Mission House has been a sort of goal all through: and here we are, by the good hand of our God upon us; and there is a restful sense of being done with our journey for the present; though, of course, we shall ere long have to start again.

We quite appreciated the cool, big, shady rooms into which they took us, and all the comforts so amply and carefully provided. The big baths seemed specially welcome; and now, after the bath, and change of clothes, and a good rest and good breakfast, we feel ready for what may come.

MAHARAJAH OF TRAVANCORE.

*(From a Photograph).*

Breakfast in the Mofussil and country places in India, means a midday meal, as on the Continent. After this was over, the Rev. Mr. Lee, from the Mission House in a compound across the road opposite, came and joined our party. We all gathered in the wide, shady verandah, a few steps higher than the garden, and filled with low chairs, when a remarkable and most intelligent man called — not a Christian —

whose story and conversation seems to have introduced us at once into the condition of things among the people here.

Travancore has been noted for its intense Brahmanism; and although it is awakening, like the rest of the land, to progress and reform, yet the enlightening comes slowly. This man is a Brahman, and was the first individual who was so enlightened and so brave as to propose, or venture to introduce, the dreadful innovation of widow remarriage. He had a little daughter who had been married as a child. The boy-husband died; and the father knew well what the little girl's fate would be as a life-long widow—a widow, though she had never been a wife. And widows are as hardly treated here as elsewhere in India. So he took the daring resolve to have her remarried. A tremendous commotion was the result; his house was pulled down about his ears, he was expelled from the Brahman quarter, put out of caste, and persecuted in every possible way. In

SISTER OF MAHARAJAH.

*(From a Photograph.)*

short, there was a great uproar. But he has braved and outlived it all. He has built a new house, and also a new well; for he could not be suffered even to draw water, and so pollute the wells sacred to the outraged Brahmans. This was a few years ago, and he has held steadily and manfully on his way, doing much to promote enlightenment, encouraging others to go and do likewise, and now seems a most contented and cheerful martyr to reform. The storm has done much good; and now innovations do not startle so much. Only a few years ago the missionaries would have been mobbed and insulted had they ventured to pass down the Brahman street; now any European may do so without fear; and the feeling of the people to the missionaries has not only become less hostile, but is generally full of friendliness. One or two other cases of widow-remarriage have occurred; and the spirit of progress is gaining sway even in caste-ridden Travancore.

As soon as it became cool enough, Mr. Duthie took us out to see something of the place. It was a most lovely evening, cool and invigorating, and we had some exquisite mountain views as the sun went down behind the glorious masses, in an ocean of brilliant yet delicate carmine.

Nagercoil is now a large village—or perhaps I should say town—nestling cosily at the foot of the grand mountain ranges, which encompass it on three sides. It opens out on the fourth, and stretches down in beautiful undulations, crowned with rich tropical vegetation, and ten thousands of the palmyra palm, away to the Southern Sea.[1] Beautiful for

[1] Of this flourishing Christian settlement, Mr. Mateer says:

A BRAHMAN AT PRAYER.

situation indeed is this famed Mission station, hidden away in its green valley, and closed in from the outer world by its own glorious natural defences. Some of the loftier peaks are five or six thousand feet high; and the Mission has a sanatorium not far away, up somewhere among these cloud-capped summits, where the coffee estates abound.

As we came home, Mr. Duthie took us through the Christian portion of the native town, where we were amused to find the streets named after the missionaries. Thus we drove down Duthie Street, Mault Street, Mead Street, and so on. We passed one or two particularly tidy little houses standing in compounds, one of which had two stories. The owner of this is a well-to-do coffee-planter, who gives most liberally to the Mission. That a man, originally low-caste, and not increased in favour by becoming a Christian, should have the audacity to build an imposing two-storied dwelling, filled the Brahmans with indignation. They threatened to pull it down or burn it. But they have not yet executed their threat. Happily, it still stands there; and its owner has returned good for evil by constructing a tank for public use.

As we got nearer home, we passed the fine large Mission church—the largest in South India; also

---

'Nagercoil was not long since the merest hamlet, connected with the Snake Temple which gives its name to the place; but having been adopted as the head-quarters of the London Mission in these parts, it is now a clean, well-built, and increasing native town. By their intelligence and industry in various ways, and especially of late years in the coffee-planting enterprise, the native Christians are becoming wealthy, and a wonderful change has taken place.'—*Native Life in Travancore*, p. 18.

the Girls' Village School, a pretty building erected only two years ago by the Christian people, all by themselves. The Printing Press, the Seminary, or English School, and other Mission buildings we also passed.

This Mission, having its chief stations at Nagercoil, Neyoor, Pareychaley, and Trevandrum, besides many smaller branches, belongs to the London Missionary Society. This noble Society, since its formation in 1795, has planted Missions in many parts of the world; but I fancy none of them have had their efforts more acknowledged of God, and more crowned with success, than this one in Travancore. It has worked for nearly the whole of this century.

It is generally believed that the eccentric but able Ringeltaube, a German, began Christian work in this province; but Mr. Duthie tells us of a native convert, named Vethananikam, who was really the first to preach the Gospel here. This man's story is very interesting. He was an earnest, thoughtful man, his soul seeking something he could not find in any heathen system. He went on a long pilgrimage to some peculiarly sacred shrine he had heard of, hoping to find the rest and peace his spirit craved. But the unrest only grew; and the questionings became more urgent. He was being led of the Spirit of God by a way he knew not. Passing through Tanjore, he heard of the white men, the missionaries, and of the new doctrines they were setting forth. Curiosity, and a certain hope, led him to the church—Schwartz's church—where Mr. John Kohlhoff was preaching.

Now, for the first time, he heard the name of Christ; and Kohlhoff, having noticed him, invited him to come and see him. From this time he had constant intercourse with the missionaries, was instructed in the way of salvation, found all he needed in this Heaven-sent faith, and eventually became a true and earnest believer.

Like Paul, he straightway began to preach. He could not keep these glad tidings to himself; he longed to make them known to his people, and begged leave to return to his home amid the palm-groves of the far south. After a weary journey, he got back to his village, called Mylādi,—a place ever to be had in remembrance in the history of this Mission. Here he began his work, and preached the truth faithfully and steadily. A small Christian community gathered round him in time; but persecution followed, and soon became so fierce and determined, that he feared the feeble light he had been honoured to kindle might be utterly quenched. So once more he set out for distant Tanjore, to beg his old friends there to send one of their number—a European missionary—to minister to his little flock in the wilderness. His request was granted; and then it was that Ringeltaube, who had just arrived from Prussia to join the Mission band, was set apart for this service. In due time he came. Some of the Christians, including Vethananikam, went to meet him as far as the pass I have spoken of, and welcomed him to their country. He settled in Mylādi, where the first Christian church was built in 1806; and thus the Gospel found entrance into this beautiful but darkly idolatrous land. Ringeltaube was eccentric, as I have said, but he was peculiarly devoted; and, judging from some deliciously quaint letters from him to his sister, he must have been a sensitive, interesting, and most original person. I cannot resist quoting one or two passages. The first is an answer to one which took thirteen months to reach him.

'My dear Hanna,—

'The letter you wrote on the 13th May, 1809, was not at all expected by me. In the very night you wrote it, I lay down sick in a travellers' bungalow, exposed to the wind and rain. I had just bought the land for the first chapel in Travancore. When I really got possession of the letter, 19th June, 1810 (thirteen months after its date), I sat in the door of the chapel, now finished; and six other chapels were almost built. The news of the life and health of our parents were unexpected by me: I thought that, after much suffering, they would have fallen asleep. As to your little Frederick, I offered him up immediately to the Giver of every good and perfect gift on the altar of the new chapel in Mylādi. Your news of our brothers and their families were of a most gladdening kind. And surely, in the troubles which I have through bad Christians, I wanted a little comfort for my soul. Now the Lord may be praised! However, I cannot approve of your conduct in this, my dear—that, in spite of the severe interdict, you dared to write to me. . . . .

'I have little hope, and almost no desire, to see once more in this world my beloved ones. I am now spoiled for a cold climate. I would always sit behind the stove, and would only be useful to terrify Frederick if he is naughty. "Beware! old Uncle William will come from behind the stove;" so you would tell him.

'I am glad that your soul has not so high expectations as formerly. It is the same with me, with the only difference that this change was wrought in me by rough means. What we lost were only beautiful blossoms, which must wither away if the fruit comes. Now these three remain, Faith, Love, Hope; but Love is the greatest among them. When we were prepared for the Lord's Supper in Warschau we learnt that together, and this is the reality.'

The following gives a most touching picture of the every-day life of the solitary man:—

'My dear!—Come, we will talk a little with one another. Do you see the house thatched with straw, and provided with ten pillars, at the foot of the rock near the three large tamarind trees? That is your poor William's dwelling-place. Come in! Though it rains heavily, we shall find perhaps a dry place. Lo! Tobias, three little dogs greet you wagging their tails! But no! their tails have been cut off. The black one with the white throat is Mr. Port; the other one with the yellow feet is Mrs. Fidelis, and the small yellow one with white feet is Miss Flora. Flora is a very jolly dog; we bark often for a quarter of an hour one towards the other, and each of us knows what the other intends to say.

'Well, what is to be seen here? Four broken chairs, two old couches made of wood and reed, a rope tied from one wall to the other, on which a coat, a gown, and some boots are hanging. Well, and what more? Shelves with books, two tables, one lamp.

'Behold, there is my old huge Maratha horse, red, with a white spot, and four white feet. He is better off than his master, for he is sleek and fat. "What have you in your box?" you ask. Clothes, books, paper. "Why do all things look so dirty and in such disorder?" Because I am a distressed, poor bachelor. "Why do you not marry, my dear brother?" *Point d'argent*, my dear sister. . . .

'My dear Hanna, there is always sorrow, fear, distress, and at last death. You ask, "Do you repent to have become a missionary?" I cannot say that. I would like to be amongst other men. However, it is all right as it is.

'Well, good-night, my beloved one! my lamp burns dimly; it is eleven o'clock: with you it is about eight. You are sitting at the table with little Fritz, Mr. R., or with our parents. How happy you are! You are their joy and comfort in their old age. Ah! might I be at once in Eternity! Kiss and embrace them and my brothers heartily. . . . . On the 16th December I shall remember you in the chapel of Mylādi. My last birthday was very *triste*, as the whole year has been. I am now over forty years old, and they call me the old Ringeltaube. Pray for your poor

'WILLIAM.'

'I live for two years past quite solitary, for the poor people are not society. I am still a bachelor; and as circumstances are, I must remain so. This life has its disagreeable side, but also its good side. As to spiritual things, I know more and more the deep corruption in myself and others, and admire more and more the Divine love, patience, and forbearance in Christ, our Saviour. That is often a very dissatisfying, bitter lesson. My poor, ragged, small congregations are still existing; but I do not observe much of the work of grace. I have now about 600 Christians who are not worse than the other Christians in India. . . . .

'My life is almost without any joy, for the soul finds nothing new, and therefore nothing that gladdens it. The artificial help of books, society, etc., is lacking here entirely. However, I am not cast down. We must go through this life full of tribulations in one way or another. It is easy for few only, and I am persuaded I get through it easier than many. I often think of what was written over the door by that shoemaker in Oels: "May things not become worse!" In the world all is now in confusion, and also here many a change may come. How happy we are if we feel that we are in God's good hand! That I feel even now. The peace of God which passeth all understanding, may it be ours! However, that is not always so, but if it is often so, it is enough to keep our hearts and minds in Christ Jesus till the life eternal!'

No wonder that Ringeltaube's health gave way. 'It is not good that man should be alone.' So pronounced He who made man. But this poor missionary was utterly alone, as far as his own people went. He seldom saw a European, and his means were not sufficient to let him marry. 'Poor, poor bachelor that I am!' he says; and how it touches one to think of that tender, affectionate nature sighing for the human companionship he so much needed, and the sympathy he craved for, and could not find! Is it not a pathetic picture?

Ringeltaube was obliged at last to leave the country. This was in 1816. But before then he had baptised 1,100 persons. Many are the stories told about him by the native Christians, with whom his work, and life, and eccentric ways are still a cherished memory. There is a church still at Mylādi—but not the original one, though built on the site of the old—and a good congregation, under the ministry of a native pastor. The Mission now numbers its converts at about 50,000, with 250 places of worship.

Before he quitted his field, Ringeltaube writes:—

'I have brought the Mission to a good standing by the assistance of our merciful God, and have given it over into the hands of an honest Englishman.'

This 'honest Englishman' was no other than our dear friend 'the General,' as we called him, whom we have revered since we were children, the late well-known General Munro, of Teaninich, Ross-shire; then Colonel Munro, Resident at the Court of His Highness the Maharajah of Travancore. He was, and is still, known as 'the good Resident;' and his name will long be remembered all over the South of India. He accepted entire charge of the infant Mission, enlarged and strengthened it, founded schools, and endowed them with grants of land. Mr. Duthie and Mr. Lee have shown us the rice-fields which are still the property of the Mission—the same that were given by the good Resident. This very house was given by him; one in which he and Mrs. Munro once lived. During all his long administration, he did everything to foster the Mission; and not only so, but promoted whatever was for the moral and physical well-being of the people over the whole kingdom. Happily this is by no means a solitary instance of missionary and philanthropic undertakings being supported and personally assisted by the servants of Government,—just such noble, disinterested Christian men as Colonel Munro.[1]

One morning, while breakfasting with Mr. Lee, he showed us a box of curious old parchments, left by the Resident, the title-deeds of the land and other property, written, in Tamil, on long slips of the

[1] When speaking of the *origin* of modern Missions in Travancore, the Rev. Mr. Mateer says in his admirable book: 'It is well known, and even apparent from some portions of the history, that it was due, if to any local patrons, to the English officers, who procured for the missionaries permission to reside and to labour in the country. Such were Colonel Macaulay, who obtained a passport for Ringeltaube, and gave personal contributions to his work; and also the distinguished Colonel Munro, who was at the same time a zealous friend of Missions and a lover of beautiful Travancore. . . . . He was the real donor of the grants referred to, which were intended for, and are still devoted, to the education of the native Christian youth. . . . . It was he who applied to the Church Missionary Society for missionaries, and helped them in manifold ways.'—*Native Life in Travancore*, p, 392.

palmyra leaf, all tied into little bundles,—this wonderful palm leaf which still provides the stationery chiefly used in the country.

We also saw the veritable cot, or couch, used by Ringeltaube; a most primitive article, suggestive rather of penance than rest. I should like to see it under a glass case in some missionary museum. Mr. Lee kindly took us all over his premises the same morning, including the Printing Press and his charming Girls' Boarding School. His wife is an invalid, and at home; but he bravely manages the fifty-six children himself, with the aid of his good Christian matron and Christian teachers. The copy-books are all made of the palmyra leaf, neatly cut into narrow long slips. The children presented me with some manuscripts of this sort, along with the neat little case of implements used in cutting up the leaf and performing the penmanship. One of the teachers had printed a text on a large card in English, and hung it on the wall of the large schoolroom, as a welcome to us. It was the first thing we saw as we entered; and the words were: 'The Lord shall preserve thy going out and thy coming in, from this time forth, and even for evermore.' Later on, as we were taking leave, after we had heard the classes read and sing, etc., one of the elder girls, with a very sweet face, came up to me, and said, in pretty English: 'Ma'am, we have learnt a text for you;' whereupon the first class repeated the beautiful words: 'The Lord bless thee, and keep thee; the Lord make His face shine upon thee, and be gracious to thee; the Lord lift up His countenance upon thee, and give thee peace!'

I think even the men had their eyes wet before the children were done repeating it; and it was entirely their own thought. Mr. Lee was as much surprised as we were. The schools are very similar to others already described, and are all admirable after their kind,—Day and Boarding Schools—Tamil and English schools. Of course the most important are the large Seminary and Preparatory School, for the education and training of young men, who are afterwards to be employed in the work of the Mission—such as teachers, evangelists, pastors, catechists, and so on. These important institutions are entirely conducted by Mr. Duthie and his son, and represent a great deal of hard thorough work. The buildings stand close to the Mission House; and it is pleasant to see the lads about through the compound at all hours. They seem specially pleased to help Mrs. and Miss Duthie in their gardening, and water the plants of an evening. There are 207 students altogether, eighty-three of whom are boarders who live on the premises. They are pleasant, intelligent lads: my husband has examined them thoroughly; and we are often out and in the class-rooms. Whenever an agent is wanted at any of the stations, the lack is supplied from the Seminary; which is thus the Christian training college for the whole Mission.

There is a first-rate Government college at Trevandrum, presided over by Professor Ross, and called the Maharajah's College, which provides both English and vernacular education for all classes and castes, Christian and non-Christian; but this one in Nagercoil is distinctively Christian, and is supported by the Mission. One thing most creditable to it—quite a feather in its cap—is, that last year the first prize in the Cator examination in Madras for Scripture knowledge was carried off by one of its students. The Seminary and the Maharajah's College in Trevandrum stand together in the forefront of all educational work in Travancore. Is not the tolerance extended to Christian Missions by this enlightened native State remarkable?

One feature in the day-schools here is quite new: they cost the Mission nothing! The teachers are all paid by the native Christian community, being simply salaried, as the pastors are salaried; but Mr. Duthie superintends the boys' schools, while Mrs. Duthie and her daughter do the same for the girls'.

Mrs. Duthie's work among the women, and her dear little daughter's, interest me profoundly; and those on the spot who know the feeling and condition of the native community thoroughly, think that no part of the Mission work is producing such valuable fruit, or telling more on the people as a whole.

## CHAPTER XIII.

### WOMAN'S WORK—SUNDAY AT NAGERCOIL.

ONE of the specialities in Nagercoil is the lace industry, which is carried on by the Christian women, superintended by the missionaries' wives. It was introduced some fifty years ago by the late Mrs. Mault, and has done wonders for the people. Hundreds of poor Christians gain a living by it. The ladies take the orders, and also all the trouble of the sale. After the women are paid for their work, the profits, whatever these may amount to, go to the support of Bible-women's work. The success of this industry is most cheering; and now it has two off-shoots: one under Mrs. Caldwell, who is a daughter of Mrs. Mault—and one at Benares. But it originated in Nagercoil; and the lace here manufactured has gained medals at three national exhibitions.

Mrs. Duthie very kindly has had an assemblage of lace-makers in the verandah, that I might see them at work. About forty women came—tidy, respectable, intelligent matrons—who sat in a row round the verandah on the floor, with their lace-pillows on their laps; and the clever, handy way they manipulated the fine thread and pins, and produced the delicate fabric, was most curious and interesting to see; and the workers seemed equally pleased to show their work.

I bought some lovely pieces off the pillows, and I would like my lady-friends to know that Mrs. Duthie has always stores of the different articles manufactured beside her, and lace in every width, and is very glad of orders for it. Any one writing to Mrs. Duthie, Mission House, Nagercoil, Travancore, would receive what they wished for by parcel post. The lace is strong as well as beautiful, and the patterns varied and delicate. I can only say it is extremely pleasant to examine the tempting boxes, and to feel that, while gratifying your taste and supplying your needs, you are all the time helping these Christian women. I must not omit to add that some beautiful specimens were offered by the workers themselves to the Prince of Wales when he visited India, for the gracious acceptance of Her Royal Highness the Princess of Wales.

I saw some of the women being paid to-day, and the money in which this was done amused me much. The coin is the smallest, I suppose, in circulation anywhere. It is called *chuckrum*, and is a wee, fat, round bit of silver, the size of a split pea, and covered with characters. The way it is counted is also droll. There are neat little boards of different sizes filled with holes, into which a handful of the coins is thrown, each coin fitting its hole. One size holds one rupee's worth, another five rupees, another ten, another twenty, and so on. There are larger coins in circulation; but the *chuckrum* is most in use.

I have had a pretty necklace and bracelet given me made of this little coin, which are quite curiosities.

Yesterday afternoon Miss Duthie drove me in the little pony-carriage to see some of the zenana and Bible-woman's work, which has happily made a good beginning here, and is specially interesting in a caste-ridden place like this. I have said how thoroughly Travancore has hitherto been under the thrall of the Brahmans—given over to superstition, and slavery, and all cruelty, and bondage untold. A very few years ago these Bible-women would not have dared to attempt the work they now are able to do. They would not only have been driven from the doors into which they now find entrance, but they could not have ventured to tread the street, far less enter the house of a good-caste family. They work chiefly among the Sudra and Vellala castes. As yet, there is not a single Brahman woman under instruction of any sort in Nagercoil. One seems to go back to old experiences, and times now happily gone by in other parts of India. One thing ought to be borne in mind, however—namely, the success of the Gospel among the low castes; and this very success is quite enough to account for the smaller progress among the higher. One may smile or be indignant at the absurdities of caste; but it is the strength of this old-world religion, which is so interwoven with the history, and affections, and the very life of the people. It is the cement which binds it all together, and makes it like a rock of adamant; which, alas! it still is, though in some places the foundations begin to shake. I believe the Brahmans are becoming afraid, as well as jealous, of the standing and influence the Christian Shanars are attaining, and are bestirring themselves in the matter of English education. God has chosen the weak and despised things of the world to confound those that call themselves mighty in this stronghold of Brahmanism and superstition.

The missionaries have had some curious battles to fight. One was to secure to the women the privilege of clothing themselves with decency. The female portion of the Shanar community are most immodest in their attire, wearing nothing on their persons above the waist. The Mission ladies were naturally determined to alter this practice—at least, among the Christians—and introduced a completer style of dress, including a jacket, in addition to the cloth which encircles the loins. The higher castes were furious at the presumption of 'the low-born.' There was the usual row; and whenever the poor women appeared outside their doors, they were attacked, and the offending garments literally torn off their backs! But the magistrates interposed, and now the poor things may go forth unmolested though decently attired. Miss Duthie took me to one house where we were received by a bright, brisk, little woman in a sort of enclosed court, open to the sky. She would not admit us quite into the house; and I was amused to notice that she took care to sit to windward of us, so that all the pollution we brought might be blown straight away without touching her. Nothing must come 'betwixt the wind and her nobility,' as Harry Hotspur puts it. Yet she was by no means a Brahman. This puts me in mind of a visit I once paid in Calcutta, at a time when the visits of European ladies were not so universally welcome in Bengali homes as they are, happily, now. I was allowed to stand for a few minutes in the verandah, but was evidently unwelcome; and, as I moved away, a metrāni, or sweeper—a menial of the very lowest description—was ordered to cleanse the place where I had stood.

Our small hostess was gorgeously attired, and was very much in the fashion as to the torn ear. The lobe was weighted with rows of thick, massive gold and silver rings, which dragged it down, in a hideous manner, almost to the shoulder. She had plenty of gold and silver on her person otherwise, which surprised me, as I knew that she was a widow; and Hindu law forbids widows to wear ornaments. A remark I made on the subject afterwards brought out some curious facts as to the customs and laws in this strange country, especially in the laws of succession to property. It seems she was the sister of a very rich man, who has lately died, and all his wealth has come to *her* son, as heir of the inheritance, not to his own! This is perplexing, and hardly to be believed; but it is true. You may be as rich a man as you please, and as great; but, when you die, your sister's children, not your own, will inherit your property, your money, your titles, your position, your very name; all must descend in the female line! In this sense one has to fight here, not for woman's rights, but for man's. I am afraid this state of things points to a very loose morality as existing somewhere. However, I am not going to enter into the mysteries of caste and custom, and the strange code they necessitate; it is much too intricate a subject. But I am thankful to say the missionaries utterly discountenance the observance of caste in any form. The Sudra and Shanar Christians do no often intermarry; and it is, perhaps, better they should not do so: but in theory, caste has no existence in Protestant Missions.

We have had an intensely interesting day. Some time ago Mr. Duthie wrote: 'Be sure you keep a Sunday for us;' which we were careful to do. At seven o'clock the great bell gave forth its invitation to service, and we all went through the cool morning air to the church, which stands close by, in a compound of its own. When we entered, I was struck with astonishment. Here was an immense building, certainly the biggest Mission church we have ever seen, filled throughout—crowded, I may say—with as decent and respectable a congregation as you could see at home. The pulpit stood a good way down from the top, with pews arranged in front of it, on either side of a wide passage to the door. These were crowded—the women to the right, and the men to the left; while on the floor, round the pulpit, up to the top, and round every pillar, the little ones of the flock were set as thickly as they could be put. The girls from the Boarding Schools sat together, and the lads from the Seminary in another group; but most of the children had come with their parents from their own village houses, and were grouped in this fashion on the floor that they might take up less of the precious space. It was a wonderfully interesting sight; they were so tidy and neat in their Sunday best; and the little creatures behaved with a quietness and propriety which would have been impossible to English children of the same age. The church is a plain, white-washed building, with an arched roof, supported by double rows of fine large pillars, and having a great number of doors and windows, all thrown wide open to admit the fresh air of the morning, while the beautiful trees which fill the compound and surround the church gave delicious shade from the glare of the fast mounting sun. Some marble tablets are set in the wall at the upper end, in memory of some of the good missionaries who have passed away. These are the only decoration. Mr. Duthie conducted the preliminary services, and then my husband preached the sermon, being interpreted by the native pastor sentence by sentence. All the service was in Tamil, except the first hymn, which was English, and sung by all the congregation. Miss Duthie played the harmonium, and the people stood during the singing, and reverently knelt at prayer, joining audibly in the Lord's Prayer, and reading every alternate verse of the Psalms for the day. Apparently all the people can read.

It was one of the most thrillingly interesting and impressive services I have ever been present at, and stirred our hearts more than I can tell. I would have come all this way, though for nothing else than to see that large congregation of devout, worshipping, intelligent, well-to-do, self-respecting people, who support their own pastor and school-masters. Besides this, they contributed last year

3,000 rupees to the general work of the Mission in operating on the outside heathen. The service lasted for two hours, and then came the slow retiring of the people—'the skailing of the kirk,' as we should say in Scotland; and this was as fine a sight as any. Many gathered round to shake hands and talk to us strangers; and then we watched the picturesque groups wending their way homeward, the fathers with the little ones in their hands, and the women in twos and threes behind. It put me in mind of similar scenes I have watched a hundred times on the hillsides at home, generally on a 'Sabbath-eve, in summer tide,' when a solemn Communion-time had gathered many grave worshippers from far and near, who, now that the services were over, and the day far spent, were reverently retiring from the moor or glen where the congregation had sat and worshipped,—where they had had their 'feast of fat things' during the long summer day.

But this was only the first of many services. The church bell seemed to ring out all day for something or other. First came the various Sunday - schools, one or two in the church, one in the verandah of the Mission House, and I think also in the girls' and boys' day-schools.

These Sunday-schools are now quite a feature —and a most important one—in every Mission. A meeting I enjoyed very much was one with the Bible-women, in the forenoon, in our wide verandah. Another, after an hour's rest—and I think the most interesting of all—was a monster Bible-class for grown-up women, in the church. The missionaries rightly regard the training of the wives and mothers as of the first importance; hence this regular catechising which is held every Sunday afternoon. And truly it was a striking sight to see the big church quite filled with women—all Christians, of course, —from the aged, grey-haired great-grandmother downwards. Many of the younger women had babies in their arms; and all had open Bibles in their hands. They were being questioned by the pastor when we went in, and every one in turn gave out her answer in a free, frank, natural way, occasionally putting a question in return. The pastor at once handed over the exercise to my husband, who catechised all round quite *con amore;* and we were delighted with the intelligence and knowledge of many of the women, especially those who had been Christians from their youth up.

A short evening service closed the busy day. Mr. Lee the while had been away in different parts of his extensive parish. He has sixty stations under his supervision, in a radius of about twenty miles. These he visits alternately, and each has its pastor or catechist, and place of worship.

We drove one afternoon into the native town of Kottar to see the church in which Francis Xavier preached so long. It is rather a large, good building, with a stone porch, and a stone floor, on which several poor-looking worshippers were kneeling, and a priest was at the high altar, engaged in some service. The house where the great missionary lived stands somewhere near. He *was* a great missionary. Whatever his errors, they were those of his Church. His zeal, his enthusiasm, his self-consecration and devotion to the Mission cause were truly heroic. It is told of him that the whole of the first night he was on Indian soil he spent in solitary prayer to God, for whose service he had given up much, or *all*, in his native land.

A NATIVE CHRISTIAN WOMAN.

## CHAPTER XIV.

### CAPE COMORIN.

OUR kind friends had promised us a sight of their Ultima Thule, the renowned Cape, the Land's End of India. So yesterday this famous expedition came off. All had been most kindly prepared the night before, and at two in the morning my husband and I stole noiselessly out of Mr. Duthie's verandah. Silently we took our seats in two light cane chairs slung between long stout bamboos. There were eight bearers to each chair, dressed, as usual, in their own tidy black skins, stalwart, civil men, half their number doing duty at a time. Thus, each 'borne of four,' we set out on our night-march of twelve miles. It was certainly a dreary, sleepy start, for the young moon had set, and it was pitch dark. I could not help casting a few longing looks back to the deep repose from which we had been roused; for one's natural rest does count for a good deal after such hot and busy days. We had no cheerful, flaming torches, either, which generally accompany the night-traveller in India; they do not seem to be the fashion here. However, the night air was very refreshing; the murky canopy overhead soon began to reveal a silver lining, the clouds gathered themselves away to the mountain-tops, and the beautiful stars gleamed out of the darkness, filling one's mind with sweet and happy thoughts. How often, in like manner, do the gracious promises of our God shine out through the deepest sorrow-clouds, making us lift up our eyes towards the heavens, from whence comes our help!

As soon as we had quite cleared the Mission compound, and were out of hearing, our bearers set up a plaintive sort of chant in a high monotone, which, on the whole, was rather pleasing. They trudged cheerily along the broad, tolerably good road, amply fringed with fine, large banyan trees, and now and then narrowing into what looked merely a bridge over the numerous bits of water gathered in tanks, and in the little rice-fields. We passed a number of hamlets, which lay silent as the dead, except for the howls of the wretched pariah dogs, of evil nature, who infest every village in the East, and the crowing of the village cocks, a cheering intimation that dawn was not far off. Accordingly, after a steady march of full three hours, a few delicate lines of pearly grey tinged faintly the eastern sky. Gradually the colour deepened; a pinky shade stole softly into the grey, which again deepened, at the horizon, to a brilliant rose; and then the sun showed himself, and the light of day triumphed gloriously over the darkness and dreariness of the night. Very soon we heard the murmur of the sea, and we found we were near our journey's end. We had left the mountains behind, and the land had gradually narrowed. The cultivation now was more rude; the soil and the roads had alike become sand, and the trees looked knotted and gnarled, with bared roots and storm-driven branches, like veteran tars, who had withstood many a tempest in the shrouds. Then came the palmyra-fringed coast, and finally the great, wide sea, looking shivery and slate-coloured, with the strangest fishing craft about, and boats and canoes close to the shore.

Mr. Lee had come out the day before to one of his stations, arranging to meet us here; and now he rode up, and took possession of us in a very restful way. He conducted us to a large empty bungalow, standing high over the sea, a perfect sort of sanatorium belonging to the Resident at the Maharajah's Court in Trevandrum. Here the happy possessor has a glorious sea-view, with perfect solitude and leisure, and good hearty whiffs, or blows rather, of the invigorating, salt-sea breeze. Mr. Lee's servant awaited us here with a tin of hot coffee, after which welcome refreshment we were able to go forth and explore. The bearers, poor fellows, threw themselves down on the sand, and were asleep in a minute.

Although Travancore as a whole is so full of natural loveliness, yet just at the Cape there is nothing very striking in the scenery. The grand mountain ranges of the Western Ghāts, though sometimes taken by navigators for the Cape, are some distance from it. The last hill we passed is a very famous one. It is said to be the same which the Monkey god, Hanumān, carried under his arm fifteen hundred miles! The story is told in the great poem, the *Ramayan*, how Hanumān was commissioned to find medicinal herbs on this mountain wherewith to restore the slain of King

CAPE COMORIN.

Rama's army. Being afraid that the morning would dawn before he had gathered the herbs, he plucked the mountain up, bore it off, and threw it down in Rama's camp, which stood in this place. The region about the Cape was the scene of other exploits of the clever god, as wonderful and credible as this one. For instance, in order to construct a bridge between Rameshwar, a sacred place on the coast, and Ceylon, he brought mountains, millions at a time, and cast them into the sea; but I can only say we did not discover the bridge.

There are no bold headlands nor precipitous crags light-house crowned just at the Land's End, only a few island-rocks with the white surf dashing over them, and always the beautiful, glittering sea stretching away to the far horizon. But there are other things interesting and new. It was curious to watch the long-shaped, narrow canoes, the catamarans of the coast, each with its most picturesque occupant, a stalwart, broad-chested, bronze fisherman, entirely innocent of clothing but for a bit of rag round his loins, standing erect in his boat, with an oar or fishing-tackle in his hand, suspending operations while he stared at the intruders. These canoes are built from the stem of a single tree, and are generally of the rudest construction.

Then another feature was the endless forests of the palmyra and cocoa palm. Along the shore on every hand there stretches a broad margin of deep, sandy waste, which is filled with ten thousands of these stately, remarkable trees. This tree, indeed, is the only thing in vegetation which could find sustenance in this unkindly soil, and it does so because it strikes its roots down deep enough until it finds what is needful to its life. The palmyra is not exactly a pretty tree, but it is exceedingly majestic, and the staff of life to the poor population of the coast.

From the palm forests we scrambled down among the rocks, until the green waves rippled to our feet, and here we found new 'treasures of the deep,' more strange and beautiful than anything we had ever seen before, in the marvellously-coloured sands which embellish this curious shore. It was chiefly to see these we came to the Cape, and they are quite as wonderful and beautiful as we had been told. Picture a great bed of fine, soft sea-sand entirely black, then close to it, but quite distinct, another of brilliant ruby-red, sparkling and shimmering in the sun-rays, like crushed diamonds and rubies; then, marching with this, another bed, much the same in size, of a yellowish white hue, large and rough-grained: this is the famous rice-sand, and it exactly resembles unboiled rice. A wild and most romantic legend is popularly told of this rice-sand, and how it originated. After the rice comes another bed of the brilliant red, and another, and another—of black, garnet, and white, alternating like beds in a flower parterre, and quite as distinct, the colours always keeping apart. It was only by digging a little way down we found the colour often underlying the yellow white, and *vice versâ*. We halted long surveying these ocean-wonders. I then filled some bottles with specimens of each colour and brought them away.

By-and-by we strolled up toward a village which crowned a little eminence over the sea. Some men had come down to look at us, and altogether our appearance seemed to create much wonderment, but the people were always pleased when Mr. Lee spoke to them in their own tongue. They are certainly the strangest-looking savages we have yet seen in this region. The women look specially wild. Their hair stands on end in a brush on the top of their heads, and they have no clothing beyond the bit of dirty rag, called a clŏth, hung round from the waist. We passed unmolested through the Brahman street; a great concession, for there is a large temple here dedicated to the god Shiva, and it is esteemed a specially holy spot. Indeed, the whole place is considered sacred, and great numbers of pilgrims visit the temple at certain periods of the year. There were many dark-visaged, naked men, much besmeared with white ashes and paint, loafing idly about, who did not seem to relish our presence, and who point-blank refused to let the gentlemen enter even the outer enclosure of the temple. The patron goddess of this great shrine is Durga, one of the wives of Shiva, and the building is said to be of very ancient date. It is completely surrounded by high walls, ornamented with stripes of colour, and there are four fine monoliths in front about twenty feet in height.

It was now getting hot, as the sun was rapidly mounting in the heavens; and, being tired, I sat down in the shade, while the gentlemen went in search of some of the villages where the Roman Catholic fishermen were to be found. There are many Roman Catholics on this coast, Xavier having commenced a Mission here in 1542, and most are fishermen. The gentlemen entered one or two villages, which were unspeakably filthy, with swarms of children, and dogs, and flies, and hideous with smells. They found in one of them two cars like those of the god Juggernath, which are drawn about during festival times; one is dedicated to St. Joseph, and the other to the Virgin Mary. So low have these poor so-called Christians sunk.

Meanwhile I was soon surrounded by a crowd of women and children, with a ring of men outside, all staring at the white-faced stranger most unmercifully, and keeping up a chorus of begging. It was a strange place. Within a stone's throw of where I sat, there was the large Hindu temple; also a *mandapan*, or temple-court, with handsome carved pillars and sculptures, and innumerable grotesque little carved deities stuck over every place. A little way off there were several white pyramidal stones used by the Shanars for their devil-worship; and, in the midst of all, a Roman Catholic church, surmounted by a cross! Behind me a noisy school of both boys and girls occupied the verandah of the *mandapan*, shouting their lessons at the top of their voice, or scratching their 'copies' in an irritating way, with a dagger-like stylus, on slips of palm leaf. These slips were very neatly cut, and the little urchins were proud to show me their accomplishment in writing on these novel copy-books. I was not sorry when the gentlemen reappeared.

We got into our chairs, and, preceded by Mr. Lee

on his good little steed as a guide, set out for the village where we were to spend the day. Mr. Lee once interrupted a devil-dance in this place. A crowd surrounded a man who was gesticulating frantically and spinning round in a kind of dance, pretending to be 'possessed.' He tried to frighten the pony, and so get rid of the rider, but Mr. Lee made the frisky little creature caper about a little, when the man bolted, terror-stricken; the fickle crowd shouted in derision, and finally heard the missionary with quiet attention for an hour while he preached to them from his saddle. Afterwards some of them came regularly to seek him, and hear him at his nearest preaching station.

Our route lay over the sand through the thick palmyra forest. Here this prince of trees, as it is rightly called, exists in all its majesty and usefulness. A proverb says of it, 'If you plant it, it will grow for a thousand years; if you cut it, it will last a thousand years.' They also say that it can supply every real need of a man's life. With its wood he can build his house or his canoe; the branches provide the thatch and the enclosures; also his punka, umbrella, rope, stationery, and a thousand things, while the sap is so nutritious he can almost live upon it.

We stopped for a little while to watch the climbers go up the tree and get some of the juice for our men to drink. It was most amusing to see them clamber up the straight, bare, branchless stems like monkeys, making skilful use of hands and toes alike, sometimes to the height of eighty or ninety feet. This they do to remove the sap or juice, which has been drawn off in a little earthen pot at the top. They have the little pot hooked on to the waist-cloth behind; they ascend with great rapidity, remove the full pot, make a fresh incision in the bark, fasten on the empty one, and descend as rapidly as they went up. There are frequent accidents, however, we were sorry to hear, and our medical missionaries have often cases in their wards of men who have fallen from their lofty perches in these tree-tops, who are often thus led to the Physician of souls. The juice is excellent when fresh, a luscious sort of drink. After it ferments it becomes intoxicating, and, I am afraid, it is most popular in this condition, and it is largely consumed by the Shanars, especially in their orgies at festival times. But its chief use is to manufacture sugar—a coarse, dark sort of soft stuff, called *jagry*, much used by the people. These climbers ascend as many as forty or fifty trees in a day; often, indeed, twice a day. This is only one of the hundred ways in which this wonderful tree ministers to the wants of the inhabitants, who but for it would be badly off indeed in these sandy wastes. We saw a great many specimens of the Umbrella tree, as it is called, a sort of acacia, with a short, bare stem, and a mass of thick, thorny bush spread out flat at the top like a Japanese umbrella. It is very curious, and gives a dense and perfect shade.

By-and-by we came to a clearing, where we found a considerable native village. Groups of neat, tidy cottages, with deep, overhanging eaves, thatched and enclosed with branches of palm leaf, stood under some large trees, and in the midst of them a little Christian church. This was a native Christian village, one of Mr. Lee's stations, and here we were to spend the day. It may be imagined with what interest we entered it, once the dwelling-place of demon-worshippers, where the horrible rites of this degrading superstition were practised, and now filled with the habitations of those who had been rescued from the miry clay of this lowest heathenism, and taught to worship the true and living God. The kind people gathered out of their homes to welcome us, headed by their pastor, and the dresser, a young medical student trained by Dr. Thomson, of Neyoor; for, besides the church, there is a small dispensary, and also a school. They took us at once to the church, and we found in a little room behind—a prophet's chamber, used by the missionary on his visits—a comfortable breakfast prepared for us.

The village is called Agusteespuram, after the Tamil sage, Agustees, who once lived here. It is one of the oldest stations of the Nagercoil Mission, and has a congregation of six hundred, who support their own pastor and pay their own schoolmaster. One interesting point to us was, that the church was built by Ringeltaube. It is a plain, substantial, barn-like structure, with white-washed walls, bare floor, and a simple rail across the upper end, where a small reading-desk stands. The windows gave the place a quaint, old-fashioned look, there being no blinds or glass, but the frames were filled with waved bars of wood, very ingenious and pretty, and the work of Ringeltaube, admitting light, and keeping out intruders, while the glare is completely softened by the shady trees without.

After breakfast, the church bell rang out, and presently the whole place was filled to overflowing, while groups stood at every window. The people sat on the floor closely packed, the men on one side, and the women on the other, while within

AGUSTEESPURAM CHAPEL.

the rails the pastors, catechists, and elders of the Church sat on chairs on each side of the pulpit. The great majority of all present were converted Shanars. There were six pastors who had come to meet us from distant stations, one of whom, a venerable, gentle-faced man, was the grandson of the first convert in this region, the one who was the means of bringing Ringeltaube to Travancore. It was most interesting to meet the good old grandson.

After the men had been introduced to us, and we had some talk, the service began, and a delightful impressive time followed, the Spirit was *felt* to be in the midst of us. The patriarchal pastor prayed in the most fervent way. Shutting my eyes, I could have fancied it was the earnest, reverential tones of one of our own men of the Highlands, pouring out his soul at a Gaelic Communion-time; a feeling which only strengthened when, at the singing which followed, the precentor read out the line before it was sung. I confess, however, that afterwards the spell was completely broken when 'instrumental music' was added. And the instrument was a fiddle, a 'genuine fiddle,' as my husband said, and not merely the *vina,* which in Western India the people love as an accompaniment when chanting their plaintive lyrics; still, it was not quite so incongruous as might have been supposed. My husband preached a good long sermon, and next gave an address; and, again like the Highlanders, the people never stirred, nor seemed to tire. Several of the pastors knew English well, and interpreted for him. Mr. Lee spoke, and some of the pastors did the same; many earnest prayers were offered, and there was deep impression. So it went on all day.

I had a most interesting hour with the women, who during a pause in the services gathered round me, bringing their lace pillows with them, and working neatly and deftly while we talked. I also visited some of the homes, which were clean and neat; and afterwards we had a great deal of talk with the men, who gave us many interesting facts regarding the condition of the people formerly, contrasting it with the improvement of the present. They spoke especially of the rise there is among the Christians in social position and standing, also in their character morally and spiritually; and we were glad to be assured that caste-feeling is decidedly declining among them. They spoke also hopefully of the change there is for the better in the heathen community generally, and gave many striking proofs that enlightenment and progress are entering even dark Brahmanical Travancore.

In former times, the oppression and cruelties practised by the high castes toward the low were fearful. If a water-bund broke, or any other calamity happened, a Pariah[1] was at once sacrificed to appease the gods. Slavery existed until quite lately, and the slaves were often most cruelly used. It was appalling to hear of the sufferings inflicted on them. For instance, one of the pastors told us that he had seen with his own eyes a woman and a buffalo yoked together in a plough! He also saw two women tied together by the hair of their heads, and then thrashed with thorns. It was an infinite relief to find that such things would not be tolerated now; though, no doubt, there is oppression enough as it is.

Altogether this was one of the most interesting 'mission-days' we have ever had; but too soon it came to a close. At five o'clock Mr. Lee announced that it was time to depart; so, after many leave-takings and kind words from the people, we got into our chairs and started. The evening was so

[1] A low caste-man.

lovely that all the fatigues of the long, exciting day were forgotten. The scenery of this Garden of South India, so famed for its beauty, is specially lovely in the softened light of evening. This is true, indeed, of all scenery, but particularly true in India. After the blaze of the glaring day has gone, the harmony, the serenity, the blended colour, the tender, sweet beauty all come out with the lights of evening. As we left the palm forests behind, and turned our faces toward the mountain-ranges which tower over Nagercoil, the views became more glorious every turn. Some of these summits, five or six thousand feet high, are superb in their rough and rugged grandeur. Some have rounded tops, and others pointed, fantastic peaks, while others lie in long, serrated ridges, or low, wavy, rolling undulations, but all are striking and beautiful. The sun was going down in a gorgeous surrounding of massive clouds in every shade of brilliant orange and crimson, lighting up the ridges and dyeing the slopes, glinting down among the green valleys, and gleaming rosy light on the still faces of the little sheets of water, which abounded all along our route, and looked like tiny lakelets. The roads are skirted by magnificent spreading trees, chiefly banyans, which now threw long, deep shadows on the grass. The scene grew more and more peaceful as the colour faded and darkness closed in, and I was glad when the bearers hushed their intoning of their own accord. Altogether the evening was a fitting close to the memorable day.

## CHATER XV.

### NEYOOR—PAREYCHALEY.

WE are busy packing up for a fresh start. A machine stands out there, beyond the verandah, in the shade, all ready for us. It is an odd little green box of a bandy, with rather a disproportionate pair of stately white bullocks standing beside. This is to carry us to our next halting-place, Neyoor, and has been provided for our use by the nice native Christians, who hospitably insist on 'speeding the parting guest,' by sending us on our way free of expense to ourselves. It is very pleasant to accept their kindness — so much of a piece with the rest. We have made life-long friends in this ideal Mission home. . . .

Here we are at this important station of the London Missionary Society, which is also the centre of the medical part of the Mission, now under the care of Dr. Thomson. It is specially interesting to us, as our friend Dr. Lowe, of George Square, Edinburgh, the well-known and able Superintendent of the Medical Missionary Society of Edinburgh, was once stationed here. He began his career in Neyoor.

When we started yesterday, Mr. Duthie drove me out a little way, while Mr. Crosbie, the Judge, took my husband in his 'trap,' to a point whence we had a glorious view of the mountains which lie about this lovely sequestered spot of earth. The scene might have been that round our own Loch Lomond or Loch Maree, if, instead of the wide, smiling valley, waving with green rice crops, and intersected with magnificent trees, there had slept a stately loch. A tiny lake did sparkle at our feet, but the beauty lay in the superb mountain ranges, with their jagged, rugged ridges, and purple, serrated sides, now veiled in a dreamy blue mist. A happy valley this expanse of green loveliness looks, and well might be in reality but for the old story that 'only man is vile.' Another of the pastors, with whom we had much talk, told us of some dreadful iniquities he saw practised in this very valley on the poor low-caste slaves, which I cannot bring myself to write. Oh, what a relief to think that now more humane counsels prevail under the influence of our own beneficent Government; also that missionaries are at work, and that the Spirit of truth and love and light is now moving over the great darkness!

About five o'clock we got into our bandy, and set off by the Trevandrum road straight for Neyoor, only some twelve miles off. It was rather rough and rutty, bumping us up and down in our primitive little machine; but we enjoyed our drive in the evening loveliness, through the picturesque scenery of this fairy-like land. A great deal of water is stored in tanks and little canals, in order to irrigate the rice-fields, so that all along the road you come on what look like lakes and serpentines, and pretty rivulets, which give a charming variety to the scenery, fringed as the banks often are with a wealth of beautiful wood. We passed a great many demon-temples, generally well-smeared with white-wash, though not with the red paint you see on idol-shrines in the Maratha country. At a little village half-way, a catechist and two or three deacons were waiting for us, sitting by their little road-side church. They escorted us the rest of the way, talking all the time, and giving much information, keeping pace with the bullocks, who thought it quite beneath their dignity to go out of a stately walk. Some of these Christians are pleasant, superior, thinking men.

We are the guests of Mr. and Mrs. Hacker, whose acquaintance we made in Nagercoil. They received us most warmly, had tea ready, and then we all went into the large church, which stands in the compound, where we found an immense assemblage of people gathered to hear the stranger-missionary gentleman. I was too tired to stay out the whole service after our not very restful drive.

The next morning we were out almost before the sun, to explore, and found a fine large compound, in which stood two good mission-houses, the church, hospital, dispensary, and other buildings for schools, with some very beautiful trees intermingling and giving beauty to the whole. There are one or two tombstones also in one place, which commemorate some of the missionaries who have died here. We breakfasted with Dr. and Mrs. Thomson, who live in one of the bungalows; but before then Dr. Thomson had shown us all his work. We first went to the Dispensary, where about thirty of the patients were assembled, and all the students, and there was a short service. Dr. Mitchell gave a short address, which was translated by one of the dressers; after which a pastor prayed, when all the patients knelt, and repeated the simple words clause by clause after him. This over, we saw the premises, including the class-rooms, where we made friends with the students and dressers. The latter are those whose studies are completed, and who will be sent forth to work at branch stations. Of these there are only six at present, and there is a great demand for dressers; but several of the students we saw will soon be ready to undertake the charge of a dispensary as full-fledged doctors. I was particularly pleased with the appearance of these young fellows; they have bright, frank, good faces, and honest expressions. Most of them support themselves, with no help from the Mission.

There were among the patients in the hospital two or three poor fellows, palmyra climbers, who had fallen from the trees; and Dr. Thomson says that accidents of this sort are unhappily of frequent occurrence. But these men often hear the Gospel in this way; they become attached and grateful to the good doctor who heals their body, and they often go out having got also health and life to their souls.

The enormous amount of work which is accomplished by this Medical Mission, and the benefit it is to the people, is shown by the fact that, during the past year, the number of patients who have been treated in the Neyoor Mission and its six branches—including those attended in their own homes—amounted to upwards of 24,600 persons. These include Christians, heathen, and Mohammedans; and the diseases, of course, are of all kinds.

It is very pleasing to hear that the Government helps the Mission considerably; a wonderfully enlightened Government it seems to be, though a heathen one. The Maharajah gave the money, I believe, which built some of the best wards in the Hospital. After breakfast, we saw some of Mrs. Thomson's admirable day-schools, of which there are four. The pupils are mostly drawn from the better castes, and there are a good many Brahman girls among them. These children attend the Sunday-school, and make no objection to the Bible as a class-book; they also sing Christian hymns and lyrics delightfully. One of the latter we heard begins with words like these: 'Sweeter than honey the name of Jesus sounds;' and such hymns they sing in their homes, and even in the streets. Thus the truth must spread, the good seed being sown here, as happily elsewhere, over the land. But, unfortunately, as in other parts, these girls leave school at the age of ten or twelve to be married, and they never return after the marriage or betrothal has taken place. Several Bible-women, however, are employed in house-to-house visitation, and follow the girls to their new homes, so keeping up the influence, and often carrying on a simple education for years after they have left school.

One of the Bible-women I saw had gone about

the country teaching, and preaching, and speaking to the women in the villages long before Bible women were appointed by the Mission. She had had her bodily ailments cured, she said; but more, 'She had been cured of her sins;' and 'the blessed medicine' which had effected this she had gone to make known to her poor sisters, who needed it as much as she did. How intensely interesting it is to sit down with a group of these humble women gathered round you, their softened, speaking countenances turned up to yours, all aglow as they hear and speak of the love of Christ which has done so much for them! A light sometimes shines on these faces, rugged and illiterate as they often are, which only the entrance of God's Spirit into the human soul could produce.

One thing I notice is, that everywhere among the women, high and low, there is a dawning knowledge of a higher sphere which has been opened for them —a something better which they might possess and which they long for, which has been 'brought to light' by the Christians' God. And I think this wins many—along with their love for the Bible; because, as they express it, 'It says kind things about us women.' Their own books 'say cruel things;' but our Book 'is kind,' and He who fed the five thousand 'is kind;' and 'did He not suffer and die for us?' So they talk, poor things! I have been much interested in the women both in Nagercoil and here; though perhaps they correspond more to the humbler orders of those I have come in contact with in Bengal and Bombay.

In the middle of the day we had another

wonderfully interesting service in the church, when all the male agents and workers of the Mission assembled to hear an address from my husband. On one side sat the teachers and schoolmasters in compact lines, of whom there were seventy-two; on the other side were fifty-three catechists and forty pastors—intelligent, well-dressed, respectable men, grave and thoughtful, truly a most striking sight! How I wished all the sceptics about Missions and their fruits could have seen it. Then there were the dressers and medical students, and students preparing for the ministry and other work (some of these were from Mr. Duthie's Seminary), also a few colporteurs; and, beyond, a goodly fringe of listeners and on-lookers, and the general public about the doors.

Dr. Mitchell spoke to them for upwards of an hour with intense earnestness. The impression was very deep; some were weeping, and every one felt that the Spirit of the Living God was in the midst of us. I never saw more intent listeners, and never felt my own heart more touched. Many of these had been devil-worshippers, and now how amazing the contrast, showing how the Gospel is taking, or I might say, *has* taken hold in this dark land.

After the service, I left my husband in earnest talk with the men, and went to meet the women in Mr. Hacker's verandah. Crowds of nice-looking women came, dressed generally in red cloths, and all, I noticed, wore the upper jackets. The three Bible-women are particularly intelligent; they work under Mrs. Thomson, who meets with them often for consultation and prayer. Among the rest were Mrs.

Hacker's embroidery workers. Instead of the lace which they make at Nagercoil, the women here are employed in making embroidery and trimmings, similar to the Irish and Swiss work; and they do it beautifully, and on good, fine calico. This industry is most helpful to the Mission, and Mrs. Hacker is very glad to receive orders. Many ladies help much in taking quantities of the embroidery for sale at other stations and on the hills; and it is of so good a quality that, like the lace, it finds ready purchasers.

Meetings with the boys and girls of the Boarding Schools followed, and filled up the afternoon; troops of them came filing into the verandah, all from the Christian schools, and we had a busy and interesting time. The boys brought us some texts written beautifully, in Tamil, on slips of the palmyra leaf. Brighter and nicer children I never saw, and they were not too shy to give out their answers distinctly and fearlessly. Many were the inquiries which were made that day about Mr. and Mrs. Lowe, and many the loving messages sent to them. They are anything but forgotten in their old sphere of labour.

The heat was intense all day, but we managed to forget it, and our fatigue also, in the absorbing interest of this true Mission-day. When it grew cooler, we had a visit from a pleasing, intelligent, native gentleman, the retired Dewān, or Prime Minister, of His Highness the Maharajah, who lives in Neyoor. After some talk, he courteously offered us a drive, and took us out in his open carriage to see something of the place. The fresher air of the evening was most reviving and restful after the stifling day, as we sped along beneath the arching trees by the cool little serpentines and rice-fields. We passed the Dewān's handsome English-looking house, standing in a garden beautifully kept, and then we came on an idol or demon temple, which we stopped to examine.

It was a most rough and rude erection, a kind of shed more than a building, about six feet square, covered over for a roof with dried branches of the palmyra tree. Inside there was the most grotesque and hideous image it is possible to conceive, a female, with glaring, staring eyes, a dagger uplifted in her hand, two tusks for teeth, between which an infant was represented as being crushed to death, and a bigger child on her arm ready to be devoured next; truly a most fiendish fiend. And the poor deluded people propitiate her! There were some now making offerings of chickens, and bowing in obeisance to this hideous object, who is called the goddess, or demoness, *Isāki.*

The legend is, that this is the evil spirit of a woman who died unmarried, and therefore, hating and spiteful and revengeful, she returned to trouble the people evermore. Small-pox is also believed to be a demoness, and now that this terrible disease is scourging the country, the price of chickens has risen alarmingly, so many are offered to appease the infuriated demoness!

*Pareychaley.*

When the kind family at Neyoor retired to rest last night we meant to have started for Pareychaley, in a country cart which my husband had engaged for the trip. Unluckily, the driver had insisted on 'an advance,' which, I believe, is the custom, and as soon as he got the rupees he disappeared into the bazaar to enjoy himself, and was no more seen. Of course, the gentlemen had taken the precaution to secure the cart and bullocks in the compound, but when the time came to start no driver could be found. Messengers were despatched in all directions, and grave consultations followed. I blush to think of the commotion and disturbance we created, and the lively night it was for our friends Mr. and Mrs. Hacker. Presently, by one of those little providences we love to recall and mark, we were rescued from all our difficulties. The kind Dewān, Mr. Nana Pillay, sent to offer his carriage to take us part of the way, so as to save us fatigue ; and hearing of the dead-lock our plans had got into, he also arranged most kindly to send on his bullock-bandy ahead, to wait until we should come up, and carry us to the end of the night journey; so our perplexities were delightfully solved. By four o'clock we had left the disturbed dwelling once more to peace, and were bowling along in comfort, enjoying greatly the beauteous awakening of the day.

The young moon had retired to rest, the fireflies had extinguished their bright little lamps, the shrill chorus of the grasshoppers and crickets from the *shola* had ceased, and the many-toned voices of night were hushed. But the cool wind sang a glad morning hymn in the palmyra plumes ; the birds were beginning to shake out their feathers in the branches, and twitter to arouse their mates; the 'fell chanticleer' was doing the same thing noisily for the villages; and the tender, twinkling stars were rapidly growing pale, and retiring before the pink flush from the advancing dawn. It was a lovely, dewy morning, and the sun had risen by the time we came up to the bandy, with a pair of splendid bullocks, which took us quickly to the end.

As we turned into the road which leads up to this Mission House we were met by a tall, fine-looking man, just turning grey, arrayed in loose, white morning costume, who accosted us so heartily and shook hands with us so warmly that we felt our welcome was more than sure. This was Mr. Emlyn, the only European missionary at Pareychaley. He soon conducted us up the slope; we turned in to the front of a large bungalow, and stood before a wide handsome verandah, commanding magnificent views of the country below. Now we were met by Mrs. Emlyn and her little girl. There is no village to be seen, and only the houses and buildings belonging to the Mission. Here this couple live, charming people, who would enjoy and adorn any society; and Mrs. Emlyn tells me she has been sometimes two years without seeing the face of an English lady, there being no other European family nearer than Neyoor. But they are as happy as they can be, thoroughly occupied and busy with their schools, and Christians, and embroidery-workers, and all their manifold work. They have their dear little girl; 'enough society in herself,' her mother says, though she sorely misses her three bright boys, who are in England at school.

The bungalow is large and handsome, and the situation exceedingly beautiful. It stands high, and at our feet lies a garden full of loveliness; beyond, there are extensive wavy undulations, wonderfully green, beautifully wooded with *shola* (or jungle) and fine trees, and the whole bounded by grand ranges of dark purple mountains in the dim, dreamy distance. This place was chosen for a station by the Rev. Mr. Abbs, a late missionary; Mr. Emlyn thinks partly for the beauty of the situation, but also because the site was easily and cheaply secured. This was because it had so evil a reputation as the abode of a demon who haunted the woods that no one would live here. At first the people thought as the white men cut down the jungle the demon would destroy them; but no! they went on unmolested. So now they have changed their opinion, and think the missionaries have conquered the demon, and he has beaten a retreat to the hills.

We sat a long time over breakfast, when Mr. Emlyn gave us many interesting and amusing, though deplorable, details of what existed among this rude, almost savage, people, when missionaries first settled among them. The place was both a natural and a moral wilderness. Demons ruled supreme. Devil dances and horrible orgies were of constant occurrence, accompanied by all the wild absurdities of this degrading worship, while ignorance, and superstition, and utter lawlessness ruled among the people. But education and the Gospel have wrought great changes. The people now admit that 'the man with the Book' is stronger than the devils. Still devil dances frequently take place, and there are a great many demon-shrines about all this neighbourhood. Mr. Emlyn told us an amusing story of the first appearance of a bicycle here. When the owner was seen riding on the novel conveyance, which ran along without a horse, the people set up a hue and cry, declaring that this was a new kind of demon, who had at length conquered the Englishman, and had run off with him!

BELL MUSIC USED AT DEVIL WORSHIP.

They believe, also, that the demoness of small-pox goes about, especially frequenting the markets, because the people congregate there. With her usual vindictiveness, she smites every one she comes near, scattering the seeds of the disease from her finger-points; and thus infection spreads, and the people die.

After hearing all these stories of the ignorant people, it was most cheering to go to the church, which stands near, and find it crammed, as at Neyoor and Nagercoil, with people rescued from this dreadful superstition. Now, like him who was possessed, they sat at the feet of Jesus, clothed, and in their right mind, ready to go and 'tell how great things the Lord had done for them,' and to seek to deliver others from this tyranny. A great proportion of those present were Mr. Emlyn's workers and assistants,—such as pastors, evangelists, teachers, and catechists. There were a good many women present, who sat on one side by themselves. The whole congregation looked most respectable and intelligent, and one could hardly believe they had ever been so sunken and degraded as the common heathen are now. The transformative power of the Gospel is indeed marvellous, and education and training have done wonders.

I ought to say that all the converts are not drawn from the Shanars. There were ten castes represented in the congregation; but few are from the higher castes, and only two Brahmans have as yet joined the Mission. The bulk of the Christians belong originally to the three divisions among the Shanars; next, to the Pariahs, who are lower; and next, to the Pulayas, who, I think, are the lowest of all; only that, in caste, it always seems as if in the lowest depth there was still a lower.

One division of the Pariahs has come over to Christianity in a body; not a man is left in Hinduism. One-fifth of the whole population of this district is now Christian. My husband, as usual, gave them a long, earnest address, which was listened to with profound attention.

After lunch, the girls from the Boarding School, and some pleasing, nice-looking women, gathered in the verandah, with a few also from the day-schools; and we had, as usual, a most interesting time. Two or three of the pastors and catechists also came, and sat and talked with us. The children look so picturesque in their bright garments, the prevailing hue of which is red; all but the torn ear, which is a terrible deformity. It is wonderful to see the weights they carry in the poor, ill-used member. The lobe is elongated in many cases nearly to the shoulder. It is as ugly and incomprehensible a fashion as the contracted foot in China; but the missionaries are successfully battling with it among the converts.

Mr. Emlyn has thirty-nine schools in his district, boys' and girls', in which, he rightly says, 'there lies the hope for the future.' In the evening, he and Dr. Mitchell walked down to the village, which is nearly a mile off. But the people did not receive them gladly. In the Brahman quarter they were treated with much rudeness, pelted with mud, and some stones were thrown. One hit my husband on the back. They returned through a heavy thunder-shower, which came down with tropical vigour. But it had quite cleared up again, with the air cooled and refreshed, when, at ten o'clock, we had once more to set out on our way.

# CHAPTER XVI.

## TREVANDRUM.

It was a pitch dark night, with heavy masses of thunder-cloud blackening the sky, when Mr. Emlyn, lantern in hand, lighted us off the Mission premises, and launched us on the public road. It felt a little eerie coming out of the brightness of the pleasant house into the mirk, escorted only by the strange, unkempt charioteer, his long naked legs dangling from his perch, and a lanky lad who sat on the step behind as a sort of guide and defence. But they knew the road, and it is wonderful how safe night travelling is. And now here is Trevandrum, another goal; and here is rest, at least for some days. We are now the guests of Mr. and Mrs. Ross. He is Principal of the Maharajah's College here. When we came in early this morning, travel-soiled and very weary, Mr. Ross himself fished us out of our dusty little den, and gave us the welcome of an old friend, though we had never actually met before.

Our excellent Joseph was here before us. He had somehow caught the recalcitrant driver, took possession of the cart and bullocks for himself and the 'kit;' and here he was, in crisp, clean, starched coat and newly-folded turban, ready to unpack and do everything for us.

As soon as it was cool in the afternoon, Mrs. Ross drove us out. Trevandrum is a most beautiful place, full of picturesqueness, and all the loveliness which knolls, and hills, and verdant undulations, with some good buildings, and the richest tropical foliage can give. The mingled rocks and hills, green valleys and lofty mountains, with the rich vegetation, the palm groves and rice-fields, and water, altogether make as lovely a panorama as one's eyes could wish to look upon.

It is the capital of Travancore, and the residence of His Highness the Maharajah and his Court. The Prince had succeeded to the sovereignty not long before our visit; and was, unfortunately for us, absent, making his grand tour through the great cities of India. The Maharajah seemed to be liked; had travelled a good deal, knew English well, and was considered an enlightened man. But I am told that his first act after his accession was to make additional grants for the repair of all the heathen temples in the State. He rejoiced in the grand-sounding title—His Highness, Sri, Patman-abhi, Dasa, Vanji Balarama Varmah Kulasahara Kridapadi Mannay Sultan Maharajah Rama Rajah, Bahadur Shamshir Jang, Fellow of the Madras University; the Maharajah of Travancore!'

This city lies only two miles from the sea. It is rather scattered, occupying a wide area, and is intersected with broad, clean, well-kept roads, richly fringed with remarkably fine trees. There is an observatory, a handsome building, which stands in a commanding position; a museum, called the Napier Museum, in the pretty park or public gardens; the College; and several other good buildings. There is also the Fort, which is surrounded by lofty walls, and guarded by sentinels, in which stand the palaces where all the Royal Family reside; the Government offices also, and a temple, which is peculiarly sacred and of great antiquity.

The whole of this little strip of a kingdom—fifty miles wide, and only one hundred and seventy miles long from the north point to the south—is full of varied interest. It is also full of natural loveliness. Every new bit we see seems more beautiful than the last. It may well be called the Garden of India. But, oh, what a moral wilderness it seems to be! Nowhere else in India is caste so strong, nor the lofty and tyrannical pretensions of the higher castes so insisted on and enforced as here.

Then to me, I confess, it is quite as despicable, and nearly as painful to contemplate the abject servility, the slavishness of the lower castes to the higher. One would not wonder so much at the calm assumption of superiority by the Brahman; but that the lower castes should have so long submitted to the oppression and all the galling indignities so unsparingly heaped upon them, is certainly a perplexity. The 'once born,' the 'low born,' the 'polluted:' by these distinguishing epithets are the low-castes designated. And the curious thing is that in this caste system, as I said, there is 'even in the lower depth a lower still.' Every low man has some one yet lower, on whom he in turn can look down and tyrannise over. And apathy is not the word to describe the utter carelessness and indifference there is among low and high alike as to the condition of others who may not be 'of their caste.' This accursed caste seems to convert the mild Hindu into a very demon of cruelty, if all the tales one hears be true—especially of the times when slavery was allowed by law. The ignorance, the superstition, the suffering, the misery, the utter degradation, are indeed pitiable to behold.

I hear so much about it all, and the marvellous complexities of the laws and customs, especially in connection with the law of inheritance, in this strangest of communities, that my brain will hardly take it all in. A Pulaya (a man of very low caste) dare not come within ninety feet of the sacred person of a Brahman. From a Nair or Sudra, also, he must keep at a respectful distance. If he sees a high caste man approach, he must creep behind a hedge, or scramble up a bank, or get off the road somehow, until the lordly 'twice born,' (the Brahman) has passed on his way. He must cover his mouth, lest his breath should taint the air; he must speak of himself as 'your slave,' never daring to use the personal pronoun. He is not allowed to clothe himself above the waist. But I need not go on with my enumeration. If you want to know more of these complexities and absurdities, read Mr. Mateer's books.

It is pleasant to turn one's gaze on the Christianised part of the population. The truth of the Gospel must come on these poor low-caste men with a joyful surprise. That any of the rights of men should ever by possibility belong to them must seem too wonderful to be true. That God should be 'no respecter of persons,' that He should think of them as His children; or that Christ, having died for 'all,' should therefore have died for them!—this wondrous story of redemption may well be 'glad tidings of great joy' to the down-trodden and despised of this once so dark little kingdom.

Christianity always raises the low castes, in civilisation, in character, in intelligence, in social standing and position, and in every way. Of course, people cannot be freed all at once from the consequences of long oppression, and the chains and bonds of superstition cannot be knocked off very easily. Apostasies have occurred; sometimes, when trouble has overtaken him, the poor ignorant convert has sought to propitiate the demon once more. The Pulaya, and even the Pariah and the Shanar, have sometimes made unsatisfactory Christians, no doubt; and who would wonder, after the ages of oppression they have undergone? It may take a generation or two to make strong, reliable men of those poor Pulayas, who were formerly slaves and treated with incredible cruelty and indignity; but when one looks at the large, noble congregations of men and women, of whom you 'can take knowledge that they have been with Jesus,' one's heart is filled with thanksgiving and joy; and who can doubt but that the Gospel will everywhere speedily triumph? Well may the missionaries take courage, and feel that the hand of God has been with them in their work, and will be so increasingly, according to His precious promise.

The Nairs whom I have mentioned, though not Brahmans, are a good caste. They form the military class, and are the aristocracy of the country. The reigning family are Nairs, although it seeks often to raise itself by matrimonial alliances with the Brahmans. This is still more systematically sought by the Royal family at Cochin. Succession among the Nairs goes in the female line; the nephew of the Maharajah being the heir-apparent,—that is, the son of his sister, not his own or his brother's. I believe this arises out of the dreadful system of polyandry, which was once largely practised here; though, happily, this is now no longer the case.

It was a special pleasure to me to renew here an acquaintance with Miss Blandford, of the Zenana Mission, begun years ago in the house of our dear friends the Robertsons in Bombay. Miss Blandford is one of the ablest and most successful of the Zenana missionaries who have ever come to India. She has laboured for many years with patience and faith, and has done a great and noble work in Trevandrum. She has been especially associated with the ladies of the Court, and she speaks of some of the princesses with the greatest affection and respect. She herself occupies a position of much and deserved influence among them, and, indeed, in the whole place, both among the natives and Europeans. Miss Blandford is a power for good. It is wonderful what the influence of this one devoted Christian woman has done for Travancore—a stronghold of superstition and caste.

*Monday, 27th.*

Early yesterday morning we attended service in the Mission Church (of the London Missionary Society). As usual, there was a good, intelligent congregation; of course, my husband preached. This now is the Malayalim Mission, as this is the Malayalim country; and the language therefore has changed. In the farther South the language was Tamil, which doubtless came in from beyond the ghāts with Tamil immigrants; but Malayalim and Tamil are closely allied, and spring from the same root as Canarese, Telugu, and Tulu—all the five being Dravidian tongues.

The Rev. S. Mateer, well-known as a missionary and an author, has long been stationed here. He has charge of Trevandrum and Quilon, but was seeking health at home at the time of our visit. Mr. Wilkinson, and Mr. Knowles who has lately joined the Mission, minister in the Gospel in his place. There are thirty-nine congregations in the district, and about 5,000 Christians, with a respectable army of teachers, village-preachers, pastors, and other agents. The work seems to be making steady progress through God's blessing here, as at the other stations; while among the churches there is a great deal of spiritual life. The meetings for prayer, Bible classes, and Sunday schools are full of heartiness; and the women seem specially earnest. There is a prayer-meeting among them, entirely conducted by themselves. Then the women who can read go to the houses of those who cannot, and read to them, and have prayer; while others collect poor children together, give them food (like our own Sunday breakfasts), and then teach them Bible lessons. The people are liberal, according to their means, and bring the first-fruits of their harvest, and other offerings, to their chapels. Of course, there are disappointments and discouragements, as I have said—where are these not to be found?—and the missionaries have a hard battle to fight; chiefly because of this abominable caste, which stands in the way of all progress.

To-day our friend Miss Blandford came for us early, and we started in her carriage to see something of her work. We first went by appointment to the Palace, entered the Fort by a huge gateway, and stood before the door of a handsome pile, where we were received by a gentleman of the Court, and straightway ushered into the presence of the senior Rāni. She shook hands with us all, my husband not excepted, and received us as any English lady would receive her guests. Her rooms are very pretty, nicely furnished, with mirrors and a few pictures, one or two couches, and a table with books, not at all crowded, nor like an upholsterer's shop, which is the usual native taste. The floor is of cool, highly-polished chunam, as smooth as marble and nearly as white, and no carpet. My first thought was, what a contrast to the usual zenana—at least, of Bengal—and how striking the difference which this lady presents with all her surroundings to those poor faded Rānis in their dreary apartments at Tanjore! Here, you see at once what education, refinement and intercourse with a cultivated Christian lady have accomplished. These influences have had a magical effect. Miss Blandford has reason to thank God for her successful work. All the ladies are much attached to her personally; and let us hope and pray that ere long the crowning joy may be hers of seeing them profess to be Christ's. The Rāni is a most pleasing person, not very young, with soft, retiring manners, perfect self-possession, wonderfully fair for a Southern woman, and having a gentle though intelligent expression of countenance. Her hair was all gathered in a great knot at one side,—a Madras fashion, and not a becoming one—and she was simply though richly attired, her chief ornament being the decoration sent her by the Queen. Of this she is immensely proud, and displayed it with the utmost satisfaction. She talks English wonderfully well; reads, writes, draws, and employs herself as educated women do. She has no children, and thus her time is all her own. She does needle-work beautifully, and showed us a group of flowers she was embroidering on velvet; she also took us downstairs, and showed us the rooms where she studies with Miss Blandford, including a room for painting, an art in which she delights. I noticed that in every apartment almost there hung a portrait of Her Majesty the Queen, of whom Her Highness speaks with the greatest reverence and affection. She is not a baptised Christian; but a Bible lay in more than one of the rooms, and Miss Blandford reads it with her constantly, and she seems to be at least intellectually a believer.

May her heart be opened to the Lord, as was Lydia's!

We were surprised to find that the man who had received us at the door in the most unpretending way, and conducted us upstairs, was the Rāni's husband—a small man about forty, without shoes or stockings, and a turban on his head. In this strange country husbands seem to be only appendages. From what I have already said of the queer laws of succession, you will see that the Maharajah's own son cannot succeed him. If he has a brother, and he is in his right mind, he can and does succeed: but the late Maharajah had no brother; he therefore adopted two nieces, his sister's children, who, by virtue of this adoption, became Rānis, and are the two ladies we have been visiting. They were married to two men chosen for them; but unfortunately the senior Rāni, as I said, has no children, which must be a great grief to her. This proved the wisdom of having adopted two ladies instead of only one. The junior Rāni has three sons now alive, and they are the heirs to the throne; so she is a person of great consequence. There was also a little princess born, at which event there were great rejoicings. How strange it is: here the joy is when a girl is born! In Bengal and other parts such an event is considered a calamity, and the attendants are afraid to go and break the sad tidings to the expectant father. But this poor little princess died, and a terrible grief it was. In consequence there must be another case of adopting; for none of the children who may be born to any of the three lads, who are themselves heirs, will be eligible for the throne. Their father is dead, but their mother is married again, and it does not matter how many different fathers the various children have so long as the mother is the same; and if she has a little girl, *her* children will be heirs. Let who can comprehend: I have made it plain as far as my own comprehension goes.

The senior Rāni and her husband are a most happy and devoted couple. He incurred the displeasure somehow of the late Maharajah, and was for years banished from the Court. But his wife was faithful to him, although they often tried to induce her to marry some one else. On his deathbed the old king relented, and the banished man was permitted to return and join his wife; and now they are living happily together, he sympathising with her in all her higher tastes. He charged himself with Dr. Mitchell's entertainment, who found him not only intelligent, but really learned in Sanscrit and other lore.

We were not so interested in our visit to the junior Rāni; she is a much more common-place woman, and yet she has a strong, good face, and was most courteous to us. Her eldest son, who is the heir-apparent, and is called the Elliah-Rajah, has an establishment to himself; but her two younger boys were with her—nice little lads, with dark olive faces, and rather heavy locks, beneath small, richly-embroidered turbans. They wore green satin coats, embroidered with gold, red silk trousers, and no shoes or stockings. Their little Royal Highnesses did everything for our entertainment: they read an English book, and recited a little; one then played on the *vina*—a small instrument like a guitar—while the other sang a monotonous strain in Malayalim. As we took leave, their mother graciously presented me with photographs of herself and her three sons.

In the afternoon we paid another Royal visit, this time to His Highness the Heir Apparent, or Elliah-Rajah. A carriage was sent for us from the Palace, in which we drove a good way to a kind of Garden-house, where His Highness resides just now. He is a mild, gentleman-like young fellow, with pleasing, quiet manners, short rather, and dressed in the simplest grey suit, English in pattern, with a small white turban twisted round his shapely head, and very becoming to his dark face. He talked English perfectly, with an excellent accent, and asked the most intelligent questions on many subjects. He seemed greatly pleased to have my husband to talk to, and begged us to prolong our visit; but when the conversation turned on religion, it was manifest that he is a very orthodox Hindu. All the reigning family seem to be the same; the Maharajah, perhaps, the most so of all. He is bringing some holy water from the Ganges, I see in a paper, to present as an oblation to the idol in one of the most sacred shrines in his dominions. It makes one's heart heavy to think that so much boasted enlightenment produces so little real light; but this only comes with the gift of the Holy Ghost. The young man was earnest, however, and thoughtful in his talk, and said with feeling as well as politeness, as we took leave of him, that he would never forget this visit, nor the food for thought the conversation had provided him. My husband next visited the Dewān, or Prime Minister; so I think we have done our duty by the powers that be.

In the evening he gave an English lecture under the auspices of the Young Men's Debating Society, and the large hall at the College was crowded in every part with both Europeans and natives. He contrasted the condition of India in 1838, when he first landed on its shores, with what it is at the present time. He showed the marvellous progress there has been, and the change for the better in a hundred ways, giving as the causes for these the efforts of a humane Government, education, missionary influence, the spread of the precepts of Christianity, and so forth. The subject was so interesting that he was listened to breathlessly; but as soon as he had finished, up started an irate Maratha Brahman, who poured forth a deluge of talk in reply. He glorified the Marathas and the Maratha dynasty, contending that the good old times of the great Shivaji were really the palmy days of India. Mrs. Ross and I had to come away in the middle of this tirade, as she was expecting friends to dinner; but the gentlemen told me afterwards that my husband had quietly answered, and in the judgment of all the audience had fairly extinguished him, at which there had been a good deal of amusement.

*Tuesday Evening.*

The belligerent Maratha, to his honour be it said, does not bear malice. He called early this morning on Dr. Mitchell, coming in state in his carriage, with scarlet-coated attendants, paid his antagonist some high-flown compliments, had a long, pleasant talk, and finally they parted the best of friends.

The Dewān has also called, and is exceedingly kind and gracious. It seems that he also is a Maratha Brahman, able and enlightened, occupying the most influential position after the Maharajah in the State.

We spent the whole of the next morning, after breakfast, with Mr. Ross, in his College and High School; a noble institution in every respect it is. Mr. Ross has an able associate in Dr. Harvey, and a good staff of native professors and teachers. There is also a Preparatory School, for which some additional premises are now being built. The College buildings are very handsome, and the rooms large, airy, and numerous. There are about a thousand pupils, taking all the departments, with one hundred and twenty in the College. We went from class to class, intensely interested. The education is thorough and excellent, and the lads bright and evidently in earnest over their studies; frank, too, and answering with a pleasant readiness you do not always find, which makes the examination animated and interesting. But what certainly had for us the chief interest, and seemed very remarkable, was to hear the Bible taught in this institution; for you must remember it is not missionary—it belongs to Government; and more than this, to a heathen Government.

The Bible classes were taught by a Syrian named Luke, an intelligent man, who is a master in the High School. Each class in the school (not College) has Bible instruction for one hour every week; and this has been the practice since it was opened, I think in 1835. The first master, Mr. Roberts, insisted on being allowed to teach the Scriptures, and the point then yielded has never since been interfered with. This man Luke is a relative of the late Patriarch of the Syrian Church, the Mar Athanasius whom we knew in Bombay a great many years ago.

Our final School visit was, perhaps, the most pleasing of all; it was to Miss Blandford's Caste-girls' school. As we drove into the compound within the Fort walls, we saw, quite close to the school building, the charred, blackened ruins of a house, evidently the scene of a late fire. 'How did you possibly escape?' we exclaimed. 'How, indeed,' said Miss Blandford, 'but by the merciful interposition of God in direct answer to prayer?'

It seems that some new Government official had set his affections on this house, which Miss Blandford had used for her school for years. She was accordingly turned out, and put to immense inconvenience. The pupils were in sore grief on account of their school, and especially for their dear lady, who had difficulty in getting other premises which were suitable. So they agreed together — teacher and taught—to pray that the old house might be given back. Then the fire occurred, the one house was consumed, while its close neighbour was spared. 'Ah,' said the children and the people also,

'God has taken care of the school-room, because it is yours. God intends you to have it; you will get it back!' And sure enough it was given back; and here they are installed, and the school is more successful, more crowded, and more a favourite than ever.

Miss Blandford's own class is composed of quite grown-up girls, pleasing and intelligent, giving very thoughtful answers to the questions put. One question was, 'What is better than gold?' 'Knowledge,' at once answered a pleasant-looking girl. 'And is there anything better than knowledge?' 'Yes,' answered another. 'What is it?' 'A pure heart!' she said.

There are three assistant teachers, but Miss Blandford is here herself all day long. She breakfasts and has her lunch here, only returning to her home when all the duties of the day are over. Do our friends at home always realise how hard often is the life of our dear Zenana missionaries?

I am always in my element in a school like this, and we stayed long, seeing all the departments thoroughly. Most of the children are disfigured by the elongated ear filled with massive rings and weights, and also by the unbecoming way they dress their hair. Some have it gathered into an untidy bunch at the left side, and others have the bunch on the forehead; a great pity, for the faces are bright and happy and pleasant, and show remarkable intelligence. They all seem fond of Miss Blandford, and also of the Miss Gahans, and to be on the most easy, familiar footing with them; 'much happier in school,' they say, 'than anywhere else.' One dear, wee child in the infant department I longed to take away to exhibit. She is remarkably small, like a doll, with innocent, big, grave eyes, which fix on yours with the most questioning gaze. She is wonderfully fair, being the child of a rich Nair family, and richly dressed in a little crimson petticoat, starred with yellow, reaching to the pretty little feet; a bright green velvet bodice edged with gold lace, and a beautiful jewel of pearls and rubies on her forehead, the hair—all that has yet grown—gathered, like the others, to the side. She sat quite happily on my lap, not in the least afraid or shy.

There were about eighty pupils in all, and among them a few Syrian Christian girls. Many seemed to be a good deal more than half Christian. They said they believed Christianity to be true, but dared not profess it, as their parents would be very angry, and they would be taken from school. This would be the saddest thing that could happen to them. And is it not wonderful that these proud, bigoted people should permit their daughters to be so completely under the influence of a Christian woman? Surely it is the Lord's doing, and shows a purpose of mercy to the next generation in Travancore.

## Note by Dr. Murray Mitchell.

*His Highness the Maharajah of Travancore.*—We much regretted that the Maharajah of Travancore was absent when we were at Trevandrum. His

Highness has often been praised as the most enlightened of Indian princes. He is a Fellow of the Madras University. He has read English literature extensively, quotes intelligently and approvingly such writers as Stuart Mill, Herbert Spencer, and Darwin, and expresses himself in English with more than correctness—with something approaching to elegance. Yet, since his accession to the throne of Travancore, His Highness has conducted himself like a bigoted Hindu. He has been prodigal in his largesses to the Brahmans. One of his latest achievements has been to get himself weighed in one scale of a balance against gold in the other. He sat in one scale, decorated with sword, shield, jewels, etc., and gold coins were heaped in the other scale, till the prince was found wanting and the gold preponderated, and then the vast sum was distributed among the Brahmans. When the last Maharajah was weighed, the sum expended amounted to £16,000. On this occasion the ceremony was still more splendid, and the gifts to the Brahmans more magnificent. Meanwhile roads, bridges, and public improvements of every kind are urgently required; but they must wait. One whole fifth of the revenues of the Travancore State is devoted to the support of Hinduism; that is to say, almost exclusively to the support of the Brahmans—especially the Namburi Brahmans. These men amount only to about 10,000; but they are omnipotent throughout Travancore. Does the Maharajah pamper these from policy, or from conviction? I came to the conclusion that it was from conviction; but in that case the mind of His Highness must be a psychological curiosity, which it would have been interesting to study.

As this sheet was passing through the press, tidings of the unexpected death of the Maharajah reached England.

## CHAPTER XVII.

### THE BACKWATER.

*March 1st.*

WE are again afloat; this time literally so. It is early morning, hardly more than dawn, and we are sitting on a sort of sofa-chair, like a garden-seat somewhat, on the roof of our boat—for we are now shooting along through the lagoons and lakes filled from the numerous rivers and streams of this well-watered land, which form the famous Backwater of the Malabar coast.

These lagoons are connected by canals, and make a grand line of water communication known as the Backwater, which is of great commercial importance to all this region. This Backwater is always smooth and navigable, and is untouched by the storms of the ocean, from which it is divided by high embankments of sand, and by a margin of cultivated and well-wooded flat country, which is generally also well populated.

The fresh morning air on the water is quite intoxicating. I could not remain any longer below in the close little cabin; and so here we are perched, enjoying the cool air, while we speed along as fast as our sixteen oarsmen can take us. The channel just now is narrow, and the banks full of beauty. We are going through a region of exquisite and picturesque loveliness too beautiful to describe. There are woods and waters, lakes and fens, rippling streams and sullen canals, stately palms and mighty monarchs of the forest, with a tangled undergrowth of dazzling, varied, gleaming *shola*, or natural bush. There are tall, wavy grasses and lowly mosses; gnarled old stems silvered with lichen, or clambered over and clothed with beauty from a hundred different delicate fern-fronds; there are climbers, and trailers, and parasites without end, which throw their gigantic arms round strong trees, and then fling themselves about with wanton frolic in loops, and festoons, and garlands of endless beauty. In short, all along the banks there is the luxuriant wealth of vegetation which belongs to the tropics, bathed in the night-dews, and gleaming and glowing in the glorious sunshine of morning.

After dinner last night we took leave of our most hospitable entertainers, who have simply loaded us with kindness. Mr. Ross drove us down about two miles in the Sircar carriage—which had been placed at our disposal from the Palace all the time of our stay—to the little pier at the head of the canal where our boat was moored. The Dewān has most considerately sent a peon (or messenger), who is to accompany us and look after the supplies of boatmen —a needful precaution. Mr. Ross sends another; so we are well off. It is indeed remarkable how carefully and wisely our whole journey has been planned for us all through; and our hearts continually swell with gratitude to our gracious God, from whose loving hands come all these benefits, and who makes our way so easy.

Joseph had our quilts and pillows spread on the narrow benches in the tiny cabin; our stalwart, dusky boatmen were ready at their oars; flags were flying gaily from stern and bow; so, waving an adieu to our friends on the bank, we struck out into the stream, and were soon gliding swiftly along in the gloom of the over-arching boughs and the thick, dark foliage which clothed the banks on either side. The moon was shining, but in a sky of very milky hue Not a star was there to be seen to cheer us on our way. The air was damp and heavy, and laden with the luscious scent of a hundred jungle flowers. Mosquitoes buzzed, and cicadas chirruped; the men were very noisy; and, tired though we were, to sleep was out of the question. The kindly visitant strove hard to come at our bidding; but the strife with the harsh voices, especially of the noisy boatmen, was quite an unequal one. When not chatting and laughing, they were singing, and kept up a monotonous chant often during the night. Coaxing and threatening were alike unavailing to keep them quiet.

We changed the men every ten miles, when we halted at some jetty, and then the hullabaloo was inconceivable. They shouted, and yelled, and woke the echoes, so as to rouse the village which had to supply the next relay; and when the unwilling, sleepy creatures came at the Sircar's hookum the strife of tongues which ensued was truly awful. So it was rather an unhappy night; but the joy of the glorious morning far more than compensated—as when does it not?—for the sorrows and weariness of the troubled night. The rejoicing, masterful

BOATS ON THE BACKWATER, TRAVANCORE.

R

sun has cleared the heavens of the cream-like veiling, or 'scuffed the clouds,' as our skipper in the China seas used to say; and how the beams dance and sparkle in the tangle of green loveliness which the banks present! It is more beautiful every moment. Some of the trees are laden with strange fruit, and others are gorgeous with bright blossoms. Looking upward you see towering, soaring cocoa palms. There are forests of them; their straight grey stems rising to the height of a hundred feet and more, crowned a-top with their beautiful plume of waving fronds, in the midst of which bright bits of blue sky peep out here and there. Then, if you keep your gaze to the level of the water, there is the *shola* I spoke of—an undergrowth of riches inexhaustible: ferns, and grasses, and shrubbery, full of greens, and browns, and brighter colours, and an infinite variety of leaf. We are just passing a thicket of bushy shrubs, with crowns of scarlet, long-shaped leaves, like the pointsetya somewhat, drooping gracefully amid the vivid green; and now another, with bunches of golden flowers, cup-shaped, a little like the beautiful chumpa. Above these the pale yellow-green, shiny, satiny leaves of the wild plantain float like flags: yards in length they seem. And now we come on some real English-looking greensward. But here is Quilon—where we are to land until the heat of the day has moderated.

We landed at eight, and were strolling up the bank, with our white umbrellas and sun-hats, having sent off our attendants in search of the Travellers' Bungalow, when we met a tall, gentleman-like man, in a suit of white flannel, who politely accosted us, and, with true Indian hospitality, invited us to his house. This was Mr. Cameron, a countryman, of course, and originally from Badenoch; so we have much in common, and were fast friends at once. We discovered afterwards that our kind friend Mr. Ross had quietly given him a hint to waylay us, if at home. He led us up by a splendid avenue of feathery casuarina trees, away toward the sea, where, high over the shore, his bungalow stands. It commands a magnificent ocean-view. How wonderful it is that the Backwater should be so quiet, so full of smiling peacefulness, and yet so near that tossing ocean; but the separation seems complete. On entering the house, we found a real bachelor abode. The verandah-room presented a delightful medley, the most prominent articles being newspapers, books, and magazines, with guns, and sticks, and fishing-tackle, and other gear of the sort in every corner. Beyond, in the inner precincts, there shone a dazzling vision of a daintily-spread breakfast-table; and beyond again, in some cool, dark, remote recesses, were to be found the crowning delight—the good old Indian bath-tub. To know the full luxury of a bath, you must come to India. Your 'tub' here means a reservoir, full to the brim, standing over-night on cool, wet slabs, into which you plunge bodily, and emerge a new being. After an experience like this, we brought very appreciative appetites to the fresh fish, and rice, and new-laid eggs, with the chillis, and chutnies, and relishes; and then the heaps of delicious fruit which always accompany an Indian meal.

After this, the gentlemen decreed that I was to repose on one of the roomy couches, which I did, with a file of the *Inverness Courier* beside me. A good hour's sleep followed to us all, and left us entirely refreshed. Mr. Carruthers, of Inverness, a grandson of the famous old editor, had joined us, and we had a charming day.

At three o'clock, after lunch, we again set sail, our kind entertainer and Mr. Carruthers accompanying us to the boat. It was still very hot; but we had a good distance, with unknown perils of waters, before us, and the supplies of boatmen, to say the least, uncertain. Our Sircar peon is very zealous, but awakens my husband's wrath by the ready knocks and cuffs he administers to the poor men when they fail in their duty. This official, with his belt, and badge, and coat of scarlet and gold, and very important ways, is quite a person of authority among the poor people, who treat him with a homage hardly less than they accord to the Sahib himself. Our own man generally departs to the stern in a sort of dignified retirement, feeling rather superseded. He has just produced, however, a most excellent curry for our dinner; how cooked in the hole in the bottom of the boat, which is all there is for kitchen, I cannot make out: but Indian servants have an amount of resource in this sort of thing which is peculiar to themselves.

The boatmen, under the darkening sky, are as like savages as if we were on Lake Tanganyika. They are wonderfully black, with shock heads, or the hair gathered into a fantastic knot over their foreheads. They have no turbans and no clothes, except the bit of rag round the loins. They chatter immensely, though now they are singing a dirge-like song. One man leads off, singing a line, and then the whole crew catch up the refrain, repeating over and over the same words to the same monotonous strain. Occasionally a clever one among them improvises, and he must say something droll, for there is a general laugh. Poor fellows! they are very enduring, and work like machines at the oars hour after hour. Dr. Mitchell often tried to talk to them; but, alas! their language was so strange that there was little mutual comprehension, and none of them could read.

The evening is exquisite, much finer than last night when we started. There is something ineffably pensive and sweet in the scene, and full of restful peace, as the golden radiance from the setting sun subdues and melts into the silvery light of the moon, not yet quite at its full, which gleams softly on the still water. The lagoon has greatly widened, and the palm trees look solemn and spectral on the distant banks. We have just been saying that such an evening, succeeding the busy, bustling, garish day, reminds one of the finished life of a chastened, happy, useful Christian, waiting calmly in the light at eventide to be taken home.

*In the Boat, 3rd March.*

Here again is the morning, full of brightness, and coolness, and exuberance of life. Our men are much quieter, so we have had some sleep. Poor fellows! they are too tired to be noisy; no wonder, for the relays have failed utterly, notwithstanding the Sircar's official and his authority. One set has brought us some forty miles. They go wearily, as we wind through the great waste of waters, and we have just told them to go to the bank and halt a little. Numbers of palm climbers are at work, scrambling up the branchless stems like monkeys, and bringing down little pots brimful of the sweet, fresh juice of the wonderful tree. We have treated our men to as much of this refreshing beverage as they can drink, with which they are greatly charmed, and they will resume their oars with more spirit. This juice is called *tādi*,[1] and by evening it will have fermented, and become intoxicating; now it is a most pleasant draught, and very invigorating

I never saw the phosphorescence on the water so glorious as last night. I could hardly lie still for gazing at its changeful beauty. The whole surface of the water sometimes looked like a lake of fire; and as the oars struck, it broke into tiny ripples and whirls of dancing light most curious and beautiful. Sometimes we seemed to go over waves and crests of light; and then again it broke into curls and twists, as if snakes of fire were pursuing us. The sounds, too, were often peculiar. Close to our stern or side there would be a sudden splash and swirl, showing unmistakably the presence of big creatures in the water, probably some monster of the deep. One time, very incautiously, I confess, I had my arm out of the window, catching the cool water in my hand, when something slimy

[1] Hence, apparently, the word *toddy*.

and cold struck it. I did not need a second warning; and when we saw a dead alligator float past on his back this morning, I thought I would not be so venturesome again. Some one, no doubt, had shot the beast.

The scenery has changed a little from yesterday. The lagoons are of wider expanse, though the channels wind and alter constantly. Now the water is a mile or two wide; a little while ago it was only a few yards. We seem to have left the palmyra tree behind, but the cocoa and other palms abound. There is a good deal of cultivation visible. There are belts of wavy, tall sugar-cane; but the crops-in-chief are always rice. The flat expanse by the water-edge is filled with the vivid green of the plant which loves the damp, warm air, and the wealth of water which a sluice opened in the embankment can pour into the fields at any moment. Away to the horizon now are to be descried hills, and dreamy, purple mountain-ranges; and on the other hand, though not always visible, there is the blue expanse of ocean; but entirely separated from us by the wall of sand I have spoken of. Nearer there is always this abounding, rejoicing vegetation, and these noble trees, with the golden rays of the mounting sun glinting through the green branches, which throw their shadows deep into the mirror-like lagoon.

There is plenty of life about, which is generally the case in the morning. A good many baggage and cargo boats are being towed, or pushed along by a pole, wielded generally by a solitary man. Other boats of quaint construction there are, though not many canoes or fishing boats. Often we came on tiny islands beautifully wooded; and hamlets are frequent now, as we get nearer Cottayam, pretty little homesteads surrounded by fences of palm branches. Pretty white churches, too, gleam amid the woods, always surmounted by a cross. Most of these are Roman Catholic, but some belong to the Syrian Christians, who are scattered over this coast. Often there is only a cross, white-washed, and raised on a

SCENE ON THE BACKWATER, TRAVANCORE.

pedestal, and occasionally ornamented with a wreath of flowers, the offering of some devout and simple worshipper. How sweet and pleasant a contrast to the shrine for the worship of demons! and how cheering! This looks almost like a Christian land. And how fairylike is the scenery: it puts us in mind, with its many waters and tortuous channels, winding among woods and islands, and low promontories, and green flats, of the lovely St. Lawrence and its thousand islands. We have just passed a tall stork, standing on one leg in a contemplative mood on a stem among some reeds; and now, a little further on, a huge crocodile lies on a bit of greensward, lazily sunning himself. It is now becoming too hot to sit on deck, and we are glad to be approaching Cottayam, where we shall stay for a few days with Mr. and Mrs. Neve, of the Church Missionary Society.

# CHAPTER XVIII.

## COTTAYAM: ITS MISSIONS — THE SYRIAN CHRISTIANS OF MALABAR.

We did not arrive here until long past noon yesterday. Our weary mariners went very dejectedly for the last few hours, and we had not the heart to urge them on, although the little cabin was like an oven, in which we were being baked and browned. Our clever chuprassie, however, knocked up a kind of awning outside the door, beneath which we sat on our quilts, cross-legged, like Oriental potentates, and endured the heat as philosophically as we could. The servants had all gone to sleep, as indeed had all nature. The dear little birds, who had been carolling to us from early dawn, found it too hot to sing any more, and hid away among the cool leaves; the giant frogs forgot to croak; the shrill voices of the untiring cicadas were happily silenced for awhile; and even the screeching, vivacious, tiresome green paroquets ceased their restless flight and chatter, and left us for awhile in peace. Only the beautiful little silver fish, which darted about us in shoals, looked cool and happy, in the clear, green depths of the still water. Voices which at midnight fill the jungle with their noisy chorus are hushed at midday, and there was not a sound but the splash of the lazy oar, and the snores of the sleeping men. The tyrant sun reigned supreme.

The water by-and-by expanded into a sea-like expanse. They say the distant banks are splendid shikār grounds, where the tiger, elephant, and leopard are to be found in the primeval forest, and also plenty of smaller game. The head-boatman pointed westward, where the large and important town of Allepy lay, with its shipping, and lighthouse, and large population; and soon thereafter we drew near to the palm-fringed shore at Cottayam.

How glad we were to step on to the jetty and take refuge from the intolerable blaze beneath the dense, delicious shade of the glorious palm forests; for here the tree abounds in every sort, and size, and species. We sat, with a cool carpet of sward beneath our feet, and the grand canopy of plumes over our heads, until the servant from the Mission House, who had watched for our arrival since morning, went for the carriage to bring us up. Mr. and Mrs. Neve had sent us a most kind invitation; and we were entertained by them, as we have been by missionaries of all Societies, in the heartiest and warmest way.

We have now left the Mission fields of the London Missionary Society behind us in the South, and have reached the borders of those occupied by the Church Missionary Society. It began its labours in the Malayalim country in 1816, at the invitation of 'the good Resident,' Colonel, afterwards General Munro, and certainly there is no region more interesting, from a missionary point of view, than this, in all India. The circumstances which give special interest to this Mission are, first, the existence here still of the ancient Syrian Church of Malabar, the history of which has been so remarkable, and has so largely stirred the hearts of Christian people everywhere; and next, the existence of a colony of Jews, who are said to have made their way to India in the first century after the destruction of the second temple. These Jews, however, are now to be found chiefly—or almost solely—in Cochin. The Syrian Christians are all about us here and around Cottayam.

Very little was known about the Syrian Church of Malabar until after 1498, when the Portuguese landed on this coast. Vasco de Gama and his people were astonished to find a colony of fellow-Christians before them in heathen India; who, in their turn, were glad to welcome the new-comers, so much more like themselves than the poor heathen round them. Three centuries later the English occupied Malabar; and it was soon after this that Dr. C. Buchanan, then a chaplain in Bengal, visited this ancient Church, and reported on its condition. He carried out his inquiry in 1806; and Colonel Macaulay, who was then British Resident in Travancore, took the liveliest interest in the matter, and aided him in every possible way. The result, every one knows, was the establishment, in 1816, of a Mission under the auspices of the Church Missionary Society, which has worked in the district ever since, chiefly among the Syrian Christians, but also among the heathen.

Is it not a most curious and striking fact, that these two communities, one of God's ancient people, and this wonderful old Christian Church, should have existed here side by side during all these ages—that a lamp of Bible truth, a double light, one might say, though a poor and feeble one enough, should have burned, however faintly, and have been kept alive amid every change and trouble, until now, when, eighteen centuries later, it is glimmering still in the midst of the deep darkness of the surrounding heathenism? [1]

Happily, now there are other lamps alight in the Mission stations, which have been planted by the different Societies, like light-houses, along the coast. Let us hope, and pray, and work, until this old Church is thoroughly revived; and God's ancient people also are brought in, and led to acknowledge Him who, with such infinite graciousness, has said: 'I am the Lord thy Saviour, and thy Redeemer, the Mighty One of Jacob.'

As to the origin of the Syrian Christians in Malabar, the missionaries generally seem to accept the usual explanation given; namely, that they are the descendants of those converted under the preaching of the Apostle Thomas in India. This is the oldest tradition, and seems to be the most

[1] I find the following in a sketch of the Syrian Christian Church by the Rev. R. H. Maddox, of the Church Missionary Society:— 'The presence of these two large and influential communities (the Jews and Christians) in the country, linked by no common tie, yet witnesses together through strange vicissitudes for eighteen centuries, to the truth of God's revelation in the midst of heathenism, is a startling as well as deeply interesting phenomenon in the history of the Church of God.'

accredited. At all events, they themselves love to speak of St. Thomas as the founder of their Church. I do not see why we should not like to do so too.

From where I sit, I can see an old, grey Syrian church peeping out from amid the woods. It is indeed a new feature in an Indian landscape, these weather-beaten, moss-marked, often dilapidated places for Christian worship one comes upon here. There is the modest grey cross rising above the trees, and pointing, like a finger of hope, toward heaven; surely suggestive of something bright and blissful in the future. These poor Christians are, no doubt, dark and ignorant enough. They were in a very sunken and degraded condition when the missionaries landed in the midst of them some seventy years ago; and still, I am afraid, they are low spiritually, and the things of God among them ofttimes ready to die. But God has not removed their candlestick out of its place; the one living and true God has been worshipped in their simple churches, and He has preserved this singular people as witnesses for Himself in a region where it may be said 'Satan's seat is,'—where heathenism in some of its foulest and most revolting aspects abounds. Our faith, then, should be equal to the certain hope and belief that a good and glorious day of grace is yet in store for them; and that the little oasis in this great moral wilderness will spread until it covers this part of India as with a garden of the Lord.

We have had quite a touching leave-taking from

our boatmen, poor fellows! who accompanied us to the Mission House, each carrying something of our effects. We retain our boat, and also the magnificent embodiment of authority, our scarlet-belted chuprassie, but we have dismissed the men meanwhile. They have been made happy by liberal *buksheesh*, including a kid for their supper, with which to make merry and recruit their exhausted energies. The salāms, down to our very feet, have been gone through, and they are off in high glee, chattering at the top of their voices. They look very much like savages. Not one of them can read; and, indeed, many of the people look wonderfully wild and barbaric for a province which boasts of schools and colleges, and English-speaking officials, and an enlightened Government.

This is a charming Mission House; and our kind host and hostess are just as charming as their dwelling. Mr. Neve is Principal of the well-known Church Missionary College of Cottayam; and along with pressing and varied work, into which both he and his wife were at once thrown on their arrival, they have to study the hard Malayalim tongue.

Near the house, and in the same compound, stands the College, a large building, in which there is accommodation not only for the education but the boarding of many of the pupils. It is a very important institution, there being no other of the kind nearer than Trevandrum on the one hand, and Cochin on the other. Mr. Neve's sphere is a most influential and important one, as it bears so much on the native Christian community, the pastors and other agents all being educated and trained within its walls. It also exercises a very elevating influence on the Syrian Church. At right angles to the house there is the College Chapel, a beautiful little building, the most church-

CHRIST CHURCH, COTTAYAM.

like, I think, I have seen in India. It is in the Old English style, with real Gothic windows,—not the usual venetian-blind pattern, which the necessities of climate have made nearly universal. Inside, it is very pretty, with stalls and pews

S

parallel to the walls, made of dark wood, the proper hue which generally comes from age. It was very pleasant to hear the bell sounding out for evening service, and now the voices of the lads came to me, led by an harmonium, in the familiar strains of the Evening Hymn.

The other missionary now at this station is Mr. Painter, who occupies a mission-house standing on a richly-wooded undulation across a valley just opposite. This valley is turned into a lake, or lagoon, in the monsoon, when the country is more or less flooded, and the members of the Mission go to each other's houses in boats.

We walked over in the cool of the evening yesterday to another compound, where a remarkable old lady resides, who received us literally with open arms. This is the venerable Mrs. Baker, widow of the Rev. H. Baker, who was one of the first missionaries to Cottayam. His noble wife worked by his side till his death, in 1866; and happily she is spared to work still. She opened a boarding-school for girls in 1818, the year after their arrival; and, wonderful to say, it not only exists still, but she conducts it. We saw it to-day. There are eighty pupils, and the dear old lady looked so busy and happy among her children. She is quite deaf; but she manages her large family marvellously, and the girls are devoted to her, and quite under her control. Many of the matrons in the native Christian homes, and the nicer women among the Syrian Christians, were trained by Mrs. Baker. Indeed, her steady, loving work of more than sixty years has had a most beneficial influence in elevating the women of the district generally. When I suggested that she ought now to rest, she said, with her brave missionary spirit: 'When I cannot have my dear girls about me, I'll lie down and die.'

There is another admirable girls' boarding-school taught and superintended by Mrs. Henry Baker and her daughters. It has about a hundred and fifty pupils, who all live on the premises, and is one of the best conducted and most successful institutions of the kind we have seen. This lady is also a widow. Her husband, the Rev. Henry Baker, son of the old lady, whose death a few years ago was a great loss to the Mission, was an able and influential man, and is known chiefly as having originated Mission work among an interesting aboriginal people, the Hill Arrians. There were some two thousand converts gathered in from among them before his death, in 1878.

Mrs. Neve has thrown herself into work for the female children of heathen families, as the other ladies work among the Christians, and already she has organised four day-schools for them. She had the little things gathered into the verandah that we might see them, and be saved a walk in the sun; and it was a very pretty sight. They look very different in feature and dress from the Christians, both Syrians and others; but they have bonnie little intensely black faces, with bright eyes and torn ears, and large chignons, and looked on the strangers with awed curiosity. They read the Bible, and answered remarkably well; and I could not but rejoice heartily that Mrs. Neve has been led to take up this branch of female work: it is of so much importance to get at the girls, the children of the heathen around. May the Master aid and bless her efforts!

Our visit would be delightful but for this consuming heat. It daily becomes more trying, and, along with the sight seeing, taxes the energies a good deal. There is a delicious sea-breeze during the afternoon, but it dies down in the evening, and you begin to pant again. Yesterday Mr. Neve took us to the library, and over the College, where my husband spent most of the morning. There are 270 lads, most of whom are Christians, and are educated up to the matriculation standard. I was much attracted by the fine, intelligent, teachers, who were themselves trained in the College, and are, some of them, Syrian Christians. As usual, Dr. Mitchell questioned the classes, and gave an address.

The further we penetrate into this wonderful little kingdom of the South, the more are we struck with the exuberance and beauty of the vegetation. Nature indeed has been prodigal of her favours. On this coast, the palm family is specially numerous and varied. The graceful areca and betel-nut abound; also the talipot; and the cocoa palm soars over one's head endlessly. Then there are the beautiful pepper trees, and other spices; also the bamboo, mimosa, casuarina, and many others; magnificent banyans, often ornamented with lovely orchids, tamarinds, and mangoes, and plantains, with plenty of the more useful woods, such as jack and blackwood, and sandalwood and teak. Different fruits you see hanging from a hundred

SOUTH INDIAN VEGETATION.

trees. The flowering shrubs are gorgeous, and so are the endless trailers and creepers, while always there is the marvellous variety of foliage, and the luxuriant wealth of green. The fine old Portuguese commanders knew what they were about when they chose beautiful and prosperous Malabar for their landing place! If it had only the beauties of holiness in equal measure with its natural beauties, it would indeed be a delightsome land.

The people seem well-to-do and comfortable, though certainly they do not need much. You see a little clearing near the water-edge; a peasant, with only his cloth for clothing, builds his hut of wood and clay there, roofs it and fences it round with dried palm branches; he owns probably a few of these useful trees, which are his revenue, and which, with his little rice-fields, and, perhaps, a few sheep or cattle, provide him and his family with everything really needful for their life. He eats, and drinks, and sleeps, and marries his sons and daughters, and he wants nothing more. It looks a peaceful picture. But there is another side to it.

My friend and I placed ourselves on the bridge by the jetty to wait; and I think we sat there for two hours, for the interest of their visit and the tortuosities of the stream had alike detained the gentlemen. But we kept a most entertaining vigil. It was a splendid chance for me to watch the people and their doings. As it grew dusk, numbers came down to bathe, and others to wash their cloths (not *clothes*). They stood up to their waists in the water, and chatted with their neighbours, or muttered their evening prayers.

They had no clothing to speak of, neither men nor women, except the universal cloth I have spoken of, which is a stripe of dirty yellow cotton wound about the loins, either hanging down, or caught up between the legs, according to the caste.

There were many passers-by on the bridge. I wished I could have sketched or photographed some of the groups. All were foot-passengers, no carts and bullocks, such as are usually seen on Indian roads. There were coolies carrying the most picturesque loads on their heads, such as bunches of cocoa-nuts tied together by the fibre, or rough, red pottery in the loveliest shapes, or a pot full of the frothy juice of the cocoa palm fresh drawn from the tree.

One or two young women passed to or from the well with water-pots poised on their heads. These they carried with wonderful grace, though the heads were sorely disfigured by a huge sort of chignon, into which the wealth of black hair was gathered at the front or side. The grace of the Grecian bend would not do here! The better-class women are erect, lithe, and often slim, the skin of a darker hue than in the West and North, the deformities being this unbecoming mode in hair-dressing, the torn lobe of the ear, and a very inadequate amount of clothing.

Soon there came a group of travellers by: an old tottering woman, wrapped and enveloped in a red cloth, and carefully led by a bonnie little girl; a younger woman, much ornamented, carrying a screaming infant on her hip; a man with a few brass drinking vessels hanging from his cloth over his back, and a betel box, a roll of matting, probably their bedding, on his head, and a small, naked boy hanging on to his disengaged hand. They looked way-worn and tired, and went wearily in single file. What was my surprise to see them hastily step aside, draw up in a line against the parapet, and bow in lowly obeisance, as a naked, fat, oily man, with a brick-dust hue of skin, a top-knot on his otherwise shaven head instead of turban, and a palm-leaf umbrella in his hand, sauntered slowly by. This was a lordly Brahman; but he condescended to bestow his benediction on the humble group as he passed on his way.

A young man, in a tidy white starched coat, whom Mrs. Neve knew, had joined us, and was very good in answering my questions. He said the wayfarers were a Soudra, or Nair family, probably respectable, well-to-do people, going to their home. The Nairs are always profoundly respectful to the Brahmans, though often a good deal jealous of them.

Presently a number of people gathered at one end of the bridge, and stuck there, for some reason or other. There was much shouting and hallooing, and we found that another Brahman, one of the Namburi caste, and therefore doubly sacred, was about to cross the road. The Namburis are the special priests of the Malayalim country, and specially holy, pretentious, and domineering to all other castes. Their laws are inconceivably absurd and strange, especially regarding marriage and inheritance, and their customs generally the same, though they have the redeeming point of being charitable and hospitable to strangers, if only these strangers are Brahmans.

Well, this sacred personage had to cross the

bridge, and the unfortunates at the other side were poor Pulayas, the lowest of the low, hardly a caste at all, from among whom the slaves usually were drawn—who are, indeed, a slave-race. Rigid law in this province forbids such inferior creatures to come within ninety feet of the high-born, holy Namburi. In former days, any infringement of this rule was punishable by death; even a Nair would cut a low-caste man down if he approached nearer than the limits allowed by law. Until within late years, indeed, the low Pulayas were not allowed to use the public roads at all! They had to go through the jungles to their work; and when they laboured in the rice-fields, their masters and owners had to shout their orders from a safe distance, to which pollution could not travel!

Watching, with intense eagerness, what would happen as the hallooing continued, we saw the waiting group break and scatter, and scamper off, it did not matter where, as if a mad dog had got into the midst of them. Some scrambled down the bank, some flew off in the direction from whence they had come, some vanished out of sight into the water; but all disappeared in a twinkling. And then the miserable man who caused it all went loftily on his way. It would have been unspeakably ludicrous if it had not been so preposterous and provoking. Fancy all these people detained and put out of their way to serve no end at all; though, of course, the man was not so much the transgressor as his system.

I must allow that the Pulayas do look low enough. Their physique is not grand. They are short and slight, with low foreheads, a mean cast of feature, exceptionally dark in complexion, and often with a depressed, vacant expression on their very plain faces. But who can wonder at this after the long ages of oppression they have worn through? The women decorate themselves with quantities of beads and strings of cowries. They also have bangles, and other ornaments made of brass and lead, for they are not allowed to wear gold or silver. They live in the most miserable huts, too bad for cattle, made of sticks and cocoa branches, and generally built near the paddy-fields where they work. Slavery is abolished by law and proclamation; but, all the same, slavery exists still. These poor creatures are slaves now—so we are assured—and are often bought and sold with the land. These low castes are not allowed to enter a shop. They supply their wants by putting their money down outside; they then retire the prescribed distance (for happily the money does not carry pollution) and shout their needs to the shopman. He takes up the money, lays the articles in its place, and departs out of harm's way, while the poor, deluded creatures take their goods and go contentedly off. Mr. Emlyn, of Pareychaley, told us so great was the ignorance formerly among the slave tribes, that they believed the missionaries were sent by Government to capture them, in order that they might be given as food to *gold-producing rats.* Nothing is too absurd or monstrous for these poor people to believe.

And yet they can be raised by the power of the Gospel. Moreover, the Gospel is the only power which has ever been able to raise them in the least, from the depth of their ignorance and degradation. A great deal of work has been done among them, and numbers have become Christians. Indeed, we are assured that the whole Pulaya caste would come over to Christianity if there were only people enough to teach them. It is natural that they should easily become converts, for they have nothing to lose and much to gain. They see the advantage the new faith brings in every way to those who embrace it. They rise at once in the social scale, have more privileges, better houses, more comforts, and become quite respectable people. Their children are received in all the Mission schools; education advances, and it has been proved beyond dispute that these outcasts are quite capable of being turned into able, intelligent, and useful citizens. Many of them are sincere and earnest, and work as catechists among their people. What a wonderful and glorious change this mighty Gospel effects! To see these poor oppressed tribes being brought in, worshipping God in the simple little churches which are springing up among the jungles, instead of practising the frightful rites of their terrible superstitions, and being considered and treated as men, is a sight which may well quicken faith, and set one's heart on fire with the longing that the work should be done thoroughly, and adequately, and at once. And there is hope in every effort put forth. The missionaries declare that the people among whom the greatest progress has been made in late years are just these poor outcast slaves.

It is a striking fact, too, that their masters often

approve of their becoming Christians. Why? because they thus become better servants. They do not steal, and cheat, and lie, as they used to do. This is a grand testimony to the moral character of these simple Christians. When shall we see both master and slave brought in together? the former saying with the prophet, 'Have we not all one Father? Hath not one God created us? Why should we deal treacherously every man against his brother?'

But I have wandered far from the bridge, as I did that night in my thoughts. Long after the sun went down, we sat there, gazing over the waters and woods, into the fading light and the silence which soon fell. Now and then a broad-winged bird, probably a kingfisher, would rise from some thicket, whirl round and round overhead, soar higher toward the heavens, until, for a moment, there seemed only a speck against the sky, and then suddenly dart down among the sedges, find there, I suppose, what he had come for, spread wing again, and disappear among the branches. It did not grow quite dark. The evening star rode high, not like a point, but a great orb, sending a broad gleam of lovely light across the calm lagoon. Sirius with his changeful sparkle hung in marvellous brilliance over us; and soon the moon, now near its full, rose like a ball of gold, and sent a flood of lovely softened radiance over the exquisite scene. By-and-by we heard in the stillness the plash, plash of the oar; our two gentlemen stepped ashore, and we sauntered home, carrying many a picture and memory in our heart, which will not easily be effaced.

NOTE BY DR. MURRAY MITCHELL.

*The Degraded Classes in Travancore.*—One of the worst things in the administration of Travancore is its merciless treatment of the lower classes. The three lowest had been from time immemorial in a state of slavery; but, in consequence of the earnest representations of the British authorities, slavery has been—nominally, at least—abolished. Of the slave races, the Pulayas were the lowest. The price of a Pulaya used to be from six to nine rupees; he was *adscriptus glebæ*, and sold with the land which he cultivated. Women were not allowed to cover their breasts till the year 1865; and when Christian women first did so they were rudely assaulted, and had the coverings torn off. These people cannot rise to be domestic servants; they would pollute every person and everything in the house!

Missionaries have all along done everything in their power to mitigate these sufferings. Recently, the Rev. A. F. Painter, of the Church Missionary Society at Cottayam, has pleaded their case with all earnestness, both in private and in public. Immediately after two letters from him had appeared in the *Madras Mail*, communicating painful facts that had come under his own notice, an official proclamation was issued by the Travancore Government, to the following effect:

[CIRCULAR.]

There being reason to believe that Pooliars, and other humble classes of the population, still find difficulty in getting free access to the public Courts and Cutcherries, and are not unfrequently obstructed in the use of the public highways and markets, His Highness's Government deem it necessary to call the attention of all public officers to an order issued from the Huzur on this subject on the 26th Panguni, 1045, and to impress upon all concerned, that the Courts and Cutcherries of the State, and all public roads and market-places, are open alike to all classes of His Highness's subjects, without distinction of creed or caste; and that no man shall be allowed to hinder another from the free use of them on any ground whatsoever, such hindrance being an unjustifiable interference with the liberty of the subject, and calculated to defeat the impartial administration of justice.

'Any public officer who may be found to deny free access to himself, on business, to any section of the population, and who may not personally receive or hear petitions from any person, or conduct investigations into cases in the presence and within the hearing of the parties concerned, on the ground that such persons are of low caste, will be visited with the severest displeasure of Government. 'V. RAMIENGAR,

'Huzur Cutcherry, Trevandrum; '(Dewān).

'21*st July*, 1884.'

For this step in advance the Travancore Government was publicly thanked by the Governor of Madras in Council, and so far, then, the right appeared to triumph. But Brahmanism was not to be tamed thus easily. True, for a few days the officials of the Native Government seemed to believe the proclamation was honestly meant; but soon afterwards a second circular, *which was not published in the Travancore Government Gazette*, was issued to the chief officials; and this practically nullified the first proclamation. In the first, all public offices, public roads, and public markets were declared open to all classes. The second proclamation strikes out of the list all those near temples, palaces, or Brahman quarters. But these are very numerous. Practically, indeed, the first proclamation is a dead letter. On the public road one still sees the wretched Pulayas driven off into the jungle or swamp. We believe there is only one market to which they are admitted—that of Cottayam; and the permission in this case has been extorted by the missionaries.

If these things are true, they are disgracefully true. After the most earnest enquiry, we believe them to be true. The attention of the Maharajah should be called to this foul blot on his administration, and should his Highness be unwilling or unable to move in the matter, the question should be taken up by the Government of Madras; or, if need be, by the Supreme Government. For these atrocities must cease.

# CHAPTER XIX.

## COTTAYAM: SUNDAY SERVICES AMONG THE SYRIAN CHRISTIANS.

My husband is certainly much in his element here, having many opportunities of declaring his message. He 'said a few words,' as he expresses it, last night to the pastors; this morning 'spoke a little' to the theological students; at one o'clock he gave a lecture to the Young Men's Christian Association; and in the afternoon he had the honour of presiding at the Annual Exhibition of the College. He gave away the prizes, and then delivered an address to the lads. An exceedingly pretty and successful display it was. The company included the whole station, and the place was gaily and very prettily decorated by the boys. But the heat! Who shall tell it? To say that we are in a perpetual vapour-bath is a mild description of what it is now.

Notwithstanding our vigils last night, we were up betimes this morning, and out. Dr. Mitchell went off with Mr. Painter to visit some of the Syrian churches; he also saw the Syrian College —empty now and silent; and then the printing press—a useful handmaid to the Mission, whence a missionary magazine issues monthly, and many useful publications. Finally he accompanied Mr. Painter to his Divinity Hall, as we should style it, where he teaches systematic theology to the aspirants for the ministry, and trains schoolmasters and evangelists. Afterwards my husband spent a most interesting hour talking to the students and getting an insight into their minds and feelings in view of their future solemn work, and then gave them an address. There were some Syrians and a few outsiders present.

I had joined him, and we breakfasted with the Painters in their pretty Mission House. I was charmed with it, and the views of the wooded, undulating country below, where one or two quaint old Syrian churches rose picturesquely among the trees. There was also the native Christian church, with its handsome tower, which put me in mind of a pretty village church at home.

I recall this morning now with peculiarly sad and tender recollection. Very soon after our visit a mournfully dark shadow fell across the sunshine of this happy home. A little child was welcomed to it to increase its joy, and then the beautiful young wife and mother was suddenly taken away to the yet better home in the mansions in the skies. It was one of those inexpressibly sorrowful events which are so mysterious also, that, not being able to comprehend, we must just meekly bow before, and accept, as simply our Father's will.

'Thy way, not mine, O Lord,
However dark it be;
Lead me by Thine own hand,
Choose out the path for me.

* * * *

Take Thou my cup, and it
With joy or sorrow fill,
As best to Thee may seem;
Choose Thou my good and ill.'

Mr. Painter had brought his young wife—a sister of his fellow-missionary, Mr. Neve—from England a few months before. There was something peculiarly attractive about her, and she seemed to us most admirably fitted, both by nature and grace, for the position she was chosen to fill. How vividly I can recall her appearance that morning as she showed me her house and school, and spoke so brightly of all the work she longed and hoped to do, and also of the sweet hope which had come into her own life! No thought of early death, or a home desolated, or work undone, or a vacant place, could ever have come into one's mind in connection with one so full of life, and joy, and hope as she was. Alas! how true it proved in her case that at the brightest 'our life is but a breath!' She only tasted the sweet joys of motherhood, and then—

'Not in darkness, but in sunshine,
Like a star she passed away!'

Sunday, as usual, was full of interest and full of work. We started early to attend some of the services in the Syrian churches, to which we had been looking forward with great expectation. Indeed, it had been a dream of mine to visit these Christians of St. Thomas, as they call themselves, ever since Mar Athanasius, the late Patriarch, used to sit in our drawing-room in

Bombay, well-nigh forty years ago, and tell us about his people. I well remember him, a man of rather low stature, with a clever, keen face, over which sat a round, low, black, turban-sort of hat, his whole person being enveloped in a long, loose, black gown. He was an able, well-educated man, who talked intelligently and well; I believe he was also earnest, and desirous of leading his Church in the direction of evangelical truth. He was consecrated Patriarch at Antioch.

Under him the Church flourished. The people became better educated, and progress and enlightenment would have been secured but for the strong conservative party who opposed him. I need not follow all the disputes which arose. Notwithstanding them all, however, the spirit of reform grew until his death, which took place four years ago. Since then the rival party—that opposed to reform—has become much stronger, and now party-spirit and division are more rife than ever.

His successor, who is also his nephew, is Mar Thomas; not equal, I am afraid, to his able relative. He seems to have little influence or power. We have not seen him, as he has gone away somewhere sick. There are several bishops, however, here, who are called Metrans, and are, of course, under the sway of the Metropolitan.

While the Portuguese were in power in this part of India, the ecclesiastics of the Romish Church tried hard to detach the Syrians from their own Eastern Church, and bring them into subjection to Rome. They did not scruple to bring all the terrors of the Inquisition, then established at Goa, to aid them in their purpose; and, of course, they were so far successful. But as soon as the Dutch took possession of Malabar, they ordered the Jesuits and priests out of the country. Then the English came, and they soon gave full liberty to the Syrian Christians, who all through had continued loyally and devotedly attached to their own Church; and they hailed their emancipation from the tyranny of Rome with great joy.

After the Church Missionary Society had commenced its work on this coast, its policy was to foster internal reform in the Syrian Church. It did not seek to draw converts from it, but to reform the whole body. However, the result was not satisfactory; and now the missionaries have altered their plan, and they receive into the Anglican Church any who may wish to enter it. So we may say there are now three parties: the reformers, the non-reformers, and the converts who have come out of both parties and have joined the Mission of the Church of England. I ought to have said that the Syrians in Travancore and Cochin who have not submitted to Rome number fully 300,000.[1] The whole country is dotted over with schools, and visited by evangelists and preachers; and may we not hope, if God's

[1] The Travancore almanac gives the number of the Syrians who have joined Rome as 136,230; about half as many are Jacobite Syrians.

people pray for it with sufficient earnestness, that ere long this ancient Church may be really reformed by a revival time of blessing from the presence of the Lord?

The Sunday services we found to be deeply interesting. We first went to the church where the reform party conduct their worship, one of the oldest in the country. It certainly has a look of antiquity; a quaint, rather poor, touching old tabernacle, in which it required no great stretch of imagination to picture the Apostle St. Thomas himself preaching from the chancel-steps to the assembled Eastern-looking groups below. Outside, the grave, grey old building looks picturesque with its surrounding of wood. A stone cross, of rather novel construction, stands not far from it, with a second cross-bar at the top, and about twenty feet in height. Buttresses support the old walls; the windows are pointed and high-set, and the roof slopes considerably. Altogether it is not unlike one of those very old churches you sometimes come on in a picturesque, out-of-the-way village in England. Inside, the building is long, narrow, perfectly simple and lofty.' The walls are sombre with decayed white-wash, and the ceiling open and arched, showing the cross-beams. At the upper end, a rail crosses the entire floor, within which, four steps up, is the altar, gaudy with yellow and green, a few unlit candles upon it, and a curtain, which is drawn across as the service requires. A large baptismal font stands at one end, the floor is carpeted, and a reading-desk, covered with red, faces you at the top of the steps. Over the altar is hung a large crucifix, and above is a domed ceiling painted with rude frescoes. A good many pictures ornament the lower part of the dome—all, of course, representing sacred scenes,—and some beautiful old bronze lamps are suspended from the beams.

We were received very kindly by some of the deacons, and conducted up a rickety old stair to a rickety old gallery made of wood, now very much worm-eaten, where I had the narrowest escape from tumbling through a great hole in the floor on to the slabs below. Within the rail, at the altar, several clergy were seated, and the congregation, composed of a good many men, a few women, and a crowd of children, sat on the stone floor below, there being no seats of any sort, not even matting. Before the service began, a woman, wrapped in a white cloth prostrated herself before the priest, to make confession, they said, in connection with her partaking of the Holy Communion for the first time.

I was very glad to have this opportunity of seeing the Syrian women, and was exceedingly struck with their superiority in countenance, and appearance, and dress to the heathen women I have seen in this place. They look intelligent, and even sweet in expression, and are wonderfully fair in complexion. The Mission schools so long conducted by the ladies here have had a most beneficial influence on these women, many of whom, indeed, have been educated in these excellent schools. The service was now begun by one of the priests, a venerable man in a white robe and red scarf, with a very long beard, who read a prayer in Malayalim, with his back to the congregation. This was succeeded by some chanting, in which two priests and eight deacons, all seated within the rail, took part. Lessons then were read from both the Old and New Testament, with lyrics between, which were sung by some boys, the people hardly joining. There were responses, however, tolerably hearty. The people stood at prayer, and at the close repeated 'Amen.' But the service, as a whole, was not impressive. The men generally were not reverent; the women, who sat separate at one side, were much more so: their heads were covered with white cloths, and they prostrated themselves occasionally, clasping their hands with much seeming devoutness. The services continued long, but there was no sermon while we stayed.

After a time we left, and went to another service, held not far off by the original, or non-reforming party. We found this going on in a verandah kind of room, narrow, unventilated and densely packed with half-clothed people, mostly men. We managed to get in; but the crush, the noise, and the terrific heat of the place, soon drove us out. I hope I shall never feel anything like that awful heat again, mingled as it was with the steam, and the breaths, and the incense which the gorgeous priest was engaged in swinging all the time we managed to remain. After this it was easy to imagine the Black Hole of Calcutta. I could only gasp and beg to be taken to the outer air, before I succumbed altogether. So we did not see much of this service, which, I believe, is full of ritual. We returned to the first place, and found worship still proceeding.

The curtain was now drawn across the altar, and the congregation much increased. Presently the curtain was withdrawn, and the priest re-appeared in a splendid robe of scarlet, with yellow hood, swinging a censer of incense, when there rose a great *shout* of prayer, I might call it, the people joining in, and making the sign of the cross repeatedly on forehead, and shoulder, and breast. The candles were now lit, the fervour of the congregation was deeper, and the responses loud and hearty. Some lyrics were nicely sung in Malayalim, and one or two in Syriac; and then all was concluded by repeating the Lord's Prayer. The Communion was to be celebrated after, when the people would sit in rows, having the bread and wine given to each, much in the same form as in the Church of England. But we could not wait for this, having to go to the Mission Church, and there join our brethren and sisters in the holy ordinance.

We found the service had already begun when we entered the cool, handsome, well-filled modern church. My first thought was, what would many a loving missionary heart at home feel, seeing what we had seen in this place? And now here was another wonderful and impressive spectacle: a large, orderly, intelligent congregation of young and old, as respectable as any you could see at home, with one from among themselves reverently conducting their devotions. These would, all of them, pastor and people, be still as the heathen outside, or at best like these poor ignorant Christians who have still so much to learn, but for the glorious work of this Mission. We have lately seen many such native Christian congregations, and been inexpressibly interested ; but our hearts seemed more than usually touched to-day : I suppose after all we had just witnessed. The large group of women and schoolgirls especially struck me, neat and tidy in their pretty, simple, white costume—such a contrast to the half-clothed, unkempt, wild-looking women of the heathen castes without. There were some Syrian women also present, who looked capable of any amount of training and work.

It need not be told how earnestly we pray and hope that the existence of this youthful, but flourishing and living native Christian Church, which, through God's goodness, has been planted in the midst of them, may have the effect of stirring up the elder sister Church to new life and vigour; and may the Spirit of the Living God be richly poured out on both, until old things have passed away and all things have become new, not only among the Christians, but among the heathen also!

After my husband had preached,—his sermon being interpreted by the pastor, we had the inexpressibly solemn joy of receiving the Holy Communion in company with the native Christians and our missionary friends, from the hands of the native ministers. In the evening Dr. Mitchell again preached, this time in the College Chapel to an English audience; and then the memorable Sabbath and our happy visit, together came to an end.

## Note by Dr. Murray Mitchell.

*Lawsuit among the Syrian Christians.*—A lawsuit which had long been going on between the reformed and unreformed Syrians, as to the possession of the College endowments, has recently been decided in the Zillah, or lower court, in favour of the unreformed. The decision has been appealed from. If, finally, the decision of the lower court should be confirmed, it will have disastrous effects. All the property of the Church will, very probably, come under the power of the Patriarch of Antioch; and the reformed Syrians will be subjected to no small hardship. Have the reformed strength enough to hold on when stripped of their endowments? We wish we could feel assured of this. Happily, the Church Missionary Society's Mission will 'keep the even tenor of its way;' and souls in quest of light will not be left in darkness. Yet when I recall the conversations which I had some forty years ago with Mar Athanasius, it is sad to think how few of his hopes seem likely to be fulfilled.

SCENE IN TRAVANCORE.

## CHAPTER XX.

### THE HILL ARRIANS OF TRAVANCORE.

In all the hill districts of India there are to be found wilder races of people, who differ in many respects from the population of the plains. These are mostly aboriginal tribes. The hill country of Travancore is no exception to the rule. In this region, in the more mountainous parts, several of these interesting races are to be found, the most notable being the Hill Arrians, who inhabit the higher slopes of the Western Ghāts.

Some of the same curious remains which have excited so much interest in other parts of India are to be found hereabout—such as cromlechs, strange circles, burial mounds, etc. The people are not idolaters; they worship demons and the spirits of their ancestors; and the rites they practise in their worship, and in the ceremonies connected with births, funerals, and marriages, are very similar to those of other wild races, such as the Karens of Burmah, the Gonds, the Santals, and others.

I must say, these wild people show most excellent taste in the selection of sites for their villages and settlements; they always choose the loveliest spots. But I had better quote what the late Rev. Henry Baker says of them in a very interesting paper he wrote on the subject of the wilder people here, and the progress of Mission work among them which he prosecuted with much vigour until his lamented death. He says :—

'There are several tribes inhabiting the Western Ghāts in the Cochin and Travancore countries, of whom the majority are divided into small wandering bodies, living for a few months in a particular spot, and then deserting it for another as soon as their scanty crop of grain is reaped. The Arrians, however, have their fixed villages, and reside generally on the western slopes of the higher range of mountains or their spurs. They number from 14,000 to 18,000 souls; and by the Government officials are called Mulla Vellens, and are considered to rank in caste above all the mechanics, and equal to Mohammedans and Jews. Their villages are often lovely spots, generally in a ravine not accessible to elephants, near to some gushing rivulet falling over rocks, and surrounded by gigantic trees and palms, rarely at a less elevation than 2,000 or 3,000 feet above the sea. Many of their houses are good substantial erections of wood and stone, built by workmen from the plains, and after the fashion common to the western coast; but in many cases they prefer temporary huts of mud, bamboo, and grass thatch, as the survivors often dislike living in a dwelling in which the head of the family has died. The whole of the hill country is owned by Brahmans or Zemindars, who receive trifling rents from the Arrians for their fruit-trees and cultivated land; and besides this, each head-man has to furnish a certain quantity of honey for the Rajah's birthday, dig a few elephant pits, and help with bark ropes to conduct the animals when entrapped into the taming cages. These people extend from Cape Comorin to the borders of Travancore in the north. A few wretched beings, called Arriars or Arrisur, are found on the eastern side of the Ghāts, near the great peak of Augustier; but they seem in a very degraded state. Their language is Tamil, and they are not allowed to be of the same race, nor have the same customs, as their richer neighbours on the western slopes. . . . . The Arrians are, many of them, rich, being large cultivators of the slopes, which they clear of jungle in the dry season, sowing during the rains. Every man, however, has to watch with guns during seed-time and harvest, to protect the crops from elephants, deer, and other animals, as well as from swarms of birds.'[1]

In character the Arrians seem to be truthful and generally moral, except that, like too many of their brethren of the hills, they are very fond of arrack. Thus drunken brawls are not unfrequent. They are manly, frank, genial and free in manner, and are well-made and athletic, the women often being fair, and even beautiful. Like many of these more manly races, they are fond of the chase, and make fearless hunters, aiming generally at high game, such as the tiger, wild elephant, and ox.

There is one remarkable difference between them and the Malayalim inhabitants of the plain: the children in a natural way inherit their father's property. It does not go away, as in the case of Hindu succession, to the children of their father's sister. Then the wife is not required to stand behind, like the Hindu women, while her lord and master eats what she has prepared for him, and then make her meal of what he chooses to leave when his appetite is appeased: the Arrian wife partakes along with her husband, eating off the same dish, namely, a shiny plantain leaf, as a loving couple ought to do. Indeed, this is a sign of their relationship, and eating together is part of the wedding ceremonial. The marriage tie among them is indissoluble, and considered sacred, and the husband has only one wife. The Arrians bury their dead—not burn them—and at their funerals

[1] *The Hill Arrians of Travancore.* By the Rev. H. Baker, jun., late Missionary of the Church Missionary Society.

have some curious ceremonies, which are repeated, and offerings made, on the anniversary of the death. All their religious rites are connected with the worship of the spirits of their dead. Missions were begun among this interesting people a good many years ago. The excellent missionary, from whose paper I have quoted, the Rev. H. Baker, was honoured to commence the work, and his account of the remarkable way in which he was led in God's providence to take it up, as well as the success given to his efforts, is so striking, that I think I cannot do better than give it in his words rather than my own. Mr. Baker was then a missionary at Cottayam. He says :—

'I had often heard of a people living in the hills, who were acknowledged to be very truthful and chaste, and were said to be the Mulla Nairs, and as ancient as the hills themselves. I had put all this down to the usual style of Indian conversation ; but during a missionary tour I met three or four fine-looking men, different from the races in the plains, both in the contour of their faces and method of wearing their clothes. We had some very interesting conversation, and they stayed the night at the tent. They left early, and I did not expect again to see them, as we were so far from their hills, but, some months after, my little daughter ran into my study, at Pullum, to say that some very curious-looking men were come to see me. This was in 1848. There were five men from as many different hills, begging me to go and open schools among them. They had a Romo-Syrian with them, named Kuppeer Curien, as guide, a man, who then, though well acquainted with the truth, did not know its power. This was my introduction to the Arrians. Again and again did they come on this errand ; but I hesitated to go so far, as I had several new but increasing congregations, some hundred children in the day-schools, and a Preparandi Class of young men, of whom I hoped to make teachers. There was no road through the forty-five miles of jungle, fever was prevalent, and coolies difficult to procure. The friends I consulted said, "Possibly you may begin the work, and may compass something, but you will have no successor." Many thought with me that the hill men were seeking for a protector, and not for Christianity; others, that no centre of operations could be made in the hills, the population being scattered, and that, even if the work of conversion did begin, the results produced by working in the plains would be more important and extensive, if a movement took place. But the heads of several villages at last came down and remonstrated on account of my delay. "Five times," said they, "have we been to call you. You *must know* we know nothing right; will you teach us or not? We die like beasts, and are buried like dogs; ought you to neglect us?" "Cholera and fever," said another, "carried off such and such members of my family; *where are they now?*" They stated that they wanted no pecuniary help, as they had plenty of rice. They wished to serve God, and not to be oppressed by any one. They offered to make over their lands as a proof of sincerity, and waited about, determined to have me in their hills; so I promised to meet them the next week on the banks of a river about thirty miles distant, whence they proposed to guide me to a principal village, and have an assemblage of their people. I sent some men a day or two before I started, in order to have a hut erected on the banks of the river, as it would be necessary to halt there for the night. On arriving there with my brother, trusting to our messengers, we found neither Arrians, hut, nor people of any kind, but a dense jungle overhanging the stream, with only a narrow track leading down to the water by which we had come. Walking in the close jungles, with a hot sun overhead, had completely knocked us up. With aching heads, and, perhaps, disappointed, angry feelings, we lay down to spend the night on boughs strewed on the ground, with a blanket overhead to keep off the heavy dews; but, before dark, some Tamil merchants who had crossed the mountains came to the river, and seeing us, crossed over on a raft, and lent us a little blanket tent, six feet square. We were thankful for this; for heavy rain soon came on. The next morning, having returned the tent to the owners, who would take no compensation, we crossed the stream, now much swollen from the rain, and, proceeding along an elephant track for an hour, found some Arrians waiting for us: they had not gone further, as they still doubted whether we would come. On entering the village of Combukuthie, so called from the hill-top beneath which it is built, having the appearance of a fallen elephant, I observed some piles of wood at the angles of a small level piece of ground. I inquired what they were for. "Oh," said they; "this is where we meet for games, settling marriages, disputes, etc. We are to have a meeting directly it is known you are come, and the piles of wood are to give the assembly light." Soon I heard men shouting from one place to another, far away up along the hill-sides: "He is arrived. Come, all!" Messages are thus conveyed from one mountain settlement to another with great rapidity. By nightfall, some two hundred men and lads, the representatives of eight hundred or nine hundred, had assembled, the piles of wood were lighted, and, with the moon also to aid, we held our conference. I told them I had at last come at their request, and it was to tell them a message I was entrusted with; that some centuries back, the people of England had the same rites and hero-worship as they had; that the Druids taught the Britons just such ideas as their Pusāries did, but that, at last, a Book was brought them which told of God—what He was, how powerful, yet the Father of His trusting children, and that He had sent this Book. . . . Further, that the God-fearing people of England had sent me with this Book to teach them the same glad tidings. They wished to see the Book; I showed them the Malayalim Testament, and read John iii., Romans i., and other passages; I said it was faith and love to God which made men happy here and in heaven. Numberless simple but very practical questions were asked by them, not in a cavilling spirit, like the Brahmans and Vedantists of the plains, on the atonement, fall of man, sin, misery, future punishment, etc. They occasionally talked among themselves, some making objections, others proposing a trial of the regulations I proposed, and a few thought the rules for the Sabbath and daily learning too severe. . . . Long after midnight, the head-man of the village said: "We have talked enough; where are the teachers we are to have?" I said: "I will send them; but we must ask God's blessing first:

*He* must *help*, or our counsels will come to grief." All knelt by the light of the blazing piles, and after a few words of prayer for help we dispersed. The strangers slept by the fires, wrapped up in their blankets, while I retired to the hut usually prepared in the village for guests. I returned, after a day or two, to Pullum, my station in the low country, after promising to send them three teachers, and to spend a fortnight of each alternate month with them.'

Thus Mission work began among these interesting simple people. Difficulties naturally arose. Enemies were busy, and the arch-enemy busiest of all; but God was working, and His hand could not be stayed. When Mr. Baker returned to his station in the low country, he summoned a meeting of his catechists and Scripture readers. He told them of the opening for Christian work among the hill people, and asked for volunteers for the service. He reminded them that men from Europe had come ten thousand miles to teach them; would they not go some forty to teach the people of their own land? The result was that thirty-seven out of the forty present offered to go; and finally it was settled that three should go together, exchanging every month or two.

This arrangement continued in force, with more or less satisfactory results, for about two years. Trials and difficulties, however, were manifold, and much discouragement had to be fought against. Some of the men were faithful and hard-working, but others were less so, and evils crept in unawares. False brethren there were, who tried to fill the minds of the people with prejudice against the missionaries, telling them also that they would lose their high standing in their tribe by becoming

Christians. Then dismal accounts were carried to the plains regarding the hill country, where fever was rife, and tigers, and elephants, and other wild beasts filled the jungles. Several times Mr. Baker and his party had to climb into trees to avoid the attacks of wild elephants. Accidents were of frequent occurrence, both from the wild creatures which abounded, and from the sudden rush of mountain torrents, swollen after every rain. Once a European gentleman fell into one of the pits, eighteen feet deep, dug for the capture of wild elephants; and though not killed he was much hurt. Fever and cholera carried off their victims, for these dread diseases always lingered about the jungles. Thus they were in 'deaths oft.' 'Why go on attempting this work?' exclaimed some who were fearful and unbelieving; and a Syrian priest assured Mr. Baker's coadjutors that the Bishop had ordered this work as a penance.

But the power of Christ rested on the faithful missionary and his little band. The good work could not be hindered. They all held bravely on, and so did the people themselves. They had been truthful and earnest in their request for Christian teaching; and soon they showed their sincerity by giving up many superstitious practices, such as burning lamps beside the graves of their ancestors, propitiating demons, and so on. They even became less addicted to arrack. The children were sent to the schools which had been opened, and some of the more intelligent young men were sent down to the plains to be trained as teachers and evangelists. There was much frank intercourse between them and the missionaries, and when they did not comprehend any part of the instruction they said so, and got it explained.

In a little over two years, upwards of three hundred Arrians had been instructed, a hundred and twenty of whom asked for baptism, and, after sufficient trial, were received into the Church. A mission church and bungalow were built, and a small Christian settlement planted ; strange to say, on the very spot on the river bank where Mr. Baker had first met the Tamil merchants. The forest was cleared, huts were built—some in trees, to avoid the risk of tigers and elephants,—and schools were opened and filled with pupils, male and female. A Christian officer from Madras came to give help, chiefly in the way of shooting the wild animals. An unknown lady in England gave twenty pounds to aid the funds, and Sir Henry Lawrence, hearing of the work, sent a hundred and fifty rupees from Lucknow, with the message, 'By all means go on; never mind obstacles, nor whence they come.' And so the Master, whose the work was, blessed and prospered it. It has been carried on vigorously ever since, and last year the converts among the Hill Arrians amounted to 2,000 souls.

## CHAPTER XXI.

### COCHIN: THE WHITE AND BLACK JEWS.

WE left Cottayam at midnight, and are now scudding along, in the light of the glorious full moon, through the shadows which lie soft and silent on the still waters of the lagoon. The moon shines so bright and clear, riding up yonder in her sweet, pure majesty, that I am writing by her light. I have been trying to read, too, sitting on our old perch, on the roof of our tidy little boat.

Good-bye, beautiful Cottayam! I suppose we shall never see it again, with all its engrossing pleasures and interests, physical, and spiritual, and moral; but we do hope to meet our kind friends again by-and-by, when we reach the Hills.

The tall cocoa-palms look spectral and weird along the banks, like sentinels calling each to the other, 'Watchman, what of the night?' The phosphorescent light is exquisite. It breaks into little wavelets of fire as the oars strike the water, and it seems to vie with the moonbeams which will make the most brilliance. The men are so noisy, so obstreperous in their mirth, that I am afraid there is little use in our attempting to go to sleep; and yet, after the day's work, and tension, and strain, sleep is desirable, and the night-air comes sweet and cool from the water through the open windows of our nice little cabin.

*Cochin.*

The night did not seem long after all, and welcome sleep at length did visit our aching eyes. Soon after dawn we got to the jetty at Cochin, and found a fine old Mussulman peon, with Mr. Seely's badge on his scarlet belt, waiting to conduct us here. And lo! he speaks Hindoostanee! I poured out a stream volubly as of pent-up waters; we had felt so tongue-tied with these Malayalim people. But the man either liked to air his English, or his Hindoostanee was not an unlimited quantity, for he soon relapsed into the gibberish his English amounted to.

Mr. Seely is the Director of Public Instruction and Principal of the Government College; and he and his wife are the embodiment of all hospitality in Cochin, and their house the centre of social amenities generally. We found a novel sort of conveyance awaiting us, something like a Japanese jinriksha, only, seated for two, and pushed instead of pulled, while the rider steers as you go along. There are no horse-gāris in Cochin; and this machine, I believe, was an importation from Pondicherry. We soon reached the house, and were cordially welcomed by Mrs. Seely, her husband having already started for his College. This is a most picturesque old house. We have leapt from the Indian bungalow-kind of abode to a Continental dwelling. I immediately peopled it with Albuquerques, and Almeidas, and Vasco de Gamas; and,

I believe, it is older than the Dutch occupation of Cochin. It is upper-storied with large rooms, and small side ones going off at every corner, and quaint little narrow stone, courts and balconies, filled by the tasteful hand of its mistress with lovely flowers, and crotons, and evergreens, and clambered over with creepers. The drawing-rooms are filled with curious and interesting things; and the whole house is a kind of museum, not the least curious and engrossing being the memories which you feel are piled up everywhere. The house opposite looks like a little fort, with flying buttresses, and ever so many queer little Dutch roofs, and a dead blue wall all round. The only drawback is the heat, which is worse than ever. The climate here is always moist and warm, somewhat like that of Bombay, but more trying; and it differs little all the year round.

Cochin is a semi-independent State, like Travancore. It has gone through many vicissitudes in its stormy history, and has had many masters; the Portuguese, Dutch, Hyder Ali, Tippoo-Sultan, and the British—all having conquered it in turn. The present Rajah is of higher caste, I believe, than the Travancore Royal family; but he is by no means so enlightened as his brother of Travancore. He is a thorough native in every sense, and knows not a word of English. We have seen his palace, but not himself. The Elliah-Rajah, or heir-apparent, however, seems a more enlightened character. Cochin is a large place, with some good buildings, chiefly Dutch, that people having done much for it. It is full of quaintness, very un-English, and also very un-Indian, except for that one thing, the heat.

It is notable as having been one of the first places in the country ever visited by Europeans. Indeed, there are many things in its past which make it an extremely interesting place to visit. Tradition says that the Apostle Thomas arrived here fifty years after Christ, and began his labours from this place. Then there are the Jews, of whom I shall speak presently, round whose history so great an interest always gathers. This remarkable colony settled here, it is generally said, in the first century; but some of the people themselves claim to have been here much earlier.

The English built their first factory here in 1660, though the State was not finally ceded to them till 1814. I think this was the date. The place now seems prosperous and to possess a lively trade, chiefly in the products of the wonderful cocoa palm, which forms the riches of this coast. There are other articles of export, such as rice, betel-leaf, and the nut of the areca palm; spices, also coffee and timber: but most of the trade and industry are connected with the cocoa-nut; for there seems to be no end to the economic uses to which it can be put. There is a large trade in cocoa-nut oil, and the coir matting one hears about so much is made from the fibre. Indeed, the fibre of the nut is most valuable, not only as an export, but the preparation of it, to send to England, and to the places where it is manufactured into matting and other articles, forms one of the most important industries of the coast. There is a very fine, large harbour, in which we saw several European vessels lying, and an immense crowd of curious native craft of every size and sort. Then there is water communication by means of the Backwater, almost to any extent; though, as yet, there is no railway.

Soon after our arrival the Rev. Mr. Wright called and took my husband to see some schools and Mission work. Mrs. Seely authoritatively sent me to bed instead of accompanying the gentlemen; but this was made up for afterwards by a visit to the grand old Cathedral, the oldest Christian church in India. It was built by the Portuguese; then turned into a Protestant place of worship by the Dutch; and it is now used by the British, having been renovated and modernised. But the original old walls remain, strong, massive and buttressed, and there are still several old tomb-stones on the flags inside. On one of these the words *de Gama* are quite legible, but whether this is the veritable tomb of the great Vasco de Gama I cannot tell. He is said to have been buried here; though the remains were afterwards removed to Goa. It is wonderful that the inscriptions are not more defaced than they are. My husband made out several. There are a good many Roman Catholic churches in and about Cochin. The East Indians are mostly of this faith, probably because the Indo-Portuguese element is strong in the population; and also because Francis Xavier visited this part, and made many converts. Mrs. Seely told me that the first book ever printed in India was published in Cochin by the Roman Catholics.

We also visited the Fort, which we were curious to see, it being the very first fortress erected by Europeans in this country. This was, of course, by the Portuguese. It was commenced by the renowned Albuquerque, and completed by others of those able commanders who sought to bring India under the sway of Portugal. The numerous and magnificent ruins of forts, churches, and monasteries which are to be found on the Western Coast, at Bassein and other places, testify to the valour and enterprise of these grand old warriors. But the Cochin fortress, as it is now, is of different dates. Not much of the original structure remains, as it has been renovated or rebuilt by the victorious Powers who succeeded the Portuguese.

The interest of our visit, however, culminated one evening when we went among the Jews, and visited both the colonies of this interesting people. After lunch, when it became cool enough, we started in the funny little jinrikshas, descriptively called 'push-push.' Mr. Wright took me in his, while Mrs. Seely accommodated my husband. We went through the long streets of the native town, which I cannot say were either clean or pleasantly odorous: but they were full of the usual picturesqueness of Eastern bazaars. The shops were quaint and curious, and the population varied. A good many Mussulmans were to be seen chiefly in the shops, squatted among their wares, many of which we recognised as old friends, having evidently come from Bombay. By-and-by the character of the population began to change. The features, costumes, complexion, everything announced that we had got to the quarter inhabited by the Jews. We alighted before the synagogue, and were received in a most friendly way by several men who gathered round, while a small crowd collected to gaze at the strangers.

This Jewish settlement, consisting of white Jews and black Jews, has existed, as I have said, for long ages in Cochin, and has always kept aloof from the heathen around. The black Jews somewhat resemble the Beni-Israel of Bombay. The two colonies live in quite separate quarters, though these are near each other. They have different synagogues, and do not worship together; but they do occasionally intermarry. If a white Jew marries a black Jewess, the children are reckoned as belonging to the black community. It has sometimes been imagined that the climate has wrought the change of complexion. But the truth is that the black Jews have by no means unmixed Jewish blood. They are descended chiefly from native proselytes. Still, the Jewish features are sufficiently marked to prove that they are of God's ancient people. The little Josephs and Rachels and Reubens who came crowding round, gazing at us with their glorious black eyes very wide open, could certainly trace their lineage up to their Father Abraham. And some of the so-called black Jews had wonderfully fair countenances and fair complexions. The black colony are much more numerous than the white. They told us that the latter only numbered fifty families, while there are two hundred and fifty of the former. There do not seem to be many wealthy men among either people. For once the Jew is poor. But they do a fair amount of trade; and they may be richer than they seem. Some of the women I saw were much ornamented with jewellery; they had some fine precious stones glittering on their breasts and foreheads.

We spent some time in the synagogue, a building quite disappointingly modern—not at all old—with tiled floor and a good deal of colour, blue preponderating. Crowds of men entered and were very friendly, talking frankly with the gentlemen about themselves and their history. They affirmed that their ancestors had settled in Cochin after the destruction of the temple by Nebuchadnezzar. Of this, however, I do not know that there is any proof. Some of them speak Hebrew fairly well, and my husband talked with them in this old tongue. He was very anxious to see any ancient manuscripts they might have; but they declared they had none. If they had, they did not care, for some reason, to show them. They said those they possessed were buried, and actually showed the place where the manuscripts were entombed! They brought out some rolls of the Law in Hebrew, which they now read in the synagogue; but Dr. Mitchell said they were not old. They showed us also some most interesting copper-plates, which they permitted us to handle and examine freely. Two are engraven on both sides with a kind of record of their past history, the language being an old form of Malayalim. The third plate seemed a cover for the other two. There is no resident Rabbi, and I am afraid there is little education among either of the bodies—the black or the white Jews.

Very little Mission work has been undertaken in their behalf. The Established Church of Scotland sent out a missionary to labour among them in 1844; but the work was soon discontinued, and has not been resumed.

While we were in the synagogue, a poor old Jew, all the way from Jerusalem, came in and asked an alms. We find that Jews do still come here from other places, and settle among their people. Is it not curious that this remnant should be found in this far corner of the earth, and so strangely preserved through the centuries? When the day of the great ingathering comes, when many nations shall say, 'Come and let us go up to the mountain of the Lord, and to the house of the God of Jacob,' let us hope and pray that these poor people may not be left out! I told them I hoped they would be of the tribes who would yet go up to Jerusalem, to the *new* 'testimony of Israel,' when the law shall again go forth out of Zion, and the Word of the Lord from Jerusalem. The poor old pilgrim who came begging touched me much. He made a most pathetic picture, his bent figure leaning, like Jacob, on the top of his staff. He wore a long Eastern robe, in stripes of bright colour, but much tattered and torn; a stiff, black cap sat on the top of his white locks, and his long white beard flowed down to his girdle. His pale, refined, and wasted features spoke of the uttermost dejection. He looked as if he had stepped forth from a group of those who sat by the rivers of Babylon and wept when they remembered Zion; as if he had 'hanged his harp on the willows' for evermore. Poor old man! he seemed touched by our sympathy, and much pleased when my husband spoke to him in Hebrew.

Some of the men had very courteously invited me to go to their houses and see their wives; so when the gentlemen went on with a company to carry their investigations into the quarter inhabited by the black Jews, Mrs. Seely and I entered some of the houses, and had some interesting visits among the women. They seemed quite delighted to see us, and crowded eagerly round. The better classes are pleasant in manner, have good features, rich olive complexions, and some of them are nicely dressed, after their own Eastern fashion, in gay colours, with plenty of ornaments. One or two spoke Hindoostanee; so that I could converse with them, and these interpreted for the others. Their language is Malayalim; the women know no Hebrew. They took me to a large, good house, where a marriage had been celebrated, and presented me to the bride, a fair, bright, very young girl, much bedizened with gold and apparel, and looking modest, as was fitting. A great deal of noisy music was going on, and evidently much feasting.

Mr. Seely now joined us; and as it was beginning to get dark, and we had a good way to go, we were obliged to take leave of the interesting people.

Mr. Wright and I shot ahead of the others, and, at the risk of being benighted, he yielded to my entreaties to be taken home through the great palm forest, which is thickly populated. There were quantities of huts and little homesteads, outside which the people sat in groups. At one part of the grove we passed through a broad street or road where only Namburi Brahmans live. How they permitted us, the impure, to pass through, I do not know; but perhaps they did not detect us in the gathering gloom, heightened by the dense masses of foliage overhead. There are many of these sacred personages, the Namburis, in Cochin; indeed, this seems to be their head-quarters; and caste is as strong and overbearing as it is in Travancore. We passed a small temple brilliantly lighted up; but we were not allowed to enter, or even look into the outer enclosure, far less into the temple itself.

I enjoyed my homeward drive in the cool night air exceedingly; and, though our friends thought we were lost, we were quite in time for dinner; at which we met some pleasant people—pleasantest of all being our intellectual, cultured host and hostess.

Next morning, some of the gentlemen who had dined with us escorted my husband to some of the factories and 'godowns,' or cellars, where he saw some of the fibre trade, and also the drying and cleaning of the coffee. I have to own that the heat has at length fairly conquered me, as now it begins to make life a burden. After breakfast, while I packed and arranged for starting, Dr. Mitchell accompanied Mr. Seely across the bay to a place with a most classic-sounding name, Ernaculum, where his College is. Here he spent a most delightful morning among the lads in airy upper class-rooms; talked and examined, and finally addressed the pupils. He then was rowed back; and by five o'clock we had started once more. I forgot to say that we have seen a talipot palm in full blossom, which is a rare sight. It blossoms, and then, alas! dies.

## CHAPTER XXII.

### TRICHOOR.

*March 8th.*

WE are now embarked for the last time on the beautiful Backwater. To-morrow morning we hope to reach Trichoor; thence a night's travel in our old acquaintance, a bullock-ghāri, will bring us once more to the railway at Shoranoor. From this point the country is intersected by the iron-road on to Madras.

We have about fifty miles of water to traverse before the sun becomes fierce in the heavens to-morrow; but we have twelve fresh, hearty, stalwart men, besides their steersman or skipper, a broad-shouldered, intensely black, cheery man, who keeps the oarsmen to their work; and they do pull with a will.

The scenery on the banks is much as before, only just at Cochin the water widens into a grand lake-like expanse, as there the Backwater unites with the sea. The harbour is a fine sight, with its ships and curious crafts, also its environment of buildings, some of them handsome, including one of the Rajah's palaces, and his public offices. The college and town at Ernaculum also lie over the water, with picturesque native villages nestling amid the palm groves and by the mangrove swamps. It is curious to see the gnarled roots arching themselves in the shallows, which are crowded with tall-necked cranes, sitting in contemplation on the stems, or stalking about with philosophic deliberation, picking up the poor little frogs and fishes, and depositing them in their pouches as a reserve-larder for their supper.

The country is a great flat, now and then transformed into a series of islets green and palm-crowned, or long strips of margin with small homesteads, and occasionally a little Christian church, generally Roman Catholic—or it may be, Syrian. They look pretty among the trees; and what a cheering sight it is to look upon that cross pointing heavenwards! You cannot see it here, at least, without feeling that your soul rises with it on the wings of hope and faith. And one needs to rise above the present, for there are temples and demon-shrines among the trees as well as churches, and Namburi Brahmans by the hundred occupy these little settlements.

The Namburis are often rich, and considerable landowners, and, of course, are all powerful. A gentleman told me (but I do not vouch for the truth of it) that the landowners of Malabar often are known by the names of their properties, as in the North of Scotland. I said I hoped they would not turn out to be Highland cousins; as I for one should utterly eschew all possible kinship with such proud oppressors as the Namburi Brahmans.

The Princesses of the Cochin Royal Family may only marry one of this high caste; and it is a curious fact that the Brahman who is chosen to be the husband of a Princess either by herself or her family, must have his funeral ceremony performed before his marriage ceremony is proceeded with! The meaning of it is that henceforward he is counted as dead to his caste. The Namburis are so much higher and more sacred than any other people on earth, that this is the law and custom, and he submits. The honour of alliance with Royalty thus involves in Cochin descent in rank, and social degradation.

Christians are numerous in the Cochin State. Counting Roman Catholics and those of all Churches, they are said to be somewhere over twenty per cent. of the whole population.

It is by no means a peaceful afternoon. Black clouds gather in heavy masses overhead, sheet lightning plays incessantly all over the heavens, the wind soughs, and wails, and makes wild sounds in the palm-tops; the water is rough, as we meet some white-crested waves coming over the barrier from the troubled sea without. I daresay a storm is coming up, which will cool the air. Meanwhile it is bleak and almost chill, as the darkness falls.

We have now had dinner, and the moon begins to show her silvery, lightsome self above the dense woods, scattering the inky clouds, and all things look more cheery. Our energetic crew took us to the bank with a few strokes of their oars; they landed, moored the boat, produced their well-burnished brass vessels, soon made a blaze with some of the dry sticks about, and cooked their evening meal, for which they had worked bravely and well. Happily all were of one caste, so they fed together, and we were so amused watching their proceedings as they sat round their fire, that we let poor Joseph's delicious curry get cold, to his great discomfiture.

The evening is now serene and sweet under the benign influence of the lady-moon, and the scene is beautiful on the banks, where everything that loves moisture and warmth seems to flourish wantonly. We lay long on the boat-roof watching the silent, peaceful scene, and then I retired 'behind the purdah' to the tiny cabin. Unfortunately the little lantern had been forgotten at Cochin, and the moon was not enough to scare nocturnal visitors. I soon saw by her light that I shared the cabin with at least one rat, a numerous family of cockroaches, and plenty of mosquitoes. I did not sleep much, therefore, and was beginning to think of a cup of tea from the spirit-lamp, as the dawn grew pink in the sky, when we stopped. Why? I inquired. For the simple reason that we had arrived. Our good men had done the fifty miles in thirteen hours. On the landing we perceived a bullock-bandy waiting, and soon after found ourselves in another pleasant mission-house, heartily welcomed by Mr. and Mrs. Bishop, of the Church Missionary Society, in Trichoor.

This is a large place, very old, and of historic interest. Moreover, it is important as the head of the Backwater, and thus the key of communication between the outer world and Cochin and Travancore. I am afraid it has also another sort of pre-eminence

A SCENE ON THE BACKWATER.

in being one of the most bigoted and evil of cities. All these cities seem to be bigoted enough, but in Trichoor you find the *crême de la crême* of Brahmanism. So we are told on every hand.

Caste is intensely and exceptionally strong, and as elsewhere stands in the way of all progress. The degradation of the lower castes, consequent on the absurd and oppressive laws of caste, of which I have already spoken, is terrible here, and hardly to be believed. For example, no native Christian, however educated and intelligent, nor any person of low caste, can obtain employment in a public office, for fear of polluting those officials who may be of higher caste! Then the school difficulties are endless. The children of some of the inferior castes dare not even approach a school where higher lads are taught. The disabilities are inconceivable, and so are the injustice and inequality of the laws. Women, too, are degraded to a degree you hardly find equalled in these days of reform in any other part of India. It is terrible to look at some of the poor miserable-looking creatures, with hardly any clothing and no sense even of decency.

The whole of this State is one of the great strongholds of idolatry and Brahmanism, where Satan still holds his seat. But, happily, Missions and Mission schools are beginning to tell. The work is going on, accompanied by fervent, believing prayer; and we may hope to see here as elsewhere, that prayer will prevail, that the prison-doors will be opened, and the captives of this terrible system go free. If the women could only be got at and elevated, there would be more hope of speedy emancipation; but ancestral superstitions and customs still have a strong hold on the people.

Namburi women are very much secluded, and guarded with the most jealous care. Even sisters and brothers are separated early. I suppose there is not a single Brahman woman of this particular caste as yet under instruction of any sort.

Two zenana missionaries (the Miss Colemans) are working here side by side with Mrs. Bishop, whose name has long been known as a successful promoter of female education. In speaking of day-schools for Hindu girls in this region, the Rev. Mr. Richards says:—'To Mrs. Bishop is due the credit of having established the first of these.' She has a boarding-school also, and altogether there seems much life in this Mission. Every one was stirring when we arrived—for morning is a busy time in a Mission-house. School work among boys and girls was going on. At eight a service was held in the church—a handsome building, which stands within the walls of the extensive compound. An hour with pundits followed, for the ladies are busy with the native language. Afterwards I was amused to see the elder Miss Coleman, who is a homœpathic doctor, enter with a great trayful of tiny bottles of globules and tinctures. She had been busy with her patients, who this week have already numbered six hundred. Some of them come great distances to be treated; and her art is already gaining for her an entrance and influence among the people. She and her sister have been here only for a few months. Mr. Bishop has procured a site whereon they are building a school, which we visited later; and a bungalow for themselves they hope also to accomplish in time.

But it is always the same story. Here, as everywhere, the Mission is cramped for want of funds. Much might be done if there was only money wherewith to do it. This is the cry everywhere, which is very sad to hear when there is so much money in our Christian country—abundance to spend on everything under the sun, except on the rescue of these perishing ones! What is an isolated Mission like this to do, for example, where there are so few Europeans to help, unless it is helped largely and liberally from home? Surely the spirit of philanthropy, not to speak of anything higher, might come in to stir men's minds in regard to what might be done to raise, and civilise, and Christianise these poor, ignorant, down-trodden people.

What, for example, can one missionary family accomplish in a place like Trichoor, to stem this torrent of idolatry and superstition which has gathered such fearful force during the ages? I am persuaded that my countrymen are only ignorant of facts when they speak of Missions as they do, and are so careless regarding them.

I am reminded of a conversation I had not long ago, in a large city in India, with a gentleman of high position, who was pleased to call upon us. My husband was out, and the gentleman told me he had heard him preach the night before, and wanted to thank him, 'for he had opened his eyes a little.' I opened mine, for he had preached on Missions.

'I have always understood,' he said, 'that Missions

are an acknowledged failure. From Dr. Mitchell's facts, however, I think I must be wrong. I wanted to ask him about it.'

I did my best to give him the information I saw he lacked; and then I asked him if he had seen none of the Mission work going on so extensively in this very city. No, he had not heard of it. I named several well-known able missionaries having schools, and colleges, and native Christian congregations: had he seen none of them? We had seen them, though only staying a few days in the place: did he know none of these men? He thought he had heard of them; but the long and short of it was, he had accepted the conclusion that Missions had failed, and so gave himself no further trouble on the subject. And then I am afraid I had the audacity to give him a bit of my mind. I told him he had seen nothing, knew nothing, had not cared to inquire, and yet he quietly pronounced the judgment, 'Missions are a failure.' Did he know that but for these despised Missions, nearly three millions of men who are now good Christian citizens would be heathen still? 'Close your eyes fast,' I said, 'and then declare that there is no sun shining out there, and your position will be quite as intelligent.'

'I deserve your reproach,' he answered; 'and when we meet again in E— you will find, I hope, that I shall be more correctly informed than I am at present.' He took leave of me with the utmost kindness, and is now one of the best friends and most liberal supporters Missions have.

A lady in Ireland said to a friend of mine the

other day: 'Do not believe a word of all this about zenanas; *it is all humbug.*' And I found that this person, although for years in India, had never once set foot within the walls of the zenanas, nor had seen anything of the dreary lives which are lived in them, nor the work our zenana missionaries seek to do; and yet she dared so to pronounce upon it! The piteous cry of India's down-trodden women had clearly reached neither the ear nor the heart of this daughter of favoured, Christian Britain.

If my countrymen and countrywomen, while in India, would only look with more interest and sympathy into the condition of the poor people among whom their lot is cast for the time; if they would seek out the missionaries, who may be too busy to seek them out, and enter somewhat into their work, taking an intelligent, Christian, or even philanthropic interest in it—I venture to promise that the benefit and pleasure would tell in two ways. In blessing, they themselves would be blessed. India would no longer look like a place of exile to them; and they would cease to long for the moment when they might quit its shores. If they shared in the sowing, they would also share in the joy of reaping.

I once knew a gentleman who hated the natives, spoke of them as 'niggers,' and judged the whole nation by a rascally 'boy' he had had in his service. He was induced by his wife one day to come to a school-gathering we had in the compound, simply because it was presented to him in the light of a garden party; and he was greatly struck with what he saw, especially with the sweet singing of the girls, and with a dear little child who repeated her verse standing on a chair:

> 'Jesus, tender Shepherd, hear me,
> Bless Thy little lamb to-night;
> Through the darkness be Thou near me,
> Watch my sleep till morning light.'

He was so struck and affected by this, that he became one of the staunchest friends of the people and of the Mission, and seemed to get a large blessing to his own soul.

This is a tremendous digression, and yet I have not the heart to strike it out.

There is a considerable body of Syrian Christians in Trichoor, and my husband has been out with Mr. Bishop interviewing some of them. They belong chiefly to the body of Romo-Syrians; that is, those who still adhere to the Church of Rome. But there is a division among them. Many began to groan under the tyranny, real or supposed, of the Vicar Apostolic, who is a European. Discontent was rife, and disputes and division followed. So a split occurred, and a strong party seceded, under the guidance and leadership of Bishop Mellus. He is unhappily absent, having left two days ago for the Persian Gulf. My husband regrets this very much.

Some say that this movement is political; I would call it national. It is *Asia* against *Europe;* so some declare. But the Bishop seems to be an enlightened man, and a reformer. He rejects the dogma of the infallibility of the Pope, wishes that the Bible should be read by the people, and is friendly with Protestants. There is no doubt, too, that he and his party long after the spiritual independence which the Syrians proper enjoy. The party is strong numerically, from five to six thousand, but they do not seem to be strong otherwise. The people lack moral force; they are weak and wavering; and the future of this movement does not seem to be very assured.

The gentlemen called on the dignitary who is doing duty for the Bishop in his absence, and found him pleasant and friendly. They had a long talk, and then he took them to the church and showed them all they wished to see. There are some good pictures, one or two images of the Virgin, and the Virgin and Child, also crucifixes, many candles, and much gilding and decoration—not at all like the simple old church and worship we saw at Cottayam.

Thus there seem to be five parties in the Syrian Church: the original Syrians, the Reforming party, the Anglican, the Romo-Syrians, and this seceding party under Bishop Mellus.

After this visit, as my husband wanted to see the Sanscrit College, which is rather a famous one, they walked on toward it. But across the entrance to the street where it stands, behold, a barrier! 'What is this?' asked Dr. Mitchell, who has had to do with Sanscrit colleges all his days. The Brahmans gathered round in great numbers, and warned the intruders off. No European had ever been allowed to set foot in these sacred courts.

It was the same in Poona, in the great Sanscrit College there, before the spirit of progress and enlightenment had entered that city, once the hot-bed of Brahmanism. But this was fifty years ago. Since then, a missionary has been asked to act as Principal of it. But now it is sad to go back all these fifty years. Trichoor, indeed, is behind its age. He spoke very kindly to the Brahmans, though with a little sarcasm, got them to laugh, quoted the Shāstras, but all to no purpose. He then requested to be shown where the Principal lived, and was escorted by crowds to a place where he was received outside by a fine old Brahman, who was naked to the waist, and shining all over with oil. He had been freshly anointed, and on his bald, unctuous head he had a sacred cord curiously arranged. He was a mild, courteous old man, and received the two gentlemen with the greatest politeness—though, all the same, he would not let them enter the college. He was learned, and showed an extensive acquaintance with Sanscrit lore, and rich withal, teaching only for the love of it.

There is a peculiarly sacred pagoda here, which we saw standing apart on its hill-top as we drove about in the evening. Like the College, no European, and no one of low-caste either, may set foot even on the hill, far less within the temple. One day, an unlucky Englishman, not being aware of his disability, walked up to the gateway, which, of course, barred his further progress. Immediately there was a tremendous commotion. The man had to take to his heels; a complaint was sent in to Government; and much money had to be expended in order that the desecrated temple might undergo purification.

One thing is pretty plain from all this—that no one has yet got quite behind the scenes, so to speak, in these curious, benighted little States. Things are still as they have been for ages. Brahmanism and Brahmans are untouched; everything connected with them being still hermetically sealed to all closer inquiry and investigation. Who would believe that, numerically, they are much the smallest portion of the population, while the Christians, who have as yet so little influence in comparison, are above a fifth of the whole people? A large field presents itself here to antiquarian research, as well as to the missionary. What curious questions there are for solution! Let who can, then, solve the problem how the barred portals are to be unlocked, and truth, in all its many-coloured lights, and its many-sided blessings, may be let in on this great darkness.

After a day of untiring interest and great enjoyment in this busy missionary abode, we prepared to resume our travels, now approaching a termination. Late in the evening, as soon as the moon rose, we took our places in three little bullock-bandies, the rough, common country sort, and made a very droll cavalcade. It did seem odd that three ghāris should be needed for three people; but when the queer little machines drew up in front of the verandah, it was quite manifest that Mr. Bishop was right in insisting that we must have one a-piece. They are very long, but very narrow and canoe-shaped, with high wheels and arched roof, thatched, as usual, with dried palm leaf. In the well-like bottom one individual could repose with tolerable comfort, but certainly not two. Joseph and his baskets were put into the first; I burrowed in a heap of straw in the second, putting myself strongly in mind of our dear old doggie, who on a Sunday used to bury himself to his nose in his kennel till church should be over, and my husband, as guardian of the party, brought up the rear. Amid the kindliest adieux from the whole assembled Mission circle—master, mistress, ladies, servants, native Christians, all—we plunged from the brightness of many candles in many hands into the darkness and silence of the night. The bullocks were meek as usual, and after one or two feeble attempts to turn their heads to their stables, at length accepted their fate, and took to the road.

Happily, it was a glorious night. The rising moon gleamed through the trees in a shimmer of silver light, throwing fairy shadows across the road. It seemed one long avenue, fringed and canopied by magnificent trees, which stood outlined against the illuminated sky with lovely effect. We sometimes passed through what seemed to be dense forests, as well as low-lying jungles; while along our route the giant forest-pillars supported a grand cathedral roof of interlacing, over-arching boughs. I do not know if it would look so fine in daylight, but now it seemed as if we were passing through one of Jehovah's most majestic temples. I am afraid I lost some of the beauty, for 'tired nature' demanded her 'sweet restorer,' and even the bumping and rattle, and general perversity of bullocks and drivers, were all alike unavailing to keep me awake. The rear-guard, my poor husband, was much worse off. He dared not sleep, or the whole cavalcade would go to sleep together; and we wanted to catch the morning train at Shôranoor. So he walked a good deal, with a formidable-looking stick in his hand, keeping the sleepy men to their duty. This seemed to consist in jerking the poor beasts' tails, for the tail to the bullock is like the rudder to the ship. On the whole, we were not sorry when at daybreak we reached Shoranoor. We got a bad and very dear breakfast, then joined the hot, dusty train when it came up; and, notwithstanding our misadventures, I confess I almost regretfully bade a last adieu to a bullock-bandy. We halted at Pothanoor for an hour, where there is a fine station; and before the day grew very hot we had arrived at Coimbatore.

# CHAPTER XXIII.

## COIMBATORE.

I AM sitting in a low chair in a huge room, shady from a deep, bowery verandah, a cool air stealing gently in, and a delicious sense of solitude and repose stealing as gently over the spirit. The sweet little birds only are astir, making music out there, talking tender things to each other and to me from among the creepers on the trellis. It is delightfully cool; such a contrast to the steamy, soaking heat of the low-lying lands and waters from whence we have come. This is a vast plain, one thousand four hundred feet higher than the sea-level; so we can breathe again, though it would be impossible to tell how tired we are. One's energies all seem to have oozed out in the great steam-bath below. Indeed, we are both so used up, in every sense, that we are making up our minds to leave part of the tour we had mapped out for ourselves, to be overtaken when, please God, we return to the plains, as soon as the hot season is over, and proceed now to the hills.

We were met at the station this morning by Mr. Hooker, a young missionary of the London Missionary Society, who has quite lately joined the band of workers here, and is by no means yet, as I tell him, out of his *griffinhood*. The older missionary, Mr. Hutchison, is now, with his wife and family, on the Neilgherry Hills. Mr. Hooker and a friend live in this bungalow, in most pleasant bachelor fashion. I confess to a strong liking for bachelor's quarters; there is the perfect freedom and unconventionality which suits people of busy habits and nomadic propensities. Mr. Hooker is full of enthusiasm about his work, and he and Dr. Mitchell are now deep in missionary economics in the library adjoining, the murmur of their voices, in chorus with the birds, breaking on the noontide silence.

There is a flourishing Zenana Mission here, conducted by two ladies from home. They spent last evening with us, and early this morning they took me to see some of their work. The schools, unfortunately, are in recess, the hot season holidays having commenced; so we hope to see more as we return. The gentlemen, who went early into the city to talk to the people and preach, through a native Christian interpreter, arranged to meet us at the native church, a fine, substantial, large building, with some interesting monuments and tablets on the walls, telling of departed missionaries. I had plenty of time to see everything, and talk to the matron of the Boarding School, for the gentlemen were long in appearing. At length they came up, walking, and very much dust-begrimed. The pony, who is as energetic as his master, had set off at a gallop round a sharp corner, upset the phaeton, and sent the poor gentlemen sprawling on to the road. Happily, it was not far to fall, as the machine is low, and they are none the worse; but Mr. Hooker cannot get over his discomfiture at the impropriety of his pet pony treating his reverend guest with such terrible irreverence!

Coimbatore is an important and beautiful station, lying on this elevated plateau, with all its grand expansiveness. In the dim distance there are great ranges of dark, purple mountains, and Ootacamund is only fifty miles off. Toward the mountains are dense forests of valuable woods. The fragrant sandalwood is there, also the mahogany, blackwood, teak, jack, and many others. In these glades the wild beasts of the forests naturally delight to disport themselves. There are great herds of wild elephants, besides the tiger, leopard, wolf, bear, and others; and altogether there are famous shikār grounds within reach. Nearer, the plain waves with fine crops of varied sorts, not now the paddy-field of the swampy, low country. There is little rice, but abundance of dāl, or pea, cotton, hemp, sugar-cane, and tobacco; while the coffee, cinchona, and tea occupy the higher grounds.

Altogether, I fancy there is no place more attractive, or better suited for European settlers in all India than this breezy, healthful plateau, with its grand neighbourhood of mountains towering yonder to the skies.

I most deeply grieve to have to add, regarding the promising young missionary of whom I have been speaking, that

'His bright and brief career is o'er.'

It was over very soon after we had seen him. It pleased God to take him away in the midst of his work and in the midst of his days. He doeth all things well; but it is inexpressibly sad to have to tell of another early death, another unexpected and mysterious call 'to come up higher' among the Mission circles in which we had so lately visited. Mr. Hooker caught fever among the swamps of the Backwater, after the monsoon had set in; the disease soon ran its course, and he went away to his Saviour before he had completed his first year in India.

The circumstances connected with his death were singularly pâthetic; but with these we will not intermeddle.

I may quote a few simple lines my husband wrote, *in memoriam*:—

So early called! How different from our thoughts
Are the deep thoughts of God!
                                        We saw him stand
In all the brightness of his early youth,
With much of culture, rich in learning's spoils,
Clothing each noble thought with eloquent speech;
Eager to serve the Master whom he loved;
His heart o'erflowing with all tender love
And pitying ruth for India's hapless sons,—
Ardent, impassioned, and his soul a-flame
With hope that soon the land would cast aside
The deep delusions of innumerous years,
And be the light of Asia and the world.
Round him how many hopes, rich-clustering, hung,
As he sped on, in buoyant energy,—
When, lo! the youthful champion falls, and we
Are stricken to the heart.
                                        We mourn; *our* loss
We mourn, of his companionship bereft
And high example.

But why mourn for *him?*
His work was finished, and his place prepared,
And the high guerdon ready; from the shocks
Of earthly circumstance redeemed, he rests—
He resteth in the bosom of his God.

He waits us yonder. When our summons comes,
May we, like him, be ready, and rejoice!
There we shall speak of shattered hopes of earth—
Of joys foregone, to be enhanced in heaven;—
There shall we see how from dark sorrow's root
There springs a flower worthy of Paradise,
Whose beauty never fades, nor fragrance wastes.

## CHAPTER XXIV.

### THE NEILGHERRIES.

*Coonoor, March 17th.*

I HAVE neglected my journal in rather a shameful way, I am afraid, since our arrival in this little earthly paradise. I can do nothing but feast on the beauty which surrounds us, and drink in the fresh scented air, and the quiet, and the perfect sense of rest, mingling with it all a deep thankfulness to our gracious God who has so lovingly watched over us and brought us in safety hither.

It is quite impossible to resist the fascination of this place, which enslaves you from the moment you set foot above the Ghāt, and only grows and grows as you explore and wander through the bewildering by-paths, and find out new charms at every turn. I confess that since we came we have both simply

> '. . . wandered away and away
> With Nature, the dear old nurse ;'

and no one would wonder, for we are on the loveliest of hill-tops, the famed Neilgherries, the Blue Mountains, as the name means.

It seemed so curious at first, and almost too good to be believed, that we had not to pack up and set out on a new tramp ; that we had actually three whole months before us wherein to be quiet here 'apart,' and rest. Yet it is wonderful how perfectly we have settled down to sedate life, after the long period we have just passed through of such delightful vagrancy.

But I must not forget that I bade you adieu at Coimbatore. After a few days' stay with our kind bachelor friends, we started one morning by an early train, and were soon speeding across the plain toward a giant wall of purple battlements, which stretched before us and towered grandly to the sky. These soon stopped our further progress, for as yet there is not a railway line scaling the wall, as on the Western Ghāts, from the Konkan to the Deccan. As we drew towards the terminus, we spied a long line of queer-looking machines drawn up evidently for the accommodation of possible travellers. These were *tongas*, a vehicle somewhat like a high - wheeled, rough dog - cart, very strong, with a capacious well situated between the front and back seats. We soon engaged one of these, and while we had our breakfast Joseph stowed our possessions in the well, mounting rugs and quilts on the splash-boards. A droll turn-out it looked. A pair of lean, small, dun-coloured *tattoos* (country ponies), with high curricle-harness, were brought out, and after much rough persuasion in the shape of kicks and blows, they were induced to let themselves be attached to the vehicle. We took our seats behind, while Joseph mounted beside the driver, and after a splutter and dash, and sundry eccentric movements from the hind legs of the cantankerous little beasts, which hurt their heels, poor things, far more than the strong machine we were off up the Ghāt like the wind. How we flew! But the driver was much too experienced in the ways of his *kittle* cattle to listen to our expostulations and let them slacken speed for an instant, even at the steepest parts. Had he done so, we should all, probably, have gone over the precipice. So he dexterously guided them round the sharp corners of the terraced ascent, and after a very short run the panting, streaming beasts were reined in at a siding, and their places taken by another pair, their exact counterpart. The little pantomime with the heels was repeated, and we were off again. This occurred every two or three miles. Thus we made the grand ascent of some six thousand feet, and a good while before darkness came we had got to the goal—the top of the delectable Neilgherries.

At first the glare was blinding, and the hot, white dust intolerable. The fiery rays of the noonday sun seemed to scorch us as they radiated from the rocky walls which rose sheer from the side of the white road. The trees and *shola* (or jungle) looked parched and drooping, every leaf was powdered with the fine, penetrating dust. We were soon as white as the bushes, and our eyes ached from the scintillating rays. But ere long we rose above all these little troubles in every sense, and got into regions where all things became new. The air grew cool and pure; the white-heat-look died out of the sky, now a deep fathomless blue, absolutely without a cloud. The upland slopes were clothed with *shola* of the freshest green. And, 'what is that low, scrubby bush which now covers the hill-sides? That is surely tea?' we inquired of our intelligent driver. We were right; it was our old acquaintance, the lowly tea shrub. Next came coffee, a larger shrub, with larger, darker leaf, but trained to grow rather low, for the better development of the berry. There was also the cinchona, with its large, beautiful leaf. All these seemed to be extensively cultivated, and covered vast reaches on the hill - sides. Occasionally we passed the white bungalow of a planter and his little settlement, including the long line of huts for the coolies who work the estate; and then a few quaint little hamlets of curiously-shaped huts, probably the villages of the wilder races who inhabit the hills.

How lovely it grew as we ascended! Noon was long past, and the shadows from rock and hill lay peaceful and soft across the road and beneath the trees. Every spur we skirted and every ascent we made the scenery became more beautiful. Giant forms near and far lay massed against the sky, glowing with the amber light of evening, while valleys and ravines, filled with dark, rich foliage, reposed in deepest shadow. Beautiful woods in every variety of tint, from the lightest green to the dark dress of the cypress and casuarina, now crowned many an eminence; while rounded hill-tops and lofty summits, or precipitous brown crags, whose rugged sides shone like burnished copper in the rays of the setting sun, reared themselves grandly over the woods. Pretty, picturesque houses, surrounded by gardens, were now more common, many of them beautifully situated. We were evidently nearing the summit. We made a long descent into a valley, crossed a pretty bridge over a brawling torrent, sped up the corresponding ascent on the other side, turned into an avenue bounded by a thick high edge of pink and white roses, which sent waves of sweet fragrance down to us, and long sprays loaded with the exquisite clusters, and stopped before a long, low bungalow. A tidy 'boy' in a clean, white, bunchy turban, and speaking English perfectly, rushed out to welcome us.

We were now in Davidson's excellent and comfortable hotel; but, to our delight, we found we had as yet a whole bungalow to ourselves. It is well named Belmont, for it stands beautifully. The house is on the top of a small plateau in the midst of an amphitheatre of distant hills. We have a terraced garden which goes to the edge of a deep ravine, across which we look at some grand summits crowned with the prettiest Swiss-looking houses and fine trees. On the left there is an undulating ridge with one or two higher points, and a lovely bit of brown-green slope, quite bare of trees. Then to the front there is a cleft, an opening through which you see a bit of the far-away plains, set in a lovely framework of many-tinted green; and then to the right we have the Droog, a magnificent headland, which I must speak about again. The *shola* and woods which fill the valley in front are not too high to obstruct our view, but make the loveliest foreground. No words can say how exquisite it is in the morning, as we stand on the steps to gaze, before setting out on our explorations; the sunbeams dance and sparkle in the foliage, and tender veils of blue vapour break and curl in airy wreaths; and the birds sing, and the butterflies flit about; and there is the sound of rippling water, which is my husband's supreme delight. Altogether 'the lines have fallen to us in pleasant places,' and our hearts overflow with thankfulness.

We have found many friends here, and much Christian work going on, into which it is a delight to throw ourselves heart and soul. The Bishop and Mrs. Speechly are here, Mr. Harcourt and Mr. Kember, of Palamcotta; also the Neves and many other dear friends. We have been specially glad to meet Dr. Jared Scudder, of the Arcot Mission, in connection with the Dutch Reformed Church in America, with his wife and family. There is a small branch of the Mission in Coonoor, and a chapel, and though there is no missionary resident all the year through, there is a young native pastor in charge, and Dr. Scudder takes the supervision and works here himself during the hot months. Every one knows the Scudders; they are a missionary family, and a remarkable one. The first missionary of the name, Dr. John Scudder, had seven sons and a daughter, all of whom became missionaries, and most have worked in the Arcot district. Several of them became doctors, and there is at least one grandson who is also a doctor and a missionary. What an honoured race! Dr. Jared Scudder is a vigorous, able, hearty man with great force of character and intensely earnest. In Arcot and Vellore the native Christians number over three thousand souls.

Mission work has also been carried on for a number of years among the aboriginal races on the hills, chiefly by the German Mission in the Kaity Valley, which lies between Coonoor and Ootacamund; but I shall be able to tell more about these interesting wild people by-and-by. The Messrs. Staines, who are owners of extensive tea and coffee estates here, are at the head of much Christian effort for the European residents; and there is a nice little chapel built by them, where we have regular service, conducted by our friend the Rev. Mr. Rowe. There is a handsome English church; also a chaplain.

*March 29th.*

It is early morning; the pure, fresh, dewy, glorious Indian morning; and, as usual, we have risen with the sun and come out to enjoy it. Indeed, the sun is hardly up yet, though the eastern horizon is flushed a rosy pink in glad anticipation of his coming. The air is crisp and invigorating, so cool that woollen clothes are comfortable, and yet so sweet and genial that you are reminded of a balmy May-day in the Riviera. We have each an armful of books, some papers and pencils, and a good glass, with broad hats and white umbrellas, for we do not breakfast till ten, and it is cool under the trees until that hour. I am also provided with a basket, to be filled by-and-by from the treasures of the woods and hedgerows, as well as from the bright flower-beds which surround our hotel doors.

What should we in India do without these delicious morning hours, when mind and soul as well as body seem awake, and able to rise a little above the earthly and material, the heat and lassitude — when one's spirit at least tries to 'mount up with wings as eagles,' and see some, thing of the glory of the great Artificer in His glorious works! It is true in a very literal sense here, that 'joy cometh with the morning.' And this 'sweet hour of prime' is especially sweet on these lovely blue hills.

Our favourite perch, where I am now writing, is a rustic seat beneath a dark spreading old cedar, on the edge of another slope to the right of the bungalow, from which we look across a deep, wide valley, through the usual feathery screen of many tinted foliage, to the grand summits which rise on the other side. At our feet, far down in the valley, a dancing stream with merry voice rattles over its rough boulder-bed; while on its banks, rising from it all over the slopes, lies the picturesque little Bazar, or native town of Coonoor. The houses, and shops, and sheds, in all the brilliance of fresh white-wash — for the season is just beginning—are scattered about as if dropped at random, perched at different elevations wherever they can find standing room. The pretty little white Mission church stands half-way up opposite to us; on another elevation there is the low structure with pointed roof which answers for both schoolroom and chapel, where we have our delightful services on Sundays and week-days. A few more pretentious buildings there are, including the Post Office, the Station Library, and a few 'stores' of the most comprehensive character. Down at the bottom of the valley two pretty bridges span the torrent, which has a handbreadth of green common on either side, where some droll little brown, tailless sheep nibble the scanty grass, ducks and geese cackle, and people begin to congregate in little groups ready for the *shandy*, or morning market.

Turning round a little, we have the tower of the beautiful Station church rising over the dark foliage of the cypress trees which surround it,—a sweet, most lovely spot, which attracts one most in the pensive, quiet hours of evening, when the sun is setting behind the western ranges. Then, far up on the crests, as well as low in the valleys, the white bungalows of European residents gleam out from amid the rich greenery of the *shola*, or beautiful natural woods—one of the chief beauties of the hills. These woods fill the hollows and clothe the slopes, mingling with fine forest trees, such as the teak, jack, sãl, and many other forest giants. The blue gum, or eucalyptus, has been extensively planted, and is to be seen everywhere in clumps and belts, or in the midst of other wood. It is here in every tint, and at every age, from the baby shrub, in its broad, bright, blue, shining leaves, to the tall, gaunt, sombre, rather tattered-looking veteran of the tribe. Fruit trees also abound, especially the peach, and we have plenty of strawberries, and also home vegetables. The hotel garden is almost a peach orchard, the branches weighed down with the wealth of ripening fruit.

The Australian 'wattle,' a kind of mimosa, very like the beautiful tree on the Riviera, spreads like a weed, resisting every effort to restrain it, and with its feathery leaves of a blue-green tint forms delicate screens through which you see the dark browns and russets and deep crimson of the rocks and ridges which tower behind. Further away the hill-sides are now white with the coffee blossom, which has burst into sudden though evanescent beauty, every plant seeming as if powdered with purest snow. In a few days this will disappear, and give place again to the unrelieved dark green of the glossy leaves. Coffee estates are now numerous over the hills; also tea gardens and plantations of the precious and beautiful cinchona shrub. Close by me now, I cannot but grieve to see the graceful *shola* disappearing fast before the planter's axe, to make room for the more profitable tea and coffee.

Then, again, beyond the nearer spurs, you look away to a never-ending succession of billowy, undulating hill-tops, absolutely irregular in shape, and now and then rising to abrupt headlands and sharp, lofty ridges. Among the former, the grand massive form of the giant Droog towers conspicuous. It is crowned with the ruins of a fort and watch-towers, which were occupied by Hyder Ali and Tippoo-Sultan during the troublous times at the close of the last century; and many are the tales still told of the wild doings of these fierce Mussulman warriors. Sheer down from the Droog we again catch a glimpse of the plains, broken into countless patches of bright colour—for this is all the fields look like 6,000 feet below. They gleam in the sunlight like a vast flooring of brilliant mosaic. But the chief charm I think, in this part of the hills is the way in which the summits are broken and intersected by clefts and ravines and the loveliest valleys, all filled with a wealth of luxuriant vegetation of the richest beauty. The variety of tint among the trees and in the *shola* is wonderful, and the delicate blue of the young gum trees gives a softness to the mass of darker foliage. It looks sometimes as if a bit of lapis-lazuli had been introduced in the rich framework of green. The effects are indescribably beautiful; especially when as now in the early morning, bright arrows of light from the rising sun pierce the green depths, and sparkle like myriad gems among the interlacing boughs. Every leaf seems to have 'its ain drap o' dew.' A tender haze floats dreamily about, enhancing the beauty, lustrous sometimes as silver sheen where it catches the dancing rays. Cloud-shadows still linger on the slopes. The sound of rippling water, from the numerous little streams and burnies which come down from the higher points, makes sweet music, mingling with the choruses of happy birds, the joyous hum of bees, and the noisy gambols of the brisk little squirrels. Small yellow butterflies flit among the dewy flowers. The irrepressible crow caw-caws, as if he was the ruler of the universe. An active little green lizard, with bead-like eyes, has just darted round the tree, wondering to find his domain invaded.

But a devoted friend of mine, a magnificent collie, has just laid his nose in my lap, and fixed his beseeching, soft eyes on mine, saying it is time to go for a stroll. The air is full of aromatic scent of the gum trees, mingled with the perfume of roses and heliotrope and 'flowers of all hue,' which abound in lavish profusion. Every house has its garden, and the verandahs are bowery with trailers, and creepers, and beautiful orchids, while the avenues and drives are adorned with rare trees, and evergreens, and flowering shrubs in endless variety. The tall tree-fern and tree-rhododendron are especially beautiful; the latter is still covered with its gorgeous blossom, at once so delicate in hue and so rich in effect. Even the public roads contribute to the beauty, being skirted by high hedgerows of China and cluster roses—pink, red, and white. As I walked to the library a little while ago with the collie, I counted thirty-four full-blown roses on one spray hanging over an old wall. Heliotrope hedges also abound, from which you can gather a sheaf of the fragrant flowers without being missed; and many a winding little by-path, leading to some bonnie bit in the woods carpeted with mosses and ferns, is edged with the scarlet and sweet-scented geranium. The whole place is intersected with capital roads—carriage roads, private roads, bridle paths, and labyrinthine tracks and trails. Oh! the will o' the wisp dances these delicious little paths lead you! Down a steep, up another, across a valley, round a spur, into a thick bit of *shola*, or the depth of a grand forest, and every moment revealing some new beauty or thing of interest. Now it is a lowly bit of moss, or a fern or wild flower, or a flower-laden shrub, or a strange bird singing a carol in the branches; or perhaps it is a single giant of the forest, which tradition says was left standing by some of the wild-hill people, because it was the residence of the genii of the place, and superstition had said, 'Woodman, spare that tree!' Then at every turn some fresh view presents itself, each one finer than the last, of these wondrous, everlasting hills. You feel you can hardly resist the impulse to kneel down and worship God in His own grand temple, among the glorious things which are His own handiwork.

One 'thing of beauty' I have never seen exactly the same anywhere else, is the fascinating, ethereal, indescribable haze or vapour I have already spoken of; I hardly know what to call it. It is as if the air was tinted a deep blue, so delicate and gossamer are its shadowy veils, which linger on the slopes, or lie in the hollows, or float low in the valleys among the foliage; and the effect amid the sunlit green is beyond description lovely.

Such is our beautiful Coonoor; though, in truth, half has not been told. Ootacamund lies some twelve miles away, on the western slopes of the Dodabetta range—the highest in South India. This well-known capital occupies a higher plateau than Coonoor, though the difference of some 2,000 feet hardly accounts for the great change in climate; Ooty, as it is popularly called, being much colder. Here the vegetation is semi-tropical, and the scenery rich and varied, as I have described. About Ootacamund there is a succession of open breezy downs, and the air is fresh and bracing, reminding one of the fine 'caller air' of our own dear heather hills at home.

There is indeed a wonderful charm about these Blue Mountains. It is not that they transcend all others in grandeur and sublimity: the Himalayas have loftier peaks and more stupendous precipices; they have also their everlasting snows. The Ghāts of Western India are more picturesque, with their jagged, pointed peaks, rocky ridges, and varied and fantastic forms; while these hills have nearly always the same blue ranges, with their rounded, undulating tops. And yet for loveliness and general fascination, for softness and all-attractiveness, the Neilgherries seem to me to surpass all other hill resorts I have seen. I yield the palm to them, and must be allowed to say in the words of the quaint old Scottish ballad:

'Of all the hills the sun kens,
Beautifullest these!'

TODAS.

## CHAPTER XXV.

### THE TODAS AND A TODA-MUND.

But the Blue Mountains have other and even higher interests than all this natural beauty I have been speaking about.

Long ages before Mr. Sullivan, then Commissioner of Coimbatore, and later, Lord Elphinstone, had conceived the happy idea of making the Neilgherries a sanatorium and a resort for Europeans from the heat of the Southern plains, these

> 'regions consecrate
> To oldest time'

had known other and very different inhabitants, some of whom remain to this day, putting forth the lofty claim to be still considered 'lords of the soil.'

Among most of the mountain ranges and more sequestered places in India—as I think I have already said—there are to be found wild primitive people, often the aborigines of the country. Among the Western Ghāts we have the Thākurs, Katkaries, etc.; in the Himalayas and other ranges, the Lepchas, Khāsis, Garos, and others; in the jungly regions of Western Bengal there are the Santals and Khols; but of all the wilder races, perhaps the Todas of the Neilgherries are the most interesting and remarkable.

Altogether there are five different races on these hills: the Todas, Badagas, Irulas, Kotas, and Kurumbers. The Badagas are a fine, manly race, and the most numerous, but they are hardly hill men; they were originally Hindus, worshippers of the god Shiva, and migrated to the hills from the Mysore country some three or four hundred years ago. They are chiefly agricultural, and acknowledge a kind of fealty to the Todas as their feudal landlords, paying them tribute in grain, which is called *goodu*. The Irulas are scarcely hill men either; they are a Tamil-speaking people, who live low down on the slopes, though they differ in many characteristics from the people of the plains.

The Todas are the least numerous of all the five tribes I have named, but they are much the most independent, as well as the most curious in their habits and ways; in their personal appearance also, and their religious observances. The question of their origin has occupied the attention of antiquarians and men interested in such matters, and much speculation has been the result; but these learned investigators are by no means of one mind on the knotty point. Some hold them to be of Scythian descent; others, that they are the descendants of some old Roman colony; others say they are Jews, and many that they are the aborigines of the Neilgherries. On this point M. Metz, of the Basle Evangelical Missionary Society, says, in his interesting little book on these tribes: 'If you ask me who are the Todas, I am obliged to answer I cannot tell. I am satisfied they are not the aborigines of the Neilgherries.' On the whole, then, I think their own account of themselves, when my husband questioned them, is the most lucid, as it certainly is the most striking: 'We have come from nowhere; our ancestors were created on these hills, and these hills belong to us!' They undoubtedly are an ancient race; and, as people of ancient race are apt to do, hold their heads very high. They look down on all the other tribes, and even on the Hindus. Indeed, I am not sure that the present lords of the soil, the masterful white people, do not come in for a share of their lofty scorn.

The hospitable kindness of some very charming people we met in Madras has just given us the pleasure of a visit to Ootacamund, and an opportunity of making the acquaintance of the Todas. The native town of Ootacamund occupies a kind of basin, formed by several spurs, one of which—and the prettiest—is Elk Hill, on which stands the beautiful house and grounds of our friends. On the first evening of our stay our kind hostess took us out to see something of the place. Crossing the beautiful little artificial lake by the willow-bund—a causeway skirted by a thick fringe of feathery willow trees—we drove up the slopes to the top of the opposite ridge. This pretty serpentine is quite two miles in length, and adds greatly to the beauty of the station. On the hill-side above are scattered many of the handsome residences of the *élite* of Madras society, among which Government House is conspicuous, surrounded by beautiful grounds and garden. On the margin of the lake stands the graceful Gothic church of St. Thomas, where the late lamented and beloved governor, Mr. Adam, lies buried. Soon, leaving the settlement behind, we drove along some upland stretches of brown moorland; then rounded spur after spur, looking down on valleys and ravines, some cultivated, and some filled with the rich dark shola. Here tea meets you everywhere; coffee does not come quite so high. Cinchona is also hardy, and grows at the height of nine thousand feet. At length, descending to a valley round a wooded shoulder, we came on one of the loveliest spots one could picture; a sort of wide hollow, sheltered by some hill-tops, clothed with the richest sward, and having some fine trees and shola about, in which the evening sunlight was glinting exquisitely. But what at once arrested our attention was that on the sward, surrounded by all this beauty, stood three or four erections, the queerest and quaintest you could conceive. It was hard to believe that they were human habitations, though some human figures sat in front, quite as strange-looking as the dwellings. They sat on the grass, basking in the sun, completely wrapped in their blankets, nothing being visible above but the heads, covered with a bush of thick, coarse black hair. One or two of the heads differed, in having a profusion of elf-like ringlets round the face and neck; these we found belonged to the women.

'You have wished to see a Toda-mund,' exclaimed our friend; 'there is one!'

Of course, we stopped, got out of the carriage, and scrambled down among the bushes for a nearer view. The figures stood up at our approach, one or two even coming to meet us, and making salāms, after their own odd fashion, by raising the right hand to their forehead and placing the thumb on the ridge of the nose.

But it was getting late and cold, and as there was not time to make any satisfactory investigations, our friend promised that we should see another of these strange settlements very soon, called the Marli Mund.

Accordingly, one lovely, clear, sunshiny day, a carriageful of big folk and little set out to make the expedition. We drove away several miles beyond Ootacamund, ascending higher and higher, and having glorious views of the two ranges, the Neilgherries and the Koondahs, and glimpses afar of the Mysore plateau. I hoped we should also see the Wynaad; but I do not think we did. We passed some planters' houses—nice, cosy, pretty bungalows; but the life these poor fellows lead, especially in the remoter parts, must often be lonely enough. Coming to the end of the carriage road, we got out and walked on by a shady path through the shola, and speedily came to the Mund, or village. As usual, the Todas had chosen one of the loveliest and most romantic spots for their down-sitting. The settlement consisted of two or three huts, erected on a small green eminence, and surrounded by a low wall of loose rough stones. We scrambled up and entered the enclosure. One hut stood at the top, another at the bottom, and a clean-swept open court between, with a fire-place of two or three stones at the side, on which a pot, set gipsy-like, was boiling merrily. A quantity of fine, dark-coloured grain lay in a heap beside a hole in the floor, wherein a damsel was pounding it vigorously with a monster pestle into a sort of meal. A third hut, standing a little apart, we found was used as a cattle-pen, and a fourth, the most pretentious and the best built, was consecrated to the Swamie, or god, and the dairy together; for with the Todas the dairy is the temple. They are altogether a pastoral people, and, like the patriarchs of old, wealth with them means the possession of herds, these herds consisting entirely of buffaloes. In this Mund, then, there were only four huts; in the first one we had seen there were five, and there are seldom more in one village. The construction of these huts is most curious. They are built of bamboos, set closely together, tied with rattan, plastered with mud, and then covered with a thick thatch. Those we saw were about thirteen feet long, and scarcely so much in height.

In shape they are an arched oval, the roof reaching to the ground, like the top of a monster waggon, whilst the ends are built up with huge logs of wood, and resemble a filled-in archway. They are substantial, and are said to be water-tight. I should think they must be air-tight too, for the only opening they possess is a tiny aperture at one end about a couple of feet square, if so much, which serves for door, window, chimney, ventilator—everything. It seemed hard to believe that a grown man or woman could squeeze through this Liliputian door. I got down on all fours to try and get a glimpse of the interior; to have crawled in would have been too daring an exploit, even if it had been possible. But I made one of the women show me the mode of ingress, and it was very droll to see her go flat down and wriggle herself in as if she had been an eel. I confess to having discovered nothing, the place was pitch-dark, especially when I filled the aperture. But my husband, who was more fortunate in his investigations, says that there is a fixed low platform at one side, covered with buffalo-skins. This is the common sleeping-place, and is all the furniture this novel habitation possesses, except a few utensils for use in cooking and eating.

In such dens the whole people of a village dwell. Two or three women were in the court when we arrived, and welcomed us with great frankness and evident pleasure. Their freedom of manner is certainly remarkable in Eastern women; they are not in the least shy or put out, even at the approach of gentlemen. The men are bold and independent, and never seem to know what fear means. They are the finest-looking wild people we have seen. The men are tall, well-formed, and athletic; and the women are undoubtedly handsome, erect, lithe, and would be attractive if, like their Hindu sisters, they were gentle and modest, and reserved in demeanour. Both men and women have strongly marked features, with good, aquiline noses. One fine old patriarch, the head-man of the village, who came forward to meet us, leaning on a staff as tall as himself, might have sat for a portrait of Abraham; and I often fancied, from the cast of countenance, that there might be something in the theory which makes their origin Jewish—only the expression is open, honest, and good-humoured. They laugh loud and merrily on the slightest provocation. Men and women dress exactly alike, if dress it can be called which consists of one garment, a long blanket, which envelopes them from head to foot. The women are much tattooed, chiefly about the neck, shoulders, and arms. Their blue-black hair is curled carefully round their well-shaped heads in long, spiral ringlets—a result produced by the skilful use of small sticks instead of curling-tongs—and has an irresistibly ludicrous effect on the top of the blanket costume. Their ornaments are very primitive; some bangles made of brass or lead, dreadfully heavy, and a quantity of cowrie-shells curiously strung into tassels, which dangle at the end of necklaces made of thread, hair, or silver, according to the wealth and position of the wearer. They are inveterate beggars, and do not look with favour on anything but white money. A display of the latter induced the women to sing us one of their songs. It was a most singular, dirge-like strain, executed with the teeth firmly set and closed—a wild, weird, mystic kind of chant, with no music in it, hardly any words, and the voices harsh and monotonous.

They are a dirty people; they never wash either themselves or their blankets; and are excessively lazy. The Toda loves to sit in his blanket in the sun, 'monarch,' he thinks, 'of all he surveys,' and eat of the produce of the soil wrought by the sweat of other brows than his own. He manages this by exacting *goodu*, or tribute, from the inferior tribes, which, by working on their superstitions in various ways, he has hitherto induced them to pay. His other and chief source of revenue is his buffaloes. Every village has its own special herd and its own pasture ground; and the sole occupation of the men is to drive the beasts to their pasture in the morning, tend them during the day, and bring them home to the Mund at night. But the operation of milking is very sacred, and can only be performed by the pujāri, or village priest. He receives the herd, joins the people in making obeisance to it, then proceeds with the milking, and finally must himself place the milk in the dairy. As I said before, the dairy is the temple, and into its sacred precincts no woman is ever allowed to enter. The milk is made into ghee and curd, and on it chiefly the people live. The buffaloes are often very fierce and dangerous. They attack strangers with great ferocity, especially white people; but, happily, they at once obey the call or whistle of their owners, and thus frequent accidents are prevented.

Although there is no caste, rightly speaking, among the Todas, they are divided into families or classes—I think five—who, though they eat together, and otherwise fraternise, never intermarry. Polyandry still exists among them, in the sense that, when a woman marries, she becomes the wife of all the brothers in the family she allies herself to; and her children belong to the husbands by seniority. I am glad to say this dreadful custom seems to be passing away, and the Todas now think it more respectable that each man should have his own wife; though morals, I am afraid, cannot yet be said to be of a high order among them. Female infanticide once prevailed, but now is said to have entirely ceased.

And what can one say of their worship and religious observances except this, that very little is known about them? Their ideas on the subject of religion seem extremely vague. They can scarcely be called idolaters, as they have no idols, or rather, images; and yet the buffalo-bell of the village is held sacred, and has libations of milk poured out and prayers made to it. It is called the Hiradeva, or Bell-god. There is also a Hunting-god, whom they propitiate. He helps them to kill the tigers, who otherwise would kill their calves. The sun is also sometimes worshipped. But, in truth, their milk and their buffaloes are their gods; and their single comprehensive prayer seems to be: 'May all be well, may the buffaloes be well!' There is a high priest among them, called a Pālal, or head milkman. He is a most sacred personage, and lives in a holy Mund, with only one attendant, called a Kāvilal, or herdsman. A few sacred buffaloes are kept for the exclusive use of this recluse, in whom Deity is supposed to dwell, and who exercises unbounded influence over every Toda. No woman may approach the sacred Mund, and no man is permitted to do so without express permission, and then he must address the holy man from a very respectful distance. None of the tribes would dare to refuse him anything he might choose to ask for, however unreasonable the demand, or some dire calamity would certainly overtake themselves or their herds.

Their ceremonies are few, the principal ones being connected with their dead. There are two funeral ceremonies, one called the 'green funeral,' which takes place immediately after death, when the body is burnt; while the other, called the 'dry funeral,' is intended to commemorate all who have died in the tribe within the year. These festivals are full of absurdity, and would take too long to describe.

Such, then, is the deep, dense darkness of this singular people. The German missionaries have tried to work among them; and from their influence, and that of other Europeans, there seems to be a gradual dawning of civilisation; but I have never heard that a Toda has yet become a Christian. A good many Badagas have accepted the truth, and there is a flourishing little congregation of Christian Badagas in connection with the Basle Mission in the Kaity valley. My husband visited this Mission, and was greatly interested with all he saw.

Our day at the Marli Mund was one not to be forgotten. After a long interview with the people, we chose a lovely spot to encamp and rest. We crept under the shade of a thick mass of thorny jungle-bush, with greensward below, carpeted with brown, dry leaves. Here we ate our lunch, after which the children lay down on rugs to sleep, and we read aloud about the Todas. The birds were frightened into silence at first, but presently began their merry little carols again, and filled the air with melody. The wild people soon discovered our retreat, and stalked up to us in their long blankets, making a ring round us, for by this time some of the men had returned from the pasture grounds. They begged hard for more white money; the *goodu*, I suppose, they thought it only right we should pay.

We stayed until the sun was beginning to get low in the west, and then turned our faces homewards. As we drove away, a gleam shone out over the picturesque little Mund, as it lay on its green knoll under the shelter of the shola; a delicate, gathering haze just then caught the ray, and was immediately alight with all the hues of the rainbow.

'Surely a bow of promise!' we all exclaimed; hope and promise, from the 'rainbow-circled throne,' even for the poor Todas.

'The people that walked in darkness have seen a great light: they that dwelt in the land of the shadow of death, upon them hath the light shined.' So may it be speedily with all the dark, degraded races of this interesting land!

## CHAPTER XXVI.

### CONCLUSION.

I MUST now take leave of my readers who have kindly accompanied us in our wanderings over some of the Mission fields of Southern India.

Very soon after our delightful visit to Ootacamund, a severe attack of illness put an end to many cherished hopes and plans. But

> ———'How sweet to know
> The trials which we cannot comprehend
> Have each their own divinely-purposed end.'

Besides—

> 'Is not His will the wisest? is not His choice the best?'

As soon as the journey to the plains was possible, my husband brought me down to Bangalore. I had long looked forward to a visit to this beautiful city of the South; but now I was here I was not able to explore it. It is one of the pleasantest and healthiest and prettiest stations in all India. It has a large native city, full of historic interest; and an expansive European quarter, where the military cantonment is, and where the English residents live in handsome houses, standing in lovely wooded grounds. The whole place is full of natural loveliness. There are the ruins of an old fort, every stone of which could tell its story of fierce struggles and warlike deeds; and, I am afraid, also of much cruelty and oppression. Every one remembers the story of Sir David Baird and his captivity, regarding which his mother made the memorable remark, 'Pity the man who is chained to oor Davie!' Well, it was here poor 'Davie' was chained; and I think it must have been even harder for the brave man to be made a show and spectacle of daily for the amusement of the ladies of the zenana, and draw water for them from a well which is still shown as one of the curiosities of the place, than even the chains and his dungeon. But I only heard of these things; I did not see them.

A far greater disappointment, however, and privation, was that I could so seldom accompany my husband in his visits to the missionaries, and saw so little of their work. Missions in Bangalore have been most successful, and the schools, congregations, and different operations carried on so extensively in the place are full of interest. We received much kindness from Mr. and Mrs. Rice, of the London Missionary Society, and from many others whose names I need not mention, including Mr. Morison, chaplain of the Scotch church.

But Dr. Mitchell paid a visit to our friend Miss Anstey's deeply interesting Faith Mission, at Colar, some distance away from Bangalore, and has given me the following account of it.

'Colar is a town of eleven thousand inhabitants, about forty miles from Bangalore. Mrs. Mitchell was not able to visit this station; and it falls to me to say a few words regarding the very remarkable work there carried on by Miss Anstey.

'Miss Anstey returned to India in the end of 1876, after being restored from what had seemed hopeless illness. Her prayer was that she might have work in training young people. Famine broke out, and it was evident that multitudes of children would be left destitute. She accordingly settled at Colar, in the heart of the district where famine was raging, and prepared to receive as many orphans as might come to her. She was in connection with no Missionary Society, had not much money of her own, and had received no promise of contributions. She felt, however, that her call was clear. She at once ordered a house to be built for the reception of seven hundred orphans. Children came to her in large numbers; from first to last she has received fully eleven hundred. Many died, famine having terribly weakened the powers of life before they arrived. Some were enticed away by relatives or friends when the famine ceased. Many, however, have been settled—generally as married couples—on little farms belonging to the Mission. At present (August, 1885), the number in the Orphanage is about three hundred and fifty. The Mission has all along been conducted—to use Miss Anstey's words—"on the principle of looking to the Lord alone for all supplies." And the supplies have been sent. The heathen have been deeply impressed by this, and a high Government servant, a Brahman, has always addressed his official letters to "God's Orphanage,

Colar." When I saw this brave woman in the midst of her labours, I feared that the burden would crush her. Not the financial burden; my question as to that received the prompt reply: "The Lord has provided, and will provide." But there was a multitude of business matters connected with the large establishment which I felt no woman should be troubled with. Still, her health has been preserved so far that a short visit to Britain seems likely to restore all her energies. He who has upheld and guided her till now will, I doubt not, uphold and guide her still.'

It had been one of my dreams—though one not to be realised—to see Miss Anstey and her large family of poor famine orphans and their Home, and all her important and most arduous work, which is carried on by simple faith in God's providing. She and her children ask in prayer for what they need. Her motto is, 'The Lord will provide'; and He *does* provide, by putting it into the hearts of His people to send her the means—and she needs large means—to feed, and clothe, and educate, and set out in life her large company of poor friendless children of both sexes. Can we not help her a little more? Can we not help *all* Missions a little more? We can surely do so by contributing more, working harder, seeking to interest others, and above all, by more *believing prayer*. 'What things soever ye desire when ye pray, *believe that ye receive them*, and ye shall have them.' Then can we not, many more of us, give ourselves to the work? For we want multitudes of workers, both men and women. May the Spirit of God so fill our hearts with love to Christ and compassion for poor India, that we shall go forth in far greater numbers, and with far more perfect consecration, until we have won the whole land for Him.

It might be done easily! The whole of India could be evangelized in a generation, if Christian people would only bestir themselves, and bring great and adequate means to bear on the great and glorious work. And let us hope that the first work of all the Churches, as it would certainly be the grandest, will more and more be the evangelization of the whole heathen world, until the idols are utterly abolished, and the name of Christ known and honoured from the rising to the setting of the sun.

Our journey from Bangalore to the Deccan was a trying one, there were so many changes; but at length, on the 16th of June, after six months' wanderings, we found ourselves once more under the hospitable roof of the Mission House at Poona. A few weeks later, and I was tossing on the wild monsoon billows of the Indian Ocean, homeward bound. I was alone, for we felt my husband must stay to complete the task he had undertaken, and also be present at the Decennial Missionary Conference in Calcutta. One thought filled my heart as our gallant P. & O. steamer, the Sutlej, swung round from her moorings and ploughed her stately way through the waves: I have bidden adieu to India! sorrowing most of all because, in all human probability, I should see her loved face no more.

# INDEX.